P9-DGJ-784

THE DEVELOPING CANADIAN COMMUNITY

The Developing Canadian Community

S. D. Clark

UNIVERSITY OF TORONTO PRESS

© University of Toronto Press 1962
Printed in Canada

To the Memory of

GEORGE E. BRITNELL

Preface

THE ESSAYS brought together in this volume are intended to serve as an introduction to the study of the Canadian community. Though *The Developing Canadian Community* is not in any strict sense a textbook, much that is contained in it has developed out of the effort of instruction over the years and it can be hoped it will do something to meet the need of the Canadian student of sociology anxious to learn more about his own society. A social science is made meaningful only when the boxes it constructs out of its theory and method come to have something in them; what is offered here can be thought of as an effort directed towards the filling of some of the emptier of sociology's boxes.

I am indebted to Mr. Jeanneret, Miss Harman, Miss Halpenny and the editorial staff of the University of Toronto Press for their encouragement and assistance in the preparation of this volume for publication. Special thanks are owing Miss Jamieson in seeing the book through the press. There is much as well for which I owe thanks to Dean Bladen, Professor Easterbrook, and Professor Burnet. The dedication of the book to the memory of the late Professor Britnell offers itself as a small way of acknowledging a debt of friendship acquired over many years.

The University of Toronto   S.D.C.
May 15, 1962

Contents

x   *Contents*

Introduction

THIS VOLUME BRINGS together papers and essays written as far apart in time as twenty or more years. Yet, what is contained herein is very much a piece. It was in 1938 that I determined to undertake a study of the development of the Canadian community. Behind this determination was the conviction that sociology had much to gain from the study of the society of the past and that the sensible place for the Canadian sociologist to begin was with the study of his own society. Thus was begun in 1938 a task which in 1962 must yet be considered far from complete.

The task might have been made easier, and more immediately rewarding, had I been able to bring to bear upon the problem of analysing the development of the Canadian community a clearly formulated theory of historical development. But I had no such theory and I have none yet. It has been my belief that any effort on the part of the sociologist to fit history into a tight, preconceived, theoretical scheme could only result in the producing of poor history—and poor sociology. If the sociologist was to turn to history it was essential that he bring to the work he undertook a spirit of free historical inquiry.

This is not to say that in turning to history he should forget about his theory. In the end, whatever the sociologist does must be judged in terms of its theoretical significance. What this means is looking at history sociologically, seeking always the sociological meaning of what is found. But this can be done without commitment to any particular theory and it certainly can be done without commitment to a theory of historical development. The sociologist can turn sociological historian without becoming a philosopher of history.

It is perhaps a crude sociological theory which got written into much that follows in this volume. Work on the development of the Canadian community was begun by concentrating on those areas of development where the sociological significance of what was happening could be seen most clearly. In the winter of 1938–9 my fourth-year honour students in sociology joined with me in the task of analysing the kind of developments which had taken place in the Klondike during the period of the gold rush. Here there was available a massive body of data and an example of a full-fledged society springing into being almost overnight. For a study of social change the Klondike during the period of the gold rush offered itself as an almost ideal sociological laboratory.

From the Klondike, the study of other areas was undertaken. The next was the backwoods society of Upper Canada. As inquiry was pushed back to the period of the old régime and forward to the period of industrialization and urban growth the complexity of the development of the Canadian community became increasingly apparent. No simple conception of development could account for all which had taken place.

In the preparation of *The Social Development of Canada* for publication, however, it seemed essential that the analysis be in terms of as simple a conception of development as possible. Otherwise, in the effort to cover such an extended period, the danger was very great that what was sociological would become lost in the presentation of a mass of facts. Thus attention was centred upon developments occurring in new frontier areas and analysis was largely concerned with the process of the breaking down of established forms of social organization and the emergence of new forms. *The Social Development of Canada* might have been described as a study of the role of the frontier in the development of Canadian society.

However it might be described, this book was intended to do nothing more than break the ground. It might have led on my part to a very much more detailed study of particular areas of development. Instead, it led to an effort to examine the development of particular forms of social organization. Religious developments attracted attention first not only because of the wealth of material available but because such developments lent themselves readily to sociological analysis. *Church and Sect in Canada* grew very directly out of *The Social Development of Canada*. In turn, the study of religious developments gave emphasis to the importance of political developments. Canadian society in important respects was a political creation. Thus resulted the study *Movements of Political Protest in Canada.*

In this shift from the study of the Canadian community in general to a study of particular forms of social organization there had come a growing realization of the complexity of the forces shaping the character of the Canadian society. The role of the frontier had given emphasis to the importance of forces developing out of the position of the Canadian community within the American continental system. The role of empire and nation gave emphasis to the importance of forces developing out of Canada's peculiar position as a society occupying the northern half of the continent.

The reader of *The Developing Canadian Community* will be made aware of this changing emphasis. The first six chapters of this volume are taken from *The Social Development of Canada.* Separated here from the documentary material which was incorporated in that volume, these six chapters assume the character of essays introductory to a study of the development of the Canadian community. The next seven chapters with the exception of the one dealing with education grew out of work on *Church and Sect in Canada* and *Movements of Political Protest in Canada.* Some of the ideas contained in these papers find fuller expression in the studies to which they are related. Many, however, might be described as in the nature of afterthoughts. One can make bold to develop ideas in a paper which might have no proper place in a book.

The reader may well feel that the final two essays of this volume should have been placed at the beginning. But they were written after the others and represent in a very real sense an effort to pull together ideas growing out of work on the development of the Canadian community, including work on a not yet completed study of the suburban community. They are perhaps something in the nature of a swan song.

In preparing the essays for publication in this volume only the slightest of editorial revision was attempted. In some of the essays statements made in the present tense have had to be changed to the past where the references were to developments occurring at the time of writing. Other references of a more general sort to the present have been let stand even though made fifteen or more years ago. The reader should bear in mind the time the different essays were written. Many of the ideas in the early essays I would today express differently. A heavy emphasis on the economic factor is particularly apparent in the essays taken from *The Social Development of Canada*. Here also there is a very considerable reliance upon the W. I. Thomas theory of social disorganization and reorganization though at no time was there an acceptance of the notion that these processes had any meaning except in terms of the particular forms of organization being analysed. The second-last essay appearing in the volume better presents the theoretical framework which was employed in the analysis of the problem of change throughout all the essays.

To give everything included in the volume the character of essays, all footnote references have been omitted with the exception of three illustrative quotations. For the sources of the data on which the essays rest the reader is referred to *The Social Development of Canada, Church and Sect in Canada,* and *Movements of Political Protest in Canada.* No attempt can be made to indicate the titles of the large number of books and articles on the economic, political, and social history of Canada upon which the essays rely. The sociologist in whatever he may attempt to do in the study of the Canadian community must place himself under a heavy obligation to the historian. To the economic historian as well the obligation cannot be a small one. Only the mention of the name of the late H. A. Innis is sufficient to give some indication of it. In Canada there is not yet a significant body of sociological literature relating to the development of the Canadian society of the past. But a beginning has been made in the building up of such a literature, particularly having to do with the early development of French Canada, and in the study of the present-day Canadian community the pioneer work done by C. A. Dawson and E. C. Hughes has been carried forward by a great number of younger sociologists.

It has never been my view that in the development of sociology all sociologists must become historians. There is much sociological work to be done in Canada of a non-historical character. Indeed, it is to the study of the contemporary scene that the major effort must be directed. But it is not unbecoming perhaps on the part of a Canadian sociologist to plead the cause of a sociology directed primarily to the understanding of Canadian problems. We have yet too few resources to dissipate them by riding off in all directions. It is to be hoped that the present volume will strengthen sociological interest in the study of our own Canadian society. There is much certainly about this society that we have yet to learn.

PART I

The Frontier in the
Social Development of Canada

CHAPTER I

Social Organization
and the Changing Structure of
the Community*

T H E   I M P O R T A N C E of the opening up of new areas of economic exploitation in the economic history of Canada serves to justify
concern with the effects of such developments upon the development
of social organization. If some of the older settled areas in Canada
early reached a state of economic maturity, and if at times economic recession halted the pushing out into new areas, these developments did little more than punctuate the sweep of frontier
economic expansion. The drying up of resources or the loss of
markets resulted in a shift to new economic activities rather than in
a prolonged economic regression; the succession of export staples
provides evidence of the importance in the economy of Canada of
new techniques of production rather than of techniques of conservation. The establishment of the fishing industry in the Gulf of St. Lawrence led to the traffic in furs with the Indians and to the settlement
of the Annapolis and St. Lawrence valleys. To fish and fur was later
added the important staple of timber, opening up for agricultural
exploitation the interior of New Brunswick and the new Province
of Upper Canada. Expansion of the fur trade to the West brought
about the sudden rush for gold in British Columbia, and eventually
in the Yukon, and the settlement of the wheat lands of the prairies,

*From *The Social Development of Canada* (Toronto, 1942), pp. 1–20.

and these developments hastened the growth of industrial capitalism in the East. The pushing out of the frontiers of manufacturing, and the exploitation of the mining and pulp and paper resources of the North, mark the final phases of the frontier expansion of economic life in Canada.

Social problems in Canada, accordingly, have been largely associated with frontier economic developments. The opening up of new areas or fields of economic exploitation made certain special kinds of demands upon social organization, and the failure to meet fully these demands resulted in disturbances in social relationships which may be described as social problems. Centres of new economic activity became the points of origin of forces of disturbance, and these forces extended to the peripheries of such activity. The areas of greatest social disturbance were to be found where the impacts of the new techniques of production were most felt, and the intensity of the disturbance reached its peak during the interval in which the new economic developments were most rapidly taking place. As the economy became more mature, the social organization adjusted itself to the conditions of production, and an approximate state of equilibrium was attained by the time the economy passed beyond the frontier stage.

Frontier economic expansion involved the recruitment of capital and labour from outside, and this growth of population made necessary the extension of institutional controls and often their establishment beyond customary boundaries. Since institutions are essentially a body of trained functionaries performing specialized services, organization had to be widened and personnel enlarged if the needs of growing populations were to be adequately served. The considerable distance which often separated new areas of development from centres of control and supply made difficult the maintenance of effective supervision from the homeland in establishing institutional agencies and also imposed severe limitations upon the recruitment of personnel. In addition, conditions within such areas discouraged the financial support of institutions which did not directly promote economic exploitation and the immigration of professionally trained workers. The drain of capital into economic enterprise left little for community services while the demand for labour meant that even those who possessed specialized training of some sort were attracted into economic vocations. The failure of churches or educational institutions to secure adequate financial support, problems of public finance, and the lack of sufficient school-teachers, clergymen, and medical practitioners were characteristic features of Canadian frontier communities. The stronger pull of economic enterprise meant that capital and labour flowed beyond the boundaries of institutional systems. Where economic development took place rapidly and considerable additions to the labour force could be immediately absorbed, as in mining frontiers, the lag of such systems was most conspicuous, but even when development took place slowly and the exploitative process did not require great numbers of workers there was a considerable interval before social organization could catch up with the movement of population.

When the economic exploitation was carried on by monopolies, controls of a political (and to some extent of a cultural) character were secured through the economic organization. Administrative obligations ordinarily accompanied the rights of monopoly, and, even when such obligations were not imposed, the monopolistic enterprise recognized the advantage of assuming considerable responsibility for at least the maintenance of law and order. The early trading companies of New France, and the Hudson's Bay Company, received extensive prerogatives of government, and even such semi-monopolistic enterprises as land colonization companies were endowed with a measure of political sovereignty. Though cultural obligations were less clearly defined, monopolistic organizations were expected to support the basic services of the community, and usually this support took the form of favours and financial assistance to an established church which in turn accepted the responsibility of such social services as education, relief, hospitalization, and recreation as well as religious teaching. For the most part, however, the economic development of frontier areas took place in terms of free enterprise rather than monopoly with the result that this agency for the transfer of social institutions was lacking. Monopoly tended to accompany the exploratory rather than expansionist phase of frontier development, or emerged later as a means of securing a greater conservation of resources. The development of new forms of economic exploitation implied the application of new techniques and skills, and this factor favoured individual enterprise. The very nature of monopoly discouraged efforts to expand the volume of production beyond an amount which the market would profitably absorb in terms of existing cost schedules, and, when abundant resources were available for exploitation as in frontiers, the restrictive policy of monopolistic enterprise led to the eventual triumph of free enterprise. As the expansion of the fur trade into the interior of the continent led to the collapse of trading companies in New France, the development of mining in British Columbia and of agriculture on the prairies marked the end of the western monopoly of the Hudson's Bay Company; land colonization companies as a means of controlling agricultural settlement were generally even more short-lived.

To some extent, the failure of economic enterprise to provide an agency for the transfer of social institutions to frontier areas was offset by efforts put forth by the state. Imperial, or later, national forces promoted the extension of political agencies into new areas of development in Canada. Frontiers have always assumed considerable strategical importance in the political organization of the northern half of the continent, and, for this reason, never became unrestricted areas of economic exploitation. The presence to the south of a rapidly expanding nation served to emphasize the need of maintaining close political contacts with the frontier. The police force and courts of law, or at any rate the army, pushed out with the frontiersmen. The maintenance of military garrisons in New France and later in the British American colonies, the construction of roads and canals to serve as military routes, the dispatch of a force of Royal Engineers to Victoria in 1859, and the organization of the North West Mounted Police in 1874 were instances of efforts to promote imperial or national interests in outlying areas of economic development. To some extent the political controls imposed by the state were paralleled by controls of a social or cultural character. Land grants to favoured individuals or organizations, financial subsidies, preferments in political appointments, or measures restricting the operation of competitive interests were means employed to build up privileged social institutions such as an aristocratic class or established church. The object was to assure the loyalty of frontier populations to the mother country, and such aids therefore served the same purpose as military garrisons or police forces. However, even when such supports of the state were extensive, there remained in new areas of development many needs not immediately taken care of by institutions. The coercive controls of the state, or of privileged social institutions, tended to be of a negative rather than positive character. The instruments of law provided no direction to behaviour outside of prohibitions, while institutions such as established churches supplied leadership only to those who were their adherents. For the large number of people who committed no infractions of the law or who did not owe allegiance to the formally constituted social institutions, authority was for the most part morally indifferent. The extension of social organization into all areas of social behaviour required the active participation of the population itself, and this involved more than simply the transfer of formal machinery.

The lack of institutional agencies securing the active participation of frontier populations increased the reliance upon individual resources, and the greater the lack the greater was this reliance. As frontier populations were left without leadership, they tended to become less dependent upon traditional institutions even after they were established. The weakened state of social organization thereby tended to perpetuate itself. Habits of independence were converted into attitudes of nonconformity, and what was first perhaps missed came later to be resented. New patterns of behaviour inevitably developed which did not fit into traditional systems of institutional control, and efforts of institutions to secure greater conformity led to a conflict of social values and to a condition which might be described as one of social disorganization. The difficulty faced by churches in reviving habits of worship after a considerable interval during which religious services were not provided and other ways of occupying the time on the sabbath day had developed illustrate the kind of problems resulting from the extension of social organization into new areas of development.

The character of the population which moved to frontier areas tended to strengthen nonconformist attitudes and to make more difficult the establishment of institutional systems. If the very fact of movement resulted in a considerable dislocation in habits and beliefs, this dislocation was greater when the population was recruited from a number of different cultural milieus. Conflicts emerged between opposing systems of control; the folkways, mores, and social codes of the various groups strove for supremacy. The efforts of some institutions to strengthen their position by privileges secured from the state were offset by the vigorous propaganda of less favoured organizations. The disturbances resulting from associations with strange people, in weakening traditional habits and beliefs, increased the area of cultural indifference and intensified as a result institutional competition. To the extent that segregation could not be achieved and long-established attachments preserved, frontier populations tended to be indifferent as to the particular institutions to which they gave their support. The effects were

evident in a large, culturally detached population in new areas of
development which floated from one institution or group to another,
their momentary attachments depending largely upon circumstances
of convenience and waves of enthusiasm.

This tendency was accentuated when the population contained
elements which had joined the movement to new areas as means of
escape from restraining influences at home. In some respects, this
was characteristic of all frontier populations in Canada. Those
people migrated who were most exposed to economic, political, or
cultural pressures. New areas of economic development provided
greater opportunities to realize potentialities of certain kinds. The
worker, peasant, entrepreneur, and the religious or political heretic
found there an outlet for their particular aptitudes or beliefs. These
types of people made more difficult the establishment of certain
forms of social organization. The extension of institutions is facili-
tated by the presence of a body of receptive attitudes and a
favourable set of social customs, and, where these were lacking,
dependence had to be placed upon the exercise of powers of
coercion or upon propaganda. The weaknesses of economic
monopolies, colonial class systems, established churches, or authoritarian systems of government, and the steady drain of the United
States upon the population of Canada, were directly related to
these characteristics of the settlers in Canadian frontier communities. When the nonconformist elements included those who sought
escape from moral codes or agencies of law enforcement, the strains
upon social organization in the newly settled areas were even
greater. Habits of resistance of such groups to authority were carried
over from the old to the new society and increased the general
tendency of frontier populations to become independent of traditional institutions. The emigration of social misfits resulted partly
from the social pressures applied to get them out of the way and
partly from the opportunities of escape or freedom from restraint
provided within rapidly growing and largely inaccessible communities. Though the nature of the frontier economy determined
to a considerable extent the particular character of these people,
in all of the newly developing Canadian communities there were
outcasts of some sort from older societies.

Similarly, the presence in frontier areas of people who had
emigrated because they were failures at home, whether because of
economic adversity, ill health, or some other reason, made more
difficult the establishment of community organization. It is true that

the rehabilitation of the individual's economic, physical, or mental condition often accompanied settlement in new areas, but this did not relieve the strain upon social organization in the interval before such rehabilitation was accomplished. The inability of such persons to provide for their needs meant that they could not fully participate in community life but were rather a burden upon frontier society. Numbers of such socially dependent persons have invariably accompanied the movement of population into Canadian frontier communities; if some found their way to such communities in the hope of bettering their state, others were sent there as a means of reducing the burdens of relief faced by local and national agencies in the home community. Efforts of France and later of Britain to secure through overseas colonization a solution to the problem of mounting poor-rates were paralleled by attempts on the part of Canadian cities to reduce burdens of relief by the promotion of settlement in the West and in recent years a back-to-the-land movement.

Other characteristics of the population served to make more difficult the establishment of orderly social relationships. Movements of people into new areas almost invariably involved disturbances in the equilibrium of age and sex groups. Though the nature of the economy largely determined the extent of these disturbances, migration ordinarily cut through the population structure to eliminate the very young and the very old and to secure a considerable predominance of men. Hazards of travel discouraged the migration of women, children, and old people, while the frontier society placed an emphasis upon productive as distinguished from service occupations and favoured as a result adult males who could take part directly in the process of economic exploitation. The age and sex composition of the population had considerable significance with respect to the stability of social organization. The absence of the older age groups in frontier areas relieved the pressure upon health and welfare institutions but removed the steadying influence of tradition and deprived the communities of the leadership of those who were not strenuously engaged in making a living. Since there were relatively few children among the early settlers, recreational and educational facilities were not required in the first years of development, but, where settlement of young persons of both sexes took place, problems of maternity and infant welfare quickly assumed considerable importance, and, in later years, an abnormally high proportion of school-age children imposed a heavy burden upon elementary educational institutions; it was not until after the passing of the first generation of settlers in frontier communities that a stable balance was secured between the school-age and total population. A predominance of men in the population raised problems of institutional adjustment of an even more critical character. Social organizations which depended upon the family unit, or which chiefly served the needs of women or children, failed to become established or remained largely ineffective. The result was that a large proportion of the normal controls of society were absent or greatly weakened. Apart from the mores of the family, religious and neighbourhood institutions were most affected. Devoutness tended to disappear when female influences were absent, while most of the niceties and refinements of social relationships depending upon companionship within the family group were disregarded or coarsened when such companionship was lacking. Where conditions were favourable, prostitution developed as a substitute for familial relationships, and the prevalence of drinking, gambling, and certain forms of crime in many frontier areas was indicative of general weaknesses of social organization resulting largely from the disproportionate number of men. In brief, the age and sex composition, like other characteristics, of the population intensified problems of institutional adjustment which resulted from the opening up and peopling of new frontier areas.

Such problems were still further accentuated by the contact of frontier populations with strange environmental influences, since adjustments to these influences were made much more quickly on the individual than on the institutional level. More strictly, adjustments took place most rapidly among that section of the population most exposed to strange environmental influences and were most resisted by that section least exposed, and it was those people least exposed who had chief voice in the direction of traditional institutional policies and activities. The dignitaries, priests, or official classes of the community were very largely sheltered from disturbing influences; the very nature of their roles meant that their employments were not directly related to frontier economic enterprise. It was the new occupational groups who faced the full force of new economic developments, and these groups had few claims upon the offices or emoluments of established social institutions. Individuals participating in frontier economic enterprise came in contact with new problems of life for which new solutions were necessary; the application of new techniques of production, and the development of new ways of living, involved a rational appraisal of the relation of means to desired ends and required the formulation of new habits of behaviour and thought. In a sense, such people moved out to the margins of society, and, while they carried with them some of the habits of thought and behaviour which had been implanted by previous forms of control, they had to leave behind, or cast off on the way, the great body of habits not fitted to the new conditions of life. Habits, like tools, were abandoned through non-usage because they failed to work. Whether this represented a failure to maintain conditions of life which had been considered desirable, or a release from social obligations which had been felt as irksome, the effect was to emancipate the individual from controls to which he had been accustomed. He was left to work out by himself a code of conduct and philosophy of life which more nearly satisfied his present needs. The immediate reaction was one of uneasiness, relieved partly by a feeling of exhilaration. The ultimate result, if new group attachments failed to be forged, was complete personal disorganization. Problems of mental health and suicide, and to some extent of intemperance, in periods of rapid social development, were an indication of the failure of individuals to resolve the personal crisis in face of radically new conditions of living.

Usually, however, some sort of adjustment was brought about. New habits developed to take the place of those discarded. But such habits were not co-ordinated within any institutional system of social control. They represented individual responses to the new conditions of life. Since social institutions, by their very nature, were established ways of doing things, cultural conflict emerged at the point of divergence between the new and old ways of life. The controls imposed by institutions had the object of making behaviour conform to socially approved standards, while adjustments to new conditions implied the emergence of kinds of behaviour which had not yet secured such approval. Thus until new social standards were incorporated within institutional systems, there existed a condition of *anomie* which was characterized by a considerable reliance upon individual effort and upon individual solutions to pressing problems. It is true that problems shared by large numbers of people called forth identical or at least similar solutions, but behind these there was little sense of obligation. Certain ways proved better than others; their approval rested upon individual experience or at most upon the immediate experiences of the group as a whole.

There was lacking any attempt to justify them within a traditional philosophy of the social good. Behaviour was in terms of a rational interpretation of the relation of means to ends lying within the range of experiences of the individual members of the group rather than in terms of past loyalties and sentimental attachments. Reliance upon such criteria meant a relaxation of previously accepted standards and a freer expression of immediately felt wants; social considerations acted only slightly as forces inhibiting behaviour.

The emergence of deviate forms of behaviour in periods of rapid social development demonstrated the failure of large sections of the population to erect successfully group codes of conduct when freed from the controls of social institutions. The breakdown of the traditional institutional structure resulted in the emergence of random types of social action which, when proceeding along certain lines, came to be defined as social problems. Such definitions of social problems, however, were necessarily subjective in that unrestrained behaviour represented nothing more than deviations from generally prevalent social norms; the mores disintegrated, but the behaviour which took place through release from their control could be termed undesirable only when assessed in terms of some set of social standards. The existence of social institutions depended upon conformity, and that behaviour was condemned which did not conform. In a sense, therefore, the emergence of social problems in periods of rapid development was a condition of the successful adjustment of individuals to the new environment. It indicated that while social institutions failed to meet new needs, solutions had been attained or at least were being sought on the individual level or within nonconformist groups.

To some extent, even though resisting or failing to make adjustments, established institutions were able to maintain their controls among certain sections of the population. This was particularly the case if they had at their disposal powerful means of imposing their sanctions. By taboos and moral restraints which carried with them punitive means of securing conformity, deviations from established norms were held in check. The criminal law of the state was the most effective instrument in securing such conformity. It was the expression of the established institutional set-up, and, supported by authoritarian sanctions, it served to check the development of behaviour patterns damaging to prevailing mores. A number of other institutions possessed some power of coercion. The compulsive attributes of religious denominations, the family, and more general communal institutions, tended to assume considerable importance when behaviour became particularly refractory. Resort to coercive measures, however, was an indication of institutional weakness; the imposition of sanctions implied that the habitual behaviour of large numbers of the population was no longer in conformity with established norms. It is true that where the deviations were not too extensive, or the forces of disturbance not too compelling, institutions were to some extent successful in re-establishing normative behaviour. The taboo preserved certain habits which, once fully accepted, converted the taboo into a moral attitude. Generally, however, the forces of adjustment could not be checked by restraints imposed by external sanctions; even the controls of the state tended to break down when faced with conditions of far-reaching social disturbance.

With the failure to maintain traditional controls, adjustments were made within the social organization, and those adjustments went furthest and proceeded most rapidly along lines which did not involve vested interests of some sort. Certain changes were readily permissible; for instance, in the case of churches, the building of places of worship with logs instead of with stones; that which proved of advantage to all the participants within an institution was ordinarily accepted without any prolonged delay. Rigidities entered at that point where certain groups, or officials, had something to lose by change. Opposition was greatest among those people furthest removed from new social conditions, while the dissatisfaction gathered greatest force among those most exposed to these conditions. Where flexibility was provided within the organization of the institution, successful accommodations often could be secured between these conflicting interests. Adjustments entered at the points of greatest disturbance even though disapproved of by those farther removed. Where such flexibility was lacking, however (and in all institutions it was lacking to some extent), attempts on the part of subordinate officials and dissatisfied members to bring about changes were promptly checked from above, and reform depended upon leadership from outside rather than within the organization.

This leadership came both from the ranks of specially trained persons dissatisfied with prevailing methods and from those who lacked any particular qualification to perform the services which they undertook to improve. The physician or judge who attempted to introduce changes at the risk of his professional reputation or employment by a public board was an example of the reformer drawn from the ranks of the technicians. Though reforms having to do with such matters as the practice of medicine or the administration of justice ordinarily were undertaken by those familiar with the techniques of these highly specialized services, in those situations where the need for improved methods was very pressing, leadership sometimes came from outside professional circles; the "quack" became a familiar figure during the cholera plagues in Upper Canada, and vigilante committees emerged (though not for long) in British Columbia and the Yukon when regularly constituted authorities of law enforcement were no longer able to maintain order. In other more legitimate ways people of non-professional status were able to make their influence felt in the advocacy of social reforms in fields where specialized training was required in the actual performance of the services. The royal commission emerged in Canada towards the middle of the nineteenth century and provided a means for the expression of opinion, although it was some time before its possibilities as an instrument of investigation and propaganda were fully appreciated. About the same time the newspaper developed as a recognized channel for the dissemination of opinions, and reform editors came to assume an increasingly important role as critics of social services. In the case of problems of a less technical nature, not only proposals for reform but participation could come from those who lacked any sort of specialized training, and, for this reason, there was a significant difference in the character of reform movements in, for instance, health and law on the one side, and morality and religion on the other. The guardians of public morals or the ministers of the gospel did not possess a body of skills which could not be quickly acquired by the layman. The temperance advocate needed to rely upon few of the findings of science to demonstrate to the satisfaction of many the evils of alcohol, while, if church bodies made efforts to establish standards of entrance to the ministry, few qualifications to preach could be insisted upon when the authority of the churches was called into question. The appointment and theological principles of the religious prophet depended upon no institutional intermediary since the truth of his version of the gospel and his charge to expound it came through special revelation; he answered an inner call, and God and his conscience were judges of the worth of his efforts. If perhaps unusual in some respects, the unlicensed religious preacher was typical in many ways of the reform leader who emerged at a time when traditional leadership was proving unacceptable.

By the very nature of their role reform leaders tended to be people devoid of "respectable" attributes. The professional person who practised unorthodox methods or advocated revolutionary changes was as likely to be denied "official" recognition as the person who lacked the qualifications required to serve within regularly constituted social institutions. Similarly, if the one type of reformer usually belonged to, the other was closely identified with, that class in the community which was without any acceptable social status. Reformers were social revolutionists in the sense that what they advocated involved an upsetting of traditional standards and very often traditional social distinctions. Thus they brought down upon themselves the full force of vested interests. In championing the cause of the unprivileged or unpopular, they challenged the privileges and accepted beliefs of the "respectable" leaders of the community. The influences which prompted people to break from established institutions and to take up the cause of reform often increased opposition against them. Desire to escape from the boredom of routine tasks, inability to secure a living or recognition in any other way, love of power which was experienced in swaying large audiences or large reading publics, and personal "grudges" against persons in authority, may have mingled, along with other motives, with the sincere conviction of doing good. But if their ideas caught on, it was because the underlying social consciousness provided a sympathetic response. The reformer differed from the "crank" in that he gave expression to genuine and persistent social needs and dissatisfactions; within programmes of reform, the vague and inarticulate feelings of large numbers of people were crystallized and identified with a clearly defined goal. It was this need for social expression rather than the character or motives of reformers which gave rise to reform movements.

If the motives of reform leaders provide no explanation of the rise of reform movements, neither do the motives of the followers. Nothing inherent within a particular reform idea determined its success in meeting the personal needs of frontier populations. The enthusiasm aroused by inspiring leadership offered to the frontier settler, perplexed by strange surroundings, a means of escape from the task of determining by himself standards of thought and behaviour. In other words, from the point of view of the individual, the movement served as a means of reorganizing the personality in terms of a particular focus of group attention. Joining or supporting the movement, particularly one of a moral or religious evangelical character but even one of health or prison reform, involved some sort of conversion which brought about a reformation of attitudes and established a set of standards depending upon group sanctions. Conversion involved the organization of habits in terms of a definite purpose and in this way it secured a stable personality. But any one of many movements would have been equally effective in meeting such individual needs. Different kinds of personal "crises," such as financial reverses, the death of a dearly loved one, or the loss of good health, caused people to endorse the cause of reform, but life histories which revealed the nature of these would throw little light upon the forces giving rise to particular reform movements. Movements developed because they provided machinery for the rationalization of individual wants on the basis of the common good. They provided an interpretation of new phenomena, and in so doing developed habits in the individual which conformed to a general pattern of social behaviour. The solution of individual "crises" was directed along channels securing the solution of social "crises"; in this way, movements became instruments of social as distinct from individual reorganization.

Similarly, cultural diffusion or environmental determinism provide no adequate explanation of the rise of reform movements. The reform movements which sprang up in Canadian frontier areas did not, of course, develop independently of outside influences. The close connection with Britain and the United States, or earlier with France, and the fact that economic developments in Canada were similar to those taking place in these other countries, meant that new ideas usually were derived from British, American, or in some cases French sources. Often local reform leaders identified their programmes with those of reform movements in outside countries; occasionally, the leaders actually came in from outside. That does not mean, however, that the development of these movements in Canada can be explained in terms of the relation with outside movements since the fact that such a relation became established (or, indeed, in many cases did not become established) requires explanation. Though related to movements outside, reform movements in Canadian frontier communities were products of forces generated from within. On the other hand, the assumption of environmental determinism that the population within these new areas of development individually readjusted their habits of thought and behaviour, and that such random adjustments explain the character of new social developments, disregards the fact that environmental forces did not act equally and in the same way upon

all the individuals of an area. These forces made adjustments necessary, but it was only through group leadership that general patterns
of social adjustment were brought about. It does not matter whether
that leadership was provided, as Walter Bagehot would have supposed, by the intellectually élite, or, as Veblen would have argued,
by the members of that class most exposed to the full force of
changing conditions; the point is that the adjustment in the first
instance was peculiar to a few, and only became generally accepted
through the unifying influence of reform movements. It is true that
where needs were fairly well defined, the nature of acceptable
beliefs was reasonably predictable. The range of choice was confined to a limited number of solutions. In most cases, however,
possible solutions were numerous and highly unpredictable as needs
were ill defined and variable in character, and here the process of
reorganization, through the establishment of dominant and generally
accepted patterns of behaviour, was more halting and painful as
competition between alternative solutions was more strenuous and
drawn-out. The ultimate form of social reorganization depended, in
the final analysis, upon the strength of appeal of rival movements or
institutions.

It was in those areas undergoing rapid change that competition
in social appeals was most apparent and keen. The weakness of
old-established forms of control meant that converts were easily
won and the field was relatively open to a great variety of social
doctrines. The "floating" character of frontier populations was
indicative of the weaknesses of social organization and the tendency
of individual grievances to find outlet in sporadic popular movements. Schisms within social institutions gave rise to new social
movements, and schisms within these, in turn, intensified still
further the disunities in the social structure. The break with old
loyalties tended to create a disposition which discouraged stable
loyalties of any sort. Sectarian religious groups, rebel trade-union
organizations, and new political parties constantly faced disaffec-
tions within their own ranks. Offsetting these schismatic tendencies,
however, there developed new stabilizing forces within reform
movements. With institutionalization, the role of reformers was
taken by that of officials, and programmes of reform became
translated into group philosophies and sets of doctrines. Vested
interests were accumulated which sought to perpetuate the organization of the reform movement by widening its area of control. In a
sense, the organization became a repository of the attitudes and

beliefs of the followers. That is to say, attitudes and beliefs, resulting from conversion, secured justification and a degree of security when officially accepted. In another sense, the organization became a repository of offices. The leaders, officials, and even the lay members were dependent upon it for their own welfare, whether it was a matter of making a living, obtaining prestige, or simply securing status in the local community. Denied leading roles in established or "respectable" institutions, nonconformists sought prestige through leadership or membership within reform organizations.

The increasing institutionalization of reform movements brought about significant changes in their role and personnel. Points of prestige tended to develop within such movements, and efforts were made to secure accommodations with older-established or traditional institutions. The nonconformists came to accept, and consequently to be accepted by, the society in which they lived, and, in return for recognition, ceased warring upon the whole social front. Greater attention was given to the qualification of officials, and even the recruitment of new followers tended to be much more selective. While these changes may have indicated an abandonment of the more advanced claims of the earlier reformers, they meant on the other hand the attainment of many of their chief objectives. With at least partial acceptance of their programmes, reform movements became incorporated within the social structure, and their controls became accepted as normative rather than revolutionary. Such changes may be described as the final phase of social reorganization, when ordered and generally recognized controls replaced those imposed, on the one hand, by authoritarian and unadjusted social institutions, or, on the other hand, by aggressive and non-accommodated social movements. The establishment of stable institutional systems, providing for such needs as those of law enforcement, health, destitution, education, recreation, cultural expression, and religion, marks the stage when the social organization had become fully adjusted to new social conditions, and mores had grown up to sustain its controls. The cycle, it is true, was never completed, as new disturbances threw up problems of social organization and adjustment, but if attention is focused upon the broad stream of development in Canada, it is possible with respect to such frontier areas as those of the fur trade in the valley of the St. Lawrence, the fisheries in Nova Scotia, the timber trade and agriculture in New Brunswick, Prince Edward Island, and Upper Canada, mining in British Columbia, the Yukon, and northern

Ontario, wheat growing in the prairies, and industrial manufacturing in the central Canadian cities to describe the process by which controls became accommodated if not thoroughly integrated.

This process may be considered as a general *movement* bringing about the establishment of a new social equilibrium. Thus with respect to social developments in Canada, the large number of different efforts to secure reform, with respect to matters of crime, intemperance, education, the class system, and religion, together with the less conspicuous changes taking place in the nature of services of medical, social welfare, and other institutions, was closely related within a general movement of social reorganization. Further, this complex of reform efforts extended beyond the purely social to include the economic and political since problems within these fields as within the social grew out of conditions of disturbance which extended throughout the society. Demands for changes in the system of government or in economic policy were indicative ordinarily of states of unrest which found expression in a wide variety of social movements. An emphasis, consequently, upon the purely social or cultural, as distinguished from the economic or political, involves a limitation to but one aspect of a much more general social phenomenon. This limitation affords a means of distinguishing sociology from economics or political science; at the same time, however, it emphasizes the close connection between these social science disciplines.

CHAPTER II

The Farming–Fur-Trade Society
of New France*

THE MOST STRIKING FEATURE in the social develop-
ment of New France was the conflict of two sets of frontier social
values, the one promoting stability and the other expansion. The
rich resources of the St. Lawrence Valley favoured the development
of agriculture while the extensive continental system of waterways
favoured that of the fur trade, and the uneasy accommodation
between these two forms of economic enterprise threatened the
stability of the society of the colony until the fur-trade frontier
pushed so far west as to be almost completely divorced from the
agrarian community. If the effects of the clash of the opposing
interests of agriculture and the fur trade were evident in the
instability of economic and political organization and were in some
measure responsible for the eventual fall of New France, they were
no less pronounced in social organization. Most of the social
problems of the community were the direct product of the pull of
these two antagonistic sets of cultural values.

The character of settlement favoured the easy transition of the
agricultural society from a frontier to a mature state. The establishment of monopoly control of the fur trade meant that early colonization was wholly in terms of agriculture and tended to take place
slowly. Lack of interest if not hostility on the part of the trading
companies, the ban upon the immigration of Huguenots, the policy
of making large grants of land to individuals who made no effort to

*From *The Social Development of Canada*, pp. 21–44.

develop them, and the constant danger of attacks from the Indians checked rapid settlement. The state itself showed little interest in colonization. The revocation of the charters of successive trading companies when they failed to fulfil their engagements in bringing out colonists indicated the concern of the French government with matters of defence more than with problems of economic welfare. In 1663, only about two thousand people were to be found in the colony. After this date, it is true, far-reaching changes in the economic organization of the colony and in the colonial relation brought about more rapid settlement. So long as the bonds of loyalty established with the Indians through commercial ties could be maintained, reliance upon trading companies and a small number of settlers had incurred no great risk to the state, but, with the alliance of the Dutch and the Iroquois, the balance of power among the Indian tribes collapsed, and the French were exposed to English competition and hostile attack. At the same time, the depletion of the fur-bearing animals in the area immediately adjacent to the colony, and the loss of the Huron Indians as middlemen in the western trade, cut the French off from any secure supply of furs; if a supply was to be obtained, it was necessary to penetrate into the distant hunting grounds of the Indians, and this western extension of the fur-trade organization and reliance upon individual traders not only imposed new strains upon defence forces but made impossible the maintenance of monopoly conditions in local trade. Changes in defence needs, and in the character of the fur trade, brought company rule to an end in 1661 and resulted in the establishment of New France as a royal colony, and the direct intervention of the state led to the institution of a vigorous policy of colonization. The dispatch of the Carignan-Salières Regiment to make war upon the Iroquois, and the settlement of the soldiers of the disbanded regiment along the Richelieu River, were means of closing up the western line of defence left exposed by the Huron defeat. The sending out of girls to marry the disbanded soldier settlers, and the encouragement of the birth rate by gifts to the heads of large families and of marriage by gifts to married couples, were designed to further the combined objects of settlement and defence. Subsidies to local industries, the introduction of an apprenticeship system, and the importation of skilled workers from France did something to widen economic opportunities in the colony. Yet agricultural settlement did not grow rapidly. Limitations in the very nature of the agricultural industry were reinforced by limitations in geography and in political and cultural controls. The western extension of agricultural settlement was halted by the closing in of the St. Lawrence Valley, while the seigneurial tenure checked agricultural expansion. By 1673, 6,705 people had settled in the colony, and by the end of the century (1706), the number had increased to only 16,417. If the increase in population represented a gain upon the rate of settlement before 1660, it could scarcely be considered sufficiently great to impose serious strains upon social organization.

Moreover, the character of the colonists made for the development of stable social organization in the rural frontier. Before 1660, the Jesuits carefully passed upon those intending to settle in the colony, and an effort was made to prevent any persons of immoral habits from embarking or to deport them if they arrived. What colonization took place during this period consisted chiefly of families rather than of detached individuals, and this meant that no serious break occurred in family attachments. Settlement involved very largely the transfer of a peasant population, and peasant social institutions, to a new environment not strikingly different from the old. After 1660, many of less desirable character did find their way to the colony in America. The disbanded soldiers were not as likely to adapt themselves to farming conditions as peasant settlers; some of the destitute of relief-burdened French parishes were dumped down in the colony; absconded debtors and criminals escaping the restraints of justice were not entirely absent among incoming settlers; and young women of undesirable moral reputation were occasionally sent, or came out of their own accord, to marry unattached men in the colony. But the numbers of those who might have been described as disreputable were not considerable, while those who had little inclination to farm would readily have adjusted themselves if the fur trade had not discouraged such adjustment. The agricultural industry, in itself, imposed severe demands upon the inhabitants and offered few opportunities to maintain habits of dissipation which the individual may have brought in with him.

Finally, conditions within the rural frontier served to favour the establishment of traditional institutional controls. The danger of Indian attacks, the difficulties of carrying on agricultural operations, and the lack of available markets, made for a considerable dependence upon the state. The organization of the rural districts under militia captains, the development of an extensive system of economic controls, and the widening of the criminal law to cover almost all forms of undesirable behaviour were indicative of the part played by the state in the rural society of New France. The establishment of the seigneurial system extended formal controls into the cultural realm, and the limited amount of good agricultural land secured the stability of this system in the rural society. The dues and acts of respect which the habitant owed to his seigneur, and the political and social prerogatives of the seigneurs, such as that of holding court, made for a hierarchical social order in which the leadership of the privileged class was accepted by the rural population. Family attachments were also strengthened by the character of settlement in the colony. The extension of settlement along the river, and the failure, as a result, of vigorous village groups to emerge, enhanced the dependence of the individual upon the family unit. The low illegitimacy rate, before the development of the western fur trade, indicated the strength of the pioneer rural family. Only one of 674 children baptized between 1621 and 1661 was illegitimate. More important still, conditions within the rural frontier of New France favoured the establishment of religious controls upon a firm basis. Within the organization of the Catholic Church, and particularly of the Jesuit Order, there had developed techniques highly adapted to the needs of a rural frontier. The Jesuit missionaries, fired with the evangelical zeal of their first leader, Ignatius Loyola, and devoted to service in distant parts from the time their order was founded, quickly secured a strong position within rural New France. The other religious orders established in later years likewise readily fitted into the community structure; the Sulpician Order of the seigneury of Montreal, the Hôtel-Dieu, the Ursuline Order, and the Congrégation de Notre-Dame restricted themselves to fields of labour in which they were specially qualified. The episcopacy, itself, particularly during the incumbency of Bishop Laval, was well adapted to serve the needs of a frontier society; Laval had been trained in one of the schools of the Jesuits and his appointment was largely the result of their influence. The geography of New France reinforced the position of the Catholic Church. The parish organization was unsuited to the needs of the extremely scattered rural population, and, until 1679, itinerant missionaries closely controlled by the Jesuit Superior, or later the Bishop, took the place of settled parish priests. Their preaching assignments required the missionaries to travel over large areas, holding mass in each place about once in six weeks, and this lack of any regular relationship between the priests and particular groups of inhabitants, and the absence of any strong feeling of local community solidarity, made for the dependence of the population upon the central authority of the church. The unifying influence of the river highway favoured centralization in the church as in the community generally. The payment of all tithes into the Seminary in Quebec, and the retention by the Superior or Bishop of full control over the appointment and pay of the missionaries were forms of centralization within the organization of the church; the influence of the church in the choice of early governors, and the right of the Bishop to appoint members of the Sovereign Council, were indicative of the extension of such centralizing tendencies into the wider organization of the community.

If the slow growth of settlement, the character of the colonists, and the nature of geographical conditions within the rural community made for the ready transition of New France from a frontier to a mature agricultural society, that is not to say that problems of social organization did not emerge as a result of frontier agrarian development. The distance of the colony from the homeland, the isolation of the settlers, the difficulty of establishing any sort of primary group life apart from the family because of the centralizing influences of geography, the dependence of the agricultural community upon military protection, the failure of the French government to adapt its restrictive economic policies to the needs of a frontier agricultural economy, and the generally paternalistic attitude of both the state and the church had effects which were evident in the inertia, extreme poverty, economic dependence, and cultural indifference of many of the inhabitants. Society in New France inevitably felt the disorganizing influence of the agrarian frontier. But it was an influence not sufficiently great to lead to any general breakdown of social organization. Rigid limitations of geography and also culture were imposed upon the expansion of frontier agricultural enterprise; the agricultural community became a closed rather than an open frontier. Forces of social reorganization, as a result, quickly asserted themselves in establishing a considerable degree of equilibrium within the rural community and in bringing about the transition from a frontier to a mature society. In terms, therefore, of the agrarian frontier in itself, problems of social organization in New France were neither extensive nor of long duration.

The opening up of a new frontier of individual economic enterprise associated with the fur trade, however, introduced far-reaching problems of social organization which extended back into the rural community and seriously disturbed society in New France throughout the latter half of the seventeenth and early part of the eighteenth century. The collapse of economic monopoly in the trade with the Indians, and the necessity of extending trading operations further inland to tap supplies of beaver, led to the increasing participation of the colonists in the fur trade, and such participation resulted in weakening the restraints of the rural society. Those engaged in the trade came to constitute a large proportion of the young men in the colony. It is possible at the peak that close to one thousand were fully employed in this occupation; Du Chesneau estimated the number as between five and six hundred in 1679, not including those who made daily excursions into nearby woods. Though there was in the life of the bush ranger much which was squalid and mean, and little which was as colourful as fireside stories suggested, it made an irresistible appeal to the youth in the colony. Traders who returned from the hazardous journey into the interior played freely upon their imaginations—like most travellers from distant lands—in recounting their experiences, and there developed as a result a romantic picture of the *coureurs de bois* which stirred the imaginations of the sons of every habitant and seigneur in the colony. It is true, on the other hand, that the drabness and bleak poverty of rural life in New France provided little inducement to young men to remain at home. The hard work in clearing and cultivating the land, the lack of interesting diversions, and the puritanical restrictions of Jesuit priests, contrasted unfavourably with the fur trader's freedom from monotonous toil, his opportunities to experience new and exciting adventures, and his seclusion from the watchful eye of the cleric. Though bush ranging involved the sacrifice of modest comforts and of a degree of security, there were few youths who did not feel that the many compensations offset the sacrifices.

By providing an outlet for the young men in the rural communities, the fur trade broke down the isolation of the scattered settlements, and quickened the tempo of social life. In this way, it probably exerted an invigorating influence in the colony. But it carried in its train social problems which seriously disturbed the rural frontier society. Those engaged in the trade came to lead a highly nomadic existence. Fur-trading parties setting out from the settlements journeyed into the upper reaches of the St. Lawrence waterways system, and were absent for as long as from one to three years. Among such groups the controls of the community broke down through the sheer impossibility of applying the sanctions upon which they rested. Always on the move, and returning to their homes for only short periods of time, the youthful traders could readily avoid the scrutiny or coercive controls of responsible community leaders. The emancipation secured through mobility was furthered by the adjustments made necessary by new conditions of life. The freedom of the woods developed in those engaged in the trade an irresponsibility which made it difficult for them to accept the discipline of rural life. The *coureurs de bois* lived recklessly, heedless of what the future held in store for them. Danger was cheerfully faced, and privation grimly accepted. Few undertakings were too fatiguing or too perilous if they offered lucrative returns from trade with the Indians. These qualities were essential in the bush ranger as such; as early a governor as Champlain had recognized the contribution which could be made by enterprising and courageous traders who found their way into the territory of the Indian hunters. But these same qualities unfitted this group of young men to settle down in and accept the controls of the rural society. A distaste for routine and steady labour and an impatience of restraints of any sort became characteristic traits of the hardened bush rangers. These traits were the product of the conditions under which they lived. Their way of life required adjustments which involved the abandonment of many old habits and the forming of many new. The chief selective agency in this process was the geographical environment of the interior of the North American Continent.

But in addition to a new geographical environment, the *coureurs de bois* came in contact with a new culture, that of the North American Indian, and the habits they formed resulted to some extent from the accommodation of the values of this new culture with those of an old. Sharing with the Indians many experiences and problems, the *coureurs de bois* readily adopted many of their ways of behaviour and with these much of their philosophy of life. Many of these acquisitions, such as techniques of travel and manner of dressing, were essential for survival under conditions faced by the traders. Even the adoption of the attitude of mind of the native, of not worrying about the future, was necessary as a means of avoiding the nervous strain of the trader's precarious way of life. But as many of the worse features of western civilization were acquired by the Indians, so many of their most dissolute habits were copied by the white inhabitants. The presence within the neighbourhood of the colony of Indian tribes, who as a result of the depletion of furs had lost their economic security, intensified the disorganizing effects of the contact with Europeans. The demands made by the French fur-trading organization upon the native culture resulted in changes in the Indians' mode of life and increased their dependence upon their European neighbours. The disorganization resulting from this loss of independence, in turn, contributed to the disorganization of the white culture through contact with these Indians. Even those habits of the Indian, however, which were not of a dissolute character took on that character when borrowed by the whites. Customs and attitudes which conformed to the Indian culture became forms of social disorganization when introduced into a different culture. Thus simple recreational and ceremonial activities indulged in by the natives tended to assume an immoral character when taken over by the *coureurs de bois*.

Through their contacts with the Indians, and because of their extreme mobility, the *coureurs de bois* came to constitute a distinct social group in which conformity to collective ways of behaviour and collective ways of thought was maintained by group loyalties. This emergence of new cultural patterns carried no threat to the traditional rural culture to the extent that the *coureurs de bois* were completely separated from the settled agricultural community. In such places as Michilimackinac, Green Bay, and Detroit, with populations consisting of western traders and transient Indians, social disorganization was wholly confined to the Indian society. But the influence of the fur traders inevitably reached back into the settled community because it was from this community that they were recruited and it was there that they made their headquarters.

Montreal became the chief centre of conflict between the settled rural and the mobile trading groups. Situated near the junction of the Ottawa and St. Lawrence rivers, it constituted the natural geographical centre for the western trade; on the other hand, situated at the point where the Laurentian and Appalachian ranges close together, it marked the western extremity of the settlements extending up the rich lowlands of the St. Lawrence Valley. In Montreal consequently trader and habitant met. Here the traders returned with their furs and secured the necessary goods to outfit another voyage. Although the importance of the fair in the town declined with the western extension of the trade, many Indians continued to frequent the place to sell their furs or for other purposes, and their presence was a further disorganizing influence in the community. The effects reached inevitably beyond the town to the rural society. Montreal provided an active labour market for farm youth. Young boys from the rural settlements, seeking an entry into the fur trade, found their way to the town; in the interval between western excursions, they often returned to their farm homes. The drift of this occupational group was the chief channel by which the values of the trading culture were transmitted to the rural. Although the truly floating population was largely confined to Montreal, the towns of Three Rivers and Quebec, and even the old-established rural settlements between, did not escape the pull of the fur-trade frontier upon their populations. The colony came increasingly to be made up of a body of traders continually on the move; the fur-trade party, in contrast to the rural neighbourhood group, exemplified the unsettled character of community life. Problems of social organization in the rural society were largely the result of the unsettlement which occurred.

Much of the destitution in the colony was indirectly if not directly related to the disturbing influence of the fur trade. The manner in which the *coureurs de bois* were paid when they returned to Montreal, and the example set them by the Indians of living from day to day, encouraged habits of extravagance which left numbers of those, too old to continue as traders, without means of livelihood. The periodic crop failures which occurred partly because of the neglect of farming through participation in the fur trade contributed further to problems of destitution. The practice of begging spread and assumed serious proportions in the town of Quebec, and, if many of the beggars were social dependants who had been shipped out by parishes in the homeland, their numbers were probably increased by the addition of persons demoralized by the fur trade. Within the Catholic Church there existed agencies adequate to deal with the wants resulting from genuine poverty as such, but the association of destitution with begging or vagrancy raised problems which required the exercise of powers of police. The establishment of poor-boards by the state, and state support of poor-houses or hospitals, were prompted by the urgency of the problem of vagabondage attributed by the sponsors of these measures to the influence of the fur trade. More extensive controls involved the intervention of the formal authority of the criminal law.

Efforts were made by the French government or the local governmental authorities to suppress some of the worst evils emerging in the rural communities as a result of the fur trade. Trading in the woods was prohibited by law or subjected to regulation. Heavy penalties were provided for those selling brandy to the Indians. Taverns were licensed, drunkenness on occasion treated as a criminal offence, and prostitution rigorously suppressed. But such coercive measures of the state were largely ineffective in securing conformity of the fur traders to the norms of the rural society. Constant violations of the law occurred among the inveterate rangers of the woods, and the ease with which they could hide in the forests, and the inclination of the inhabitants to assist them in escape, made it almost impossible to effect arrests. The influence of the traders resulted in an increasing problem of crime in the settled community as well as on the fur-trade frontier. Acts of violence, armed robberies, and murders were not infrequently committed, while sex crimes were sufficiently widespread to attract attention and call forth measures of suppression. A number of taverns along the river front became hangouts of robber gangs, and the existence of the open frontier to the West made difficult effective policing. Criminals could readily escape into the interior, and, like the *coureurs de bois*, were often aided by local inhabitants, such as the tavern keepers, in making such escapes. The lack of respect for authority which the conditions of the fur trade encouraged gave rise to some extent to attitudes of indifference on the part of the public to general problems of order and crime. The *coureurs de bois* who disregarded regulations of the fur trade became popular heroes in the eyes of many of the inhabitants, and this partiality for the outlaw traders asserted itself in a tendency to take the side of violators of the law in general. The fact that most forms of crime in the colony, apart from unlawful participation in the fur trade, involved little threat to the rights of private property but were rather acts of personal violence contributed further to the unconcern of many of the colonists with matters of law enforcement.

The fur trade not only encouraged attitudes of disrespect for the authority of the law, but introduced discordant interests into the councils of the state itself. There developed a set of problems respecting which there were serious conflicts between governmental and ecclesiastical officials, and even between the various governmental officials; and the divided jurisdiction, and the failure of the government to follow a consistent policy, weakened efforts to enforce the law. Some of the governors, and a number of the local

councillors, under the influence of the ecclesiastical party, were
prepared to go to considerable lengths in carrying out a policy of
rigorous control of the fur trade, but their restrictions usually met
with a cool reception from the Minister of Colonies in Versailles.
The vacillation of official attitudes led to a policy wavering from
stern oppression to mild tolerance.

The failure of governmental controls, however, reflected more
fundamental weaknesses of the colonial organization than simply
that of the conflict between secular and ecclesiastical authorities.
Efforts to suppress the evils of the fur trade by confining it to
Quebec, Three Rivers, and Montreal failed in face of economic
forces pushing it westward. Competition from the English in the
south and north could be met by the French only through the
extension of the fur-trade organization into the interior. The
coureurs de bois played a vitally necessary role in the maintenance
of French control over the western trade. The disorganizing
effects of their activities were an inevitable result of the contradictions within the economic organization of the colony.
The weakness of the state in controlling the *coureurs de bois* or
checking the brandy trade lay in its dependence upon the fur trade
as its chief source of revenue. Expansion westward, in response to
English competition, involved increasing governmental outlays, and
the heavy fixed costs of the trade made necessary a policy of promoting still further expansion. In the long run, expansion was
economically as well as socially disastrous to the colony, but the
burdens of overhead costs made impossible a policy of curtailment.
Problems of social disorganization were the immediate effects of
economic contradictions which led evenutally to political collapse.

Expansion of the fur trade involved the weakening of the moral
and cultural controls of the local community and primary groups.
The effects upon the family were the most immediate, and, in the
eyes of those concerned with the welfare of the colony, the most
readily discernible. The opportunity of joining at a very early age
fur-trading parties going west gave to young boys a feeling of
independence of their parents. Sex mores as well suffered from the
participation of so many young men in the fur trade. The domestic
requirements of the fur traders encouraged the legitimate employment of Indian squaws; but demoralization of the natives, and their
impoverishment with the decline in returns from hunting and
increasing dependence upon European goods, led to a reliance upon
such employment as a means of subsistence. Such contacts with the

Indians resulted in sexual irregularities. Cohabitation with Indian squaws was common among the single young men, and even those who were married often had native mistresses. Illegitimacy, encouraged by the Indians as a means of establishing ties with the whites, increased in the Indian villages, and prostitution developed in the chief centres of trade. The fact that the economic relationships of the French with the Indians were of a bargaining character favoured the commercialization of sexual relationships. The traders possessed commodities readily available to the natives, and the desire for these commodities resulted in a willingness on the part of Indian women to engage in prostitution. The small number of white prostitutes in the colony increased the dependence of the traders upon the natives, and there developed a regularized if not extensive trade of prostitution in Montreal and Michilimackinac in which Indian women were employed. The effects of the fur trade extended back to weaken the family organization of the rural communities. Relationships with the Indians, and the free and easy life, made the *coureurs de bois* reluctant to accept the responsibilities of marriage. To acquire a wife meant settling down in the colony or at any rate making some provision for her maintenance. Efforts of the colonial governors to encourage marriage largely failed with respect to this group, and many of the daughters of the habitants were left without husbands. The prolonged absence of married men on excursions to the West further served to weaken the family and to give rise to problems such as adultery. Family disorganization, to the extent that it emerged, reflected the wider disorganization in the rural mores of New France. The pull of the fur trade made more difficult the establishment of a stable community life, and the family suffered from the general unsettlement which obtained.

The weakening of family controls in the colony was not offset by the strengthening of other primary group attachments. Inherited cultural values associated with the ethnic background of the population had quickly weakened in face of forces of geography, and the fur trade checked the development of new cultural attachments to take the place of those transmitted from the homeland. As a result of the influence of the traders, no group emerged with a strong sense of collective interest in, and a consciousness of, its obligations to the rural community. The attractions of the fur trade led to the neglect of agriculture and prevented the development of distinctions of social worth resting upon successes achieved in husbandry or rural public life. The enterprising but reckless *coureur de bois* tended to command, particularly among rural youth, more respect than the hard-working and patient habitant, while the swashbuckling leader of fur-trading parties won a position of prestige denied the public-spirited leader in the rural community. The agricultural class lacked definite social status so long as farming remained subordinate to the occupation of fur trading. Other social classes in the community were little more able to provide cultural leadership. The centralized character of the overseas trade in furs checked the growth of a well-to-do merchant class within the colony. The large merchants who reaped the really substantial profits from the fur trade by providing the necessary provisions for carrying on the trade with the Indians and by marketing the furs brought down to Montreal did not become settled inhabitants. Often they were represented in the colony by agents, and, if they personally transacted their business, they returned to France when their affairs were wound up. This outside control of the fur trade resulted in a heavy cultural loss to New France. In effect, the only group which secured large material benefits from the fur trade made no contribution to the cultural life of the colony. The local bourgeoisie, petty traders, innkeepers, and others, did not acquire wealth and consequently failed to acquire attributes of social worth which would have separated them off from the great bulk of the inhabitants. Instead of providing leadership within the colony, they were subject with the rest of the population to the demoralizing influences of the western trade. The official class, likewise, failed to develop any strong sense of being a distinctive social élite. Though the members of this group were least exposed to the influence of the fur trade, their occupation was not sufficiently attractive to offset the prestige of the *coureurs de bois*. Salaries of the councillors were extremely small and did not induce the immigration of persons trained in jurisprudence; most of the local officials found it necessary to engage in petty trade to supplement their meagre incomes.

If, of all classes in the colony, the seigneurs were the most securely established, a number of factors limited the effectiveness of their leadership in resisting the disorganizing influences of the fur trade. The Crown, jealous of the royal prerogative, took care not to endow them with powers which would have made possible the erection of a genuine feudal order on the American frontier. They were deprived of privileges of a military character, and were not endowed with any real political power. Limitations imposed by the Crown were reinforced by the forces of geography. Defence from Indian attacks required the centralization of the control of the army in the hands of the Governor, the building up of a mobile military force to wage war upon the Indians, and the appointment of militia captains throughout the rural districts who were directly responsible to the chief executive. As a result, the patriotism which was aroused by the fear of the Indian enemy was directed towards the Governor rather than towards the local seigneurs, while the militia captain in many respects became the most important person in the local community. Furthermore, expansion of the fur trade westward resulted in the emergence of a distant frontier in which problems of criminal and civil jurisdiction could not be handled by the seigneurial courts. The heavy burden imposed upon the Sovereign Council with the increasing number of cases relating to trading matters or to the activities of western traders led to the erection of a system of royal courts throughout the colony and this development brought about a steady decline in the influence and prestige of the seigneurial courts. The result of this combination of pressures of a political and geographical character was to divest the seigneurial system of New France of many of the attributes of feudalism.

The direct influence of the fur trade led to a further loss of such attributes. The interest of the seigneurs was wholly identified with the land since their economic welfare depended upon returns from agriculture, and the diversion of much of the resources and energies of the colony into the fur trade and the small returns from agriculture left them in a state often bordering on penury. At the same time, the little interest taken in rural problems, and lack of prestige attached to rural leadership, lowered their status in many cases to little more than that of debt-ridden farmers. The attempt to lead the life of gentlemen on incomes derived from feudal dues which from the circumstances of a new country could scarcely ever be profitable inevitably rendered the economic position of this class insecure. To reduce their standard of living to conform to their meagre incomes was as objectionable to their tastes as to increase their incomes by engaging in trade was disastrous to their social position. Some accepted the inevitable, and became little more than substantial farmers, working side by side with the habitants in the field; by such an adjustment the seigneurial institution was to survive and become an established feature of rural life in French Canada. Commercial vocations in the colony provided a more happy means of adjusting to economic demands, but petty trade offered little in the way of remuneration or prestige, and the seigneurs were ill qualified to engage in the more lucrative exploits of commerce. They lacked the capacity and financial resources to compete successfully with merchants who came out from France; the bourgeoisie which attained a position of supremacy after the British conquest recruited few from the ranks of the seigneurial class. The participation of many of the sons of seigneurs, and even of seigneurs themselves, in the fur trade, to the extent of becoming *coureurs de bois*, was indicative of the disintegration of the class rather than of its adjustment to the conditions of a fur-trade–agrarian society. Some of the more adventurous of the seigneurs, it is true, were able to place themselves in charge of fur-trading parties made up of their own habitants, and thus achieved a position of leadership as fur lords which they failed to achieve as lords of the land. For the most part, however, the conditions of the fur trade favoured more rugged qualities of leadership than those possessed by the seigneurs. The fur trade gave rise to a type of hierarchical organization which made no provision for such attributes of worth as those to which the *gentilhommes* could lay claim. It was *coureurs de bois* like Du Lhut who were able to assume charge of trading parties or military expeditions. The result was that the entry of seigneurs into the fur trade meant the loss of those distinguishing marks of superiority derived from the system of landholding.

Intendants and priests, in denouncing the *coureurs de bois*, made little distinction between the sons of seigneurs and other followers of this vocation. The social background of the former made them if anything more difficult to control. They shared with the common bush rangers a dislike for discipline of any sort, while their aristocratic ties gave them an exalted opinion of their own worth. For this reason, the more spectacular forms of disorder and dissipation of the *coureurs de bois* were likely to be indulged in by these scions of the colonial nobility. The demoralization of a large number of the sons of seigneurs, in combination with the abject poverty of many of the seigneurs themselves, destroyed the vestiges of aristocracy which the feudal system in the colony was intended to create. A few of the seigneurs, it is true, with more favourable holdings or other means of subsistence achieved a position of influence and prestige in the community. A very great number, however, fell hopelessly into debt, and were constantly facing difficulties in relations with their creditors. Appearances were often kept up though it meant doing without the decencies of life. In many cases the condition of their families was so critical as to make them objects of charity from the government. Appeals of the governors or intendants seeking assistance from the King for distressed seigneurs became increasingly frequent, and such appeals were usually accompanied by urgent pleas to bring to an end the creation of new seigneuries, or at any rate to give grants only to those who would not become a burden to the government. A variety of aids was designed to relieve the situation of hard-pressed seigneurs. Some secured political appointments, while others were granted the privilege of selling licences for the fur trade. Such expedients, however, offered little in the way of a solution to a problem, the existence of which was inherent in a social system torn between farming and fur trading. As the prestige of the class declined, a less desirable type of persons sought seigneurial grants. Originally intended to attract the lesser nobles of France, the seigneuries tended increasingly to be occupied by adventurers who had made money following other pursuits or by retired officers of the army who lacked other means of support. The seigneurial grants became for a certain class of persons a speculative venture and, for another class, a government sinecure. This disintegration of the colonial class structure would have been no great loss if conditions in the colony had given rise to a genuine rural social élite. But the attractions of the fur trade rendered this impossible until after the turn of the seventeenth century. The *coureurs de bois* came to constitute in the period 1660–1700 the aristocracy of the colonial society, and it was this class which set to some considerable extent the standards for the community as a whole.

The absence of any group able to assume a position of cultural leadership increased reliance upon the church. Vigorous efforts were made by the local bishops to check evils emerging in the colony as a result of the fur trade, and these efforts were ably supported by the Jesuit missionaries and by the Sulpicians in Montreal. Every opportunity was seized by the missionaries to denounce the trade in brandy, and *mandements* promulgated by the Bishop carried the penalty of excommunication for this offence. Religious and moral prohibitions were widened to embrace a great variety of evils associated with the fur trade. But these efforts were largely ineffective so far as the *coureurs de bois* were concerned. Though Jesuit missionaries were stationed at the various trading posts, and very often went along with the traders to and from the settlements, this intercourse seldom led to the establishment of relationships such as ordinarily exist between priests and their parishioners. The *coureurs de bois* could readily escape from the watchful eye of the missionaries, and on occasion successfully contrived to leave them behind when setting off on trading excursions. Once in the woods, the traders were too far removed from the influence of the church to observe their religious duties seriously, and tended to develop attitudes of careless indifference to things sacred which were mitigated only by a fund of superstitious beliefs made up of a mixture of Indian mythological and Catholic theological tenets. The irreverence of the sceptic and the superstition of the pagan became combined in the outlook of the bush rangers.

Consequently the Jesuits and the higher ecclesiastical authorities recognized that the secure establishment of the church in the colony and of successful missionary enterprises among the Indians depended upon checking the development of the western fur trade. In their eyes, most of the evils in New France lay in the practice of young men going off to the woods to engage in trade with the Indians. The *coureurs de bois* sensed this threat to their economic welfare; encroachments of the missionaries, and controls of the church, as a result were met with suspicion and no little hostility. This conflict between the church and the traders turned mostly about the brandy trade. While the traders may have had no strong religious feelings, they viewed with alarm the possibility of excommunication; few of even the boldest *coureurs de bois* were prepared to accept with equanimity the prospect of being turned adrift from the church. Accordingly, many of them developed a conscience which permitted their engaging in the brandy trade without feeling the necessity of confession, and to meet this threat to its control the church undertook to determine guilt outside the confessional, and upon such external evidence to apply its sanction of excommunication. Exercise of virtual police powers involved the ecclesiastical authorities in conflict with the secular, and gave rise to violent protests against any exercise of the power of excommunication in relation to the brandy trade. Early governors such as Argenson and Avaugour, though under the influence of the ecclesiastical party, found themselves opposed to the clergy in their treatment of the brandy trade as a crime, and Mésy, likewise, broke with the Bishop over this question. But it was under the vigorous leadership of Talon and later Frontenac that the controversy was finally brought to a head. The Recollets, absent from the colony from

1629, were brought back in 1672 to offset the influence of the Jesuits, and the protests of the governors to the home government forced the local Bishop to modify his policy. If the recall of Frontenac in 1682 and his succession first by Le Barre and then by the religiously minded Denonville represented a victory for the church, Frontenac's return in 1689 marked the failure of the church to put an end to the brandy trade. This failure was a measure of the weakening of the controls of the church with respect to the activities in general of the fur traders.

The brandy trade, and the disorderly conduct of the bush rangers generally, were in themselves serious deviations from those norms which the church sought to uphold. But the influence of the fur trade upon religion to some extent extended back into the settled rural communities. The irreverent and superstitious attitudes of the *coureurs de bois* infected the thinking of a considerable number of the colonists. Church obligations ceased to be taken as seriously, particularly by the male members of the population, as they would otherwise have been, and there was evident throughout the colony a weakening of religious fervour. Though poverty provided a legitimate reason for the failure to contribute sufficiently to the support of the clergy, the opposition to increasing the tithes expressed, in slight measure at least, an underlying feeling of indifference to the welfare of the church. Sacred attitudes, fostered within the simple life of a peasant society, were weakening in face of the increasing importance of secular interests, represented in the fur trade. Such a tendency did not involve any general resistance to Catholicism— the habitants remained passionately attached to the church—but it did mean an indulgence in forms of behaviour strenuously opposed by ecclesiastical leaders. The concern shown by a zealous priesthood for the morals of the inhabitants, and bitter denunciations by the bishops of immorality, drunkenness, impiety, and the vain and immodest manner in which women dressed, may be considered indicative of the attitudes of strict Catholic disciplinarians, but these efforts to secure reform found justification in the prevalence of kinds of behaviour which represented deviations from the strict code of a peasant society. It was such tendencies in the behaviour of many of the inhabitants of New France which chiefly aroused the concern of the leaders of the church. If these leaders represented the most evangelical of European movements of Catholicism, this evangelism was increased by developments within the colony. Though defining the issue in moral terms, the church's emphasis upon the virtues of frugality and plain living expressed a desire to maintain the conditions of a simple, peasant society. So long as the fur trade flourished and exerted a strong influence upon the rural communities that desire could not be fully realized.

The challenge to the church's ideal of a peasant society was simply a part of the larger challenge which involved the mores of the rural family, the prestige of the seigneurial class, and (in so far as it expressed rural rather than trading interests) the formal law of the state, and to the extent that this challenge could not be successfully met the colonial society was left without any single focus of cultural values. What values emerged tended to relate to the immediate needs of the inhabitants, and, in those areas outside the province of individual self-interest, they were in some degree morally indifferent. The confusion of values extended furthest, of course, among those actively engaged in the fur trade, and the *coureurs de bois* might be described as culturally marginal in all respects, but to some extent this confusion was general throughout the colonial population. Though no complete, nor perhaps even considerable, break from the traditional rural culture occurred, the increasing weakening of traditional cultural ties was apparent during the interval in which the pull of the fur trade was strongest.

The socially disorganizing influence of the fur trade was greatest in the years 1660–1700 during which period the *coureurs de bois* played the chief role in the trade. After the turn of the century, depletion in the supply of beavers in the Great Lakes region led to the extension of the fur-trade organization into the Saskachewan area, and this change in the location of the trade involved a shift from individual economic enterprise represented by the *coureur de bois* to large commercial enterprise employing a steady labour force. Those engaged in the trade became increasingly differentiated from those engaged in agriculture, and, seldom finding their way into the rural communities, they exerted no such disturbing influence as that which had been exerted by the *coureurs de bois*. Montreal remained the centre of the trade, but it became now a metropolitan centre independent to a considerable extent of the resources of the rural communities in so far as the actual carrying on of the fur trade was concerned. The break did not become complete until about 1783, but after 1720 the trend had become definitely marked. For the first time, there emerged a clear distinction between *urban* and *rural* society, and, as the urban became more sharply defined, the rural attained a greater degree of maturity. There developed a distinct agricultural group with its distinctive set of social mores. It was this development within the agrarian society which paved the way for the moral solidarity which became pronounced after the British conquest.

Immediately, however, after the turn of the century, new disturbing influences made themselves felt within the colony. As the organization of the fur trade became more complex and far flung, government came to play an increasingly important role and a greater dependence came to be placed upon military forces to defend the lines of trade and to resist the rapidly growing colonies to the south. A powerful bureaucracy emerged in Quebec, and the colony tended to be converted into something of an armed camp. The growth of a "smart set" in the capital, engaged in a round of dinners, balls, and theatrical entertainments (and in political corruption), carried threats to the simple virtues of a pioneer rural society. Scepticism found its way into the colony through the contacts of officials with liberal elements in Europe, and society in New France after 1750 felt to some extent the effects of the *philosophes* emerging in old France. These influences were confined to small circles in the towns, but the increase in military forces had much more general effects upon moral standards; the growth of problems of adultery and illegitimacy in the colony was closely related to the new demands being made by defence and war. In the end, some sort of satisfactory accommodation would probably have been made between interests identified with the rural society and official and military interests; even before 1760 the seigneurial class was becoming more closely identified with bureaucracy, and the church was beginning to lose much of its evangelical pioneer attitude—the Jesuits were coming into disrepute—and was tending to adopt a more tolerant outlook. But other developments after the turn of the century carried much more serious threats to the rural way of life. The western extension of the fur trade served to promote the growth of a group of local merchants, and the challenge of this class to the leadership of the seigneurial class and of the church was beginning to make itself evident before 1760. Ultimately, the strengthening of commercial interests would have meant a dominance of pecuniary values through the society of New France. Such developments, however, were sharply arrested by the British conquest. Both the tightening grip of colonial officialdom and the growing power of local French commercial interests were destroyed by the Treaty of Paris which transferred the administration and defence of the colony to British officials and military forces and made possible the dominance in commerce of American and Scottish merchants. With political and commercial control in the hands of a "foreign" group, the seigneurial class and more particularly the church emerged as the dominant institutions of the new social order of French Canada.

In some ways the conquest and the assertion of supremacy of the rural way of life were the inevitable consequences of developments which had taken place throughout the French colonial period. If the growth of commercial interests before 1760 involved a threat to traditional authority, these interests did not become sufficiently powerful to bring about a modification of colonial policy and avert the disaster of military conquest. The dominance of the fur trade, and the highly centralized character of its organization, had led to the failure to develop a diversified economy, and this dependence upon a single staple made necessary increasing support from the state. The inevitable concentration of control checked the development of a powerful and independent commercial class as a support of the colonial system, and, involved in the contradictions of the economic order, the state collapsed with the decline of the fur trade upon which it depended. Traditional cultural institutions, such as the church, on the other hand, weakened during the long period when the fur trade was supreme, benefited when it declined and eventually passed under foreign control. Whereas the state, in the end, broke down because it lacked supports outside the interests of the fur trade, the church obtained a dominant position largely because of the lack of other strong interests in the colony.

CHAPTER III

The Rural Village Society
of the Maritimes*

IF THE DISORGANIZING FORCES in the early social
development of the Maritime region were less far-reaching than
those evident in New France during the period of rapid expansion
of the fur trade, they were considerably more diversified in character.
The kind of socio-economic unity secured in New France by the
St. Lawrence Valley was conspicuously lacking. Flexibility in economic organization resulted from the variety of resources and from
the number of points of entry by which they could be exploited.
Early development took place in terms of the fisheries, and the
large number of different bases in the region and of centres of
supply in Europe emphasized the diversity of economic interests.
The result was the emergence of several widely separated settlements each of which gave rise to its own kinds of social problems.
The different social heritages of the population and economic
and technological conditions of life led to different sorts of social
adjustments and different forms of cultural development. Only
slowly did there emerge integrated social organizations for larger
areas which became organized as provinces. The persistence of
diversity made impossible any real cultural unity for the whole
Maritime region.

Although the colonization of the Maritimes began about the same
time as that of the St. Lawrence Valley, the character of economic
development checked any considerable settlement. Exploitation of
the Gulf fisheries by the French led to trade with the Indians and

*From *The Social Development of Canada*, pp. 95–119.

to the establishment of a settlement about the Bay of Fundy as well as along the banks of the St. Lawrence, but the hunting hinterland of the Maritime Indians was not sufficiently extensive to support any profitable trade in furs. The rapid destruction of the fur-bearing animals within the region, and the absence of any approaches to the interior of the continent, reduced the fur trade to a secondary interest of the inhabitants. Both the Indians and the whites found it necessary to depend very largely upon other means of livelihood. The raising of cattle became the chief industry of the French colonists about the Minas Basin. The Bank and Newfoundland fisheries developed as the dominant interest of French and English trading-capitalist organization.

The nature of the fishing industry discouraged the promotion of settlement. Unlike the fur trade which came increasingly to depend upon the participation of local colonists, the fisheries were exploited by interests operating from a large number of European bases from which the necessary labour and supplies were secured. Attempts to promote colonization met with the vigorous opposition of these interests which feared the competition of local capitalists and labour. The long struggle to prevent the establishment of fishing settlements in Newfoundland was indicative of efforts to preserve the ship fisheries carried on from European bases. The policy of carrying on the fisheries from home bases was favoured particularly by the British who looked upon the development of this industry as a means of strengthening the navy. In the French Empire, emphasis upon land garrisons led to a greater interest in permanent colonization. Settlement on the mainland, accordingly, took place slowly, and was more in relation to the overseas-controlled fishing industry than in response to a genuine desire for the development of colonies. The retreat of France from most of Newfoundland and from Acadia with the Treaty of Utrecht in 1713 led to the establishment of a fishing base in Cape Breton and of an agricultural settlement in what later became known as Prince Edward Island. The British, in turn, established a military garrison at Annapolis to police the rural Acadian settlements and to check the considerable smuggling trade growing up in Louisbourg. Encroachments of the French upon the English base near the Strait of Canso and upon the New England fisheries led to the capture of Louisbourg by a party of New Englanders in 1745, and, when the post was returned to France in 1748 and heavily fortified, Halifax was founded to offset its military importance. Growing concern on the part of the British government with respect to the French settlements in the Minas Basin gave rise to the project of establishing a number of German protestant communities among them, and, when this failed through the danger of Indian attacks, and the Germans were settled at Lunenburg, the evacuation of the Acadians was undertaken.

The subordination of the interest of these scattered communities to that of the fishing industry weakened their social organization. The rich marshlands of the Minas Basin favoured the development of an agricultural industry in Acadia, and settlement spread down the Annapolis Valley and around the Bay of Fundy to the head of Cobequid Bay, but, though an uncertain market for livestock was early secured in New England and a smuggling trade with Cape Breton later developed, the Acadians remained largely isolated and became increasingly dependent upon their own resources. The lack of economic opportunities, and the ease with which agricultural operations could be carried on, destroyed any spirit of enterprise and made them content with their drab existence. To some extent this indolence was a protective device in resisting the demands of an aggressive commercialism. Security could be gained only through exerting a stubborn independence in face of governmental pressures. The hostile attitude of French and English officials was the price paid for the refusal to serve the needs of the fishing industry of either France or Britain. The reluctance of the settlers to move to French-controlled areas rendered their production of less value to the French fishing base of Cape Breton, while their opposition to taking the oath of allegiance made them a threat to the English fishing interests. If heavy cultural losses, and eventual evacuation, were the prices paid, the Acadians were able to secure, by clinging to isolation, a degree of economic self-sufficiency and thus to avoid the immediate disaster of commercial exploitation.

Problems of social organization of the French settlement in Prince Edward Island, in contrast, reflected very clearly the effects of commercial exploitation and displayed the weaknesses of the precarious relation between agricultural and fishing interests. The colonization of Prince Edward Island, in the end, contributed little to the economic organization of the French colonial Empire. Frequent and disastrous raids by field mice, and other misfortunes, rendered the colony of little value as a supply base for the fisheries of Cape Breton, while the prohibition by the French government of the right to fish prevented the inhabitants from seeking other means of livelihood. Many of the colonists brought out to found the settlement were of an unenterprising character, while those Acadians induced to move to the island were unwilling to engage in the difficult task of clearing the land. The result was that the settlement remained largely dependent upon assistance from the home government. Supplying Cape Breton with such products as beef, this provisioning trade deprived the colony of sufficient livestock to establish the agricultural industry on a firm basis. The problems of the settlement were indicative of the failure to establish healthy relations between agricultural and overseas-controlled fishing communities. The burden of military support for the fisheries imposed increasing strains upon the agricultural community, while the influence of military garrisons checked the development of stable social organization in the fishing community.

In the case of the British colonization ventures there was a similar failure to relate settlement to the dominant economic interest of the fisheries. Promotion came for the purpose of securing the strategic lines of empire and thereby removing any naval menace to the fishing industry. The choice of the site of Halifax emphasized considerations of strategy rather than of economic resources. Situated in an area of poor soil, a profitable agricultural industry could not be developed, and, until the province could support a considerable trade, the only source of wealth of the town was in its function as a governmental centre and naval base. Its economically dependent character was enhanced by the type of colonists brought out to found the settlement in 1749. While the influx during the winter of 1749–50 of a number of families from New England served to promote a local fishing industry, the German colonists after 1750 and the Acadian French who drifted into the town were useful only in providing labour in building fortifications. A system of municipal relief early developed to meet problems of destitution, and the presence of large numbers of physically unfit persons, vagrants, disorderly characters, and homeless children gave rise to institutional methods of treatment. A hospital was erected in 1750 to care for the destitute ill, an orphanage established in 1752 to provide for the large number of homeless children among the German settlers, and a workhouse founded in 1759 for the confinement of vagrants and disorderly persons. The drinking of rum assumed major proportions in the habits of the population, while theft, smuggling, usury, and libel were common in the roll of crimes. The presence of naval garrisons gave rise to problems of illegitimacy and desertion. The economic and social dependence of the population upon institutions of the state checked the development of any vigorous cultural life. Governmental and military officials, and the few merchants, constituted something of a local aristocracy, but until the functions of government were broadened, and trade developed, there were lacking the supports of a true social élite. The large number of ethnic-religious groups within the town gave to it a cosmopolitan air, but the cultural effects were evident in the absence of a spirit of community or a pride in local undertakings. Although plans had been made for the recruitment of teachers, no schools were established before 1760. The interests of religion were almost as neglected as those of cultural welfare. Two places of worship, St. Paul's Anglican and Mather's Congregational, were constructed, and a resident Church of England clergyman secured, but neither of these religious denominations exerted much immediate influence in the province. The Society for the Propagation of the Gospel provided missionaries to Annapolis and Lunenburg, but for the most part, with the exception of Catholicism, the formal organization of religion was confined to military and official circles and, in the case of Congregationalism, to the small merchant group in Halifax.

The German settlement in Lunenburg did little to strengthen the social organization of the colony. Though Lunenburg was favourably situated with respect to the fisheries, neither the policy of the colonial administration nor the inclination of the German colonists encouraged their prosecution. Farmers rather than fishermen had been recruited with the intention of forming a number of agricultural settlements interspersed among the French Acadian population. The abandonment of this plan and the final selection of Lunenburg as the site of the German settlement involved the heavy social costs of promoting an agricultural industry in an area more adapted to the fisheries. In addition to the failure to select the occupational types suitable to settlement in such an area, there was a failure to discriminate properly between those able and unable to face the conditions of pioneer life. The activities of the over-zealous colonization agent in Germany resulted in the recruitment of large numbers of persons hopelessly incapable of supporting themselves in the New World. The imperial government as a result found it necessary to make annual grants for the relief of the settlers and efforts to discontinue these allowances were vigorously resisted by the colonial governors on the ground that in no other way could order and harmony be maintained. Riots in Lunenburg, and the desertion of some of the Germans to join the French in the interior, indicated that the fears of the governors had foundation in fact. The German settlement remained on the cultural fringe of the English colony, and yet lacked sufficient means to develop any independent cultural life of its own. Most of the settlers were Lutherans or Calvinists, and the failure to provide them with ministers of their own persuasian while supporting in the community an S.P.G. missionary did little to keep alive religious interests and much to antagonize the population against the Church of England. The weaknesses of the social organization of Lunenburg, like that of the French agricultural settlement in Prince Edward Island, resulted from the tenuous ties between agricultural colonization and the overseas or New England controlled fishing industry. Local industry and trade were alike discouraged, and this check to free economic enterprise not only reduced the agricultural communities to a state of economic self-sufficiency but prevented the rise of any towns except those which were the centres of government and military garrisons. Thus the English like the French settlements in the Maritime region before 1760 failed to develop any secure cultural life. Intended primarily to supply fishing bases or to check foreign encroachments, they remained little more than outposts of empire or temporary bases of New England.

Settlement in terms of free economic enterprise took place only after 1760 with the collapse of the French empire in America and the expansion of New England into Nova Scotia. A close relation between settlement and the fisheries had emerged in New England with changes in the nature of the fishing industry involving the use of smaller units and the employment of local labour, and with the growth of trade which depended upon local bases of supply. Though the decline of French interest in the Maritime region strengthened the hold of the west county interests of England upon the fisheries of eastern Nova Scotia, it made possible the extension of New England's control over the fisheries of western Nova Scotia, and the growth in importance of New England commercial interests resulted in the promotion of schemes of settlement. Anxiety in Britain respecting the danger of depopulation resulted in a policy of discouraging emigration, and settlement after 1760 was largely of people from the Atlantic seaboard. Nova Scotia shared in a general movement of population which greatly extended the frontiers of New England.

The New England migration brought new sources of strength to the social organization of Nova Scotia. The settlements which grew up shared in the economic expansion of New England. The origin of the settlers, the advantages of the direct transportation route to Boston, and the character of economic production favoured the close relationship with the Atlantic seaboard colonies. The New Englanders were pioneers from a pioneer community, and they possessed all the advantages of familiarity with their environment. Fishing, farming, or, later, shipbuilding, was undertaken, and the products of their labour found a sale in the markets opened up by commercial interests in New England from which necessary manu- factured goods, largely imported from England, were received in return. The result was the absence of any considerable problem of social dependency, though some of the settlers had to be given provisions during the first year or two in the province. Destitution was associated very largely with the individual hazards involved in fishing or farming, and those people who found themselves without means of support were readily assisted by local agencies of the community. The town meeting inherited from New England provided available machinery for poor relief. The nature of problems of crime and morality likewise reflected the influence of the New England social heritage. Few of the settlers were without their vices, such as the drinking of rum, but these vices represented deviations from, rather than any general breakdown, of the mores. The New Englanders inherited the close village organization developed in the older colonies. The town meeting and the congre- gational organization of the church moved with the settlers, and the transfer of these institutions did not involve the intervention of secondary and thereby more rigid social agencies. Settlement in villages followed the pattern established in New England, and, to the extent that whole communities emigrated, there was no break in social continuity. Even movement of individual families involved little adjustment, as all the inhabitants were familiar with the form of community organization and readily participated in its erection in the new homeland. The result was that the New Englanders in Nova Scotia were not to any considerable extent emancipated from the moral controls of the communities from which they emigrated. The strict puritanical attitudes of the inhabitants of the older colonies were brought over without any serious impairment, and their preservation was secured through the sanctions imposed by the close village group and religious congregation.

The town meeting provided an effective agency of cultural leader- ship in the villages settled by New Englanders. Though many of the privileges claimed by the town proprietors such as the appointment of town officers, the levying of local taxes, and the surveying of land were assumed by the provincial government to the indignation of people highly jealous of the rights of local autonomy, these constitutional limitations upon their functions did not render them wholly unimportant in the pioneer communities. On the one hand, means of communication were not sufficiently developed to enable Halifax to maintain effective controls in outlying areas, and, on the other hand, the feeling of local autonomy on the part of the New Englanders was too strong to be suppressed by administrative devices erected in the capital. The result was that many of the vestiges of the proprietary system persisted in the village organization of these settlements. The proprietors provided the nucleus of an upper social class. As substantial farmers and tradespeople or persons of superior education, they gained a position of influence in the local villages, and, when located in the larger towns such as Horton, Falmouth, and Cornwallis, their influence extended throughout the larger community. The "Esquires" and "Gentlemen," such as Simeon Perkins in Liverpool, enjoyed a standard of life somewhat above that of the ordinary inhabitants, but in return they provided the leadership so necessary in the pioneer settlements. These settlements, consequently, were not exposed to levelling influences which led to a complete disregard of class distinctions, while at the same time their economic progress was not retarded by a rigid class system.

Only in the failure to provide education were the cultural limitations of the village organization much in evidence. More extensive machinery than the town meeting was required for the erection of educational institutions and the recruitment of teachers. Many of the effects of inadequate educational institutions, however, were postponed until the neglected generation reached maturity, and in the meantime local pride and a consciousness of the worth of the group's inheritance preserved those cultural values which did not depend upon such secondary services as those of education. Most of the demands of the pioneer society could be met within the village organization. It was only when this primary group relationship became insufficient, and the support of the tie with New England was lost, that the need for more effective agencies to preserve cultural values became acute.

Religious interests during the early period of settlement were likewise strong among the New Englanders. These settlers inherited the attitudes of devoutness typical of the population of the older Atlantic colonies, and the persistence of these attitudes was secured through the strong link between the church and the local community. The village settlement and town meeting provided the framework of the congregational organization. The prominent citizens of the community served as elders of the church, and the town meetings assumed the responsibility of erecting meeting houses. The result of this close tie between the church and the village was that devotional services were carried on even when ministers were not available, a situation which obtained in a large number of the early settlements. That is not to say that Congregational clergymen were not eagerly sought and that their ministry was not essential for the ultimate survival of the church, but only that the character of Congregationalism made it possible to keep alive religious interests during the interval when regular services could not be provided. Eventually ministers were secured for the chief settlements of New Englanders with the conspicuous exception of Halifax where Mather's Congregational Church was left unsupplied. If difficulties were still being faced in a number of communities, the church appeared to be firmly established in the province as a whole by 1775.

Though New Englanders comprised the great bulk of the population settling in Nova Scotia during the period 1760–75, a number of other groups found their way into the province. Ulster Irish from New Hampshire, Boston, and from overseas settled in Truro, Onslow, and Londonderry at the head of Cobequid Bay and a few along the banks of La Have River beyond Lunenburg. During the years 1773–5 a large number of Yorkshire English families came out and settled among New Englanders at Amherst, Cumberland, and Sackville in the Chignecto peninsula. The first group of Highland Scots arrived just before the American Revolution and joined a number of Pennsylvania settlers in Pictou. Irish Catholics from Newfoundland and French Acadians from the mainland located along with transient New England fishermen in Cape Breton. Because of their isolation, however, these various settlements contributed little to integrating the social organization of the province.

The Ulster Irish, most of whom were from the older American colonies, brought with them much the same heritage of village organization as the New Englanders, and they tended to accept the leadership of this larger group. The fact that the principles of church government of American Presbyterianism were very similar to those of Congregationalism strengthened the ties. The Yorkshire English, locating in communities containing numbers of New Englanders, were likewise influenced to some considerable extent by the cultural values of this group. Though followers of John Wesley, no missionaries came out before the Revolution, and the form of religious worship followed by the Yorkshiremen within their Methodist societies was not radically different from that followed by the New Englanders within their Congregational organizations. The Highland Scots of Pictou had no time to establish any sort of settled community life before the outbreak of revolution led to their recruitment in Highland military regiments. In the case of the settlements in Cape Breton, what cultural ties existed were mostly with New England, but for the most part the population of the island became detached from outside centres of influence almost entirely. Here Channel Island interests employing bilingual labour dominated in the control of the fisheries, and most of the local fishermen engaged in the industry without licences. In contrast with the South Shore, temporary stations took the place of settled villages, and the New England fishermen returned to their homes in the winter after spending the summer in Cape Breton. The isolation from Halifax made impossible effective policing, and when the British garrison was removed in 1768 the local authorities were left without support in maintaining law. The large number of inlets, and the proximity to Newfoundland, provided means by which the population could evade officers of the law sent to apprehend them, and a condition of almost general disorder prevailed along the coastline.

The New England migration, and the smaller settlements in the interior and in Cape Breton, did little to strengthen the position of Halifax or extend her influence. The capital shared in few of the economic advantages from the extensive *entrepôt* trade being developed with Nova Scotia as an important base. Lacking an immediate hinterland of her own, she did not possess the resources or organization to compete with the powerful commercial interests in New England in providing markets for the fishing and farming settlements along the South Shore, the Annapolis Valley, and in the interior, while the costs of policing Cape Breton were offset by few economic gains. Some industries were established in the town—a brick factory, distillery, and sugar factory—but the government and military base continued as the chief means of support. When the strategy of imperial defence made necessary the stationing of a large military force in the province, the town prospered, but when it was withdrawn local trade declined and there were few alternative occupations to which the population could turn. The lack of economic opportunities, and the attractions of the town as the centre of governmental institutions and military forces, accentuated problems of destitution which had emerged before 1760. Hangers-on of the army fell on the relief roll when the army was withdrawn, while a continual influx of transient workers and indigent persons from outside added to the responsibilities of local authorities. In 1759, and again in 1768, the Nova Scotia legislature attempted to check the immigration of socially dependent persons by means of legislation, but on both occasions the Act was disallowed by the British government. In 1770, chiefly as a means of relieving Halifax of the burden of supporting transient workers from the country districts, an Act of the provincial legislature introduced a residence qualification for relief. Efforts to check the influx of undesirable population elements, however, failed to provide any real solution to a problem which resulted from the weakness of the town's economic and social supports, and the result was a continuance and elaboration of the aids found necessary in the fifties.

Other forms of social life in the town were strengthened little more by the developments which took place in the province after 1760. The army and navy continued to set the moral standards of the community, and the puritanism of the New England settlements exerted no conspicuous influence. Similarly, the leavening effect of the New England migration upon cultural organization was not greatly felt within the capital. The exclusiveness of the colonial aristocracy tended to be maintained, and as a result the economic isolation of the capital found emphasis in its cultural isolation. Intervention by the colonial administration in matters of local government in the out-settlements was indicative of the extension of political controls in the province, but these efforts found little support in the cultural influence of the governing classes. The predominant interests of these classes remained sharply divorced from the interests of the large fishing and farming population in the colony, and there was a failure to develop a social class equipped to provide leadership for the whole province. Ethnic differences increased the cultural particularism of the various settlements, and Halifax failed conspicuously to give a lead in establishing some sort of cultural integration.

This failure was also conspicuous in the field of religion. Apart from the Congregationalists, a number of religious denominations became established in the province—Presbyterians, Methodists, Roman Catholics, and a few Baptists and Quakers—emphasizing the autonomy of the out-settlements, and the established Church of England proved unable to provide leadership to offset their decentralizing influence. With the growth of settlement after 1760, the church, with the support of the government, undertook to win the adherence of the large nonconformist population lacking the services of regular ministers. The promotion of the interests of the church had the important object of securing more firmly the political allegiance of the new settlers in the colony. A corresponding society made up of prominent members of the government as well as of the church in the colony was organized to supervise missionary activities and to seize opportunities of extending Anglican influence, and, paid by the Society for the Propagation of the Gospel and the British government, missionaries were located at the chief centres of settlement, Annapolis, Windsor, Cumberland, Prince Edward Island, and Lunenburg. The record of achievement, however, was not noteworthy. In spite of efforts to make the church a truly provincial denomination, it remained representative of only the official and military interests in the colony, drawing its chief support from within the town of Halifax. The tie with the government proved in the end as much a weakness as a strength of the church. Identity with the ruling minority divorced the church from the great mass of the population. The bulk of the people were of religious persuasions other than that of Anglicanism, and, while the problems of the pioneer society made difficult the maintenance of their denominational connections, they showed little inclination to support a church almost completely lacking in an understanding of their needs. The failure to develop an itinerant missionary organization, and its reliance upon holding services in the chief centres of population, contributed further to its lack of influence in the rural settlements. The weakness of the Church of England in the society of Nova Scotia before 1776 was a measure of the weakness of the economic and cultural interests of Halifax. Efforts to extend the controls of the provincial capital met with the stiff resistance of the out-settlements, and the lack of support of the Church of England was simply one expression of these resistant attitudes.

The effects of the failure of Halifax to provide leadership did not result in any serious breakdown of controls in the provincial society so long as the local village organizations remained strong.

The socially vigorous and community-conscious New England settlements provided an element of strength to the whole social organization of Nova Scotia before 1776. It is true that the failure of Halifax to integrate the out-settlements within the provincial system of government weakened the colonial administration and institutions identified with this administration, but the effects of lack of leadership from the capital were offset by the strength of local organization and by the leadership provided from New England. The town meetings and Congregational churches derived sufficient support from the older colonies to function without the co-operation of the provincial government. But this dependence upon outside aids and detachment from Halifax involved dangers which became conspicuous when the American Revolution cut these settlements off from their established lines of communication. Failure to retain cultural ties with New England was to reveal weaknesses in the organization of the local community while the aggressive feeling of local autonomy was not sufficient to withstand completely the centralizing influence of war and trade after 1776. Largely independent of the provincial capital before the outbreak of revolution, the New England settlements after 1776 were to become to some considerable extent an economic hinterland of the rapidly expanding metropolis.

The shift of trade routes and the growing importance of commercial interests in Nova Scotia resulting from the Revolution led to fundamental reorientations in community organization. Whereas Halifax before 1776 had been divorced from the main stream of development, the Revolutionary War tended to emphasize her strategic position and thereby enhance her economic as well as political importance. She seized the trade with the out-settlements and with the British West Indies which formerly had been controlled by New England. But the activities of American privateers in raiding coastal towns and of American traders in smuggling commodities into and out of the province, during the Revolution, were an indication that economic integration in terms of the dominance of Halifax was not readily brought about; efforts of the provincial authorities to police the waters of Cape Breton were only partially successful in preventing contraband trade in this area, and little more success attended similar efforts to restrict the trade of the rural settlements with the revolutionary colonies. After the Revolution, the aggressive commercialism of New England continued to provide a serious threat to the new *entrepôt* trade being developed by Nova Scotian interests, and the advantages secured in the imperial Navigation System were offset by restrictions upon the trading operations of British vessels in American ports and by smuggling carried on by American ships in the Maritime and West Indian waters. Efforts to meet this competition by a policy of bounties to the fisheries when export took place in British boats led to conflict between Halifax and the outports which secured expression in the secession of Cape Breton from Nova Scotia in 1784 and in the increasing opposition of the Assembly to the Council in provincial politics.

This tendency towards centralization and increasing regional conflict was equally apparent with respect to social organization. Although the relief machinery developed in the early years of settlement continued, apart from Halifax, to meet problems of individual destitution as they occurred in the local communities, the Revolution and movements of population after gave rise to problems of destitution for which local agencies were wholly inadequate. The influx of refugees with the evacuation of Boston in 1776, the large migration of Loyalists at the conclusion of war, the periodic arrival of boatloads of destitute colonists during the eighties and nineties, and the immigration of Highland Scots, many of whom were poverty-stricken, towards the end of the century, taxed the resources of local communities and led to efforts on the part of the provincial government (supported in the case of the war refugees and Loyalists by the imperial Parliament) to provide relief. The intervention of provincial authorities emphasized centralizing tendencies in the colonial society, and the shift of the function of relief brought with it a decline in the importance of local organizations. That is not to say that the colonial administration succeeded in building up any permanent organization of poor-relief. Particular problems of destitution called forth some sort of action, but there was no attempt to regularize such activities within a general system of relief. The nearest approach to the development of institutional methods of action was the establishment of boards to determine among what Loyalists and disbanded soldiers assistance was required. Agencies of relief still remained institutions of the local community, and aids from the provincial authorities were in the way of emergency measures. But the increasing reliance upon such aids emphasized the inadequacies of the local machinery.

With respect to matters of order and morality, the immediate effects of the Revolutionary War and the expansion of trade were felt most fully by Halifax, but the developments of this period unloosed forces which extended throughout the rural society. The close group controls of the village settlements tended to disintegrate in face of the influences of war and trade, and these tendencies were considerably accentuated with the Loyalist migration. The new population elements cut across established community lines and introduced habits of behaviour which had an unsettling effect upon moral standards and social order. The most independent of the Loyalists settled at Shelburne and in the St. John Valley, and the difficulties of administration in the latter area resulting from its remoteness hastened the organization of the province of New Brunswick. Apart from these two settlements, disorganization was greatest in those areas where a large number of the Loyalist settlers were disbanded soldiers. Long association in army camps had developed habits of heavy drinking and dissipation, and intemperance became increasingly prevalent in the rural districts. The importance of molasses and rum in the trade of Nova Scotia fostered the traffic in liquor and discouraged efforts of reform such as stringent licensing laws and temperance movements. Crime increased as pecuniary relationships assumed greater importance, and the change in its character was evident in the shift from a reliance upon primary group controls to a reliance upon controls of a secondary and impersonal nature. Gaols were erected in the various towns, and the formal law came to play a greater part in the maintenance of order in the community.

More far-reaching still were the adjustments which took place in cultural organization. The break with New England, the growth of commerce, and the war led to the disintegration of those ethnic and social bonds which had grown up in the local communities before the Revolution. Some of the more respectable members of the local communities, particularly those communities settled by New Englanders, identified themselves with the revolutionary cause of the American colonies, and, if they did not withdraw from the province, they lost considerably in prestige. The Loyalist migration served to weaken still further rural leadership in Nova Scotia. The Loyalists challenged established status relationships while they failed to achieve, except in New Brunswick, a privileged social position. These tendencies of disintegration of the rural class structure were accentuated by the expansion of trade which resulted to some extent in rural business men being overshadowed by those in large centres. The efforts of the new trading interests to integrate the economic life of the province in terms of the dominance of Halifax were paralleled by efforts to integrate the cultural life. But the resistance of the out-settlements to the controls of the metropolis evident in the economic sphere was even more evident in the cultural sphere. The tenuous commercial ties provided no solid cultural bond between the capital and the rest of the province. As the forces of centralization increased subordination to Halifax, forces of decentralization, together with the incapacity of the governing aristocracy to provide effective leadership, checked the establishment of a stable equilibrium in the relations between Halifax and the hinterland.

The pull between forces of centralization and of local autonomy was even more apparent within religious movements. The developments resulting from the Revolution and expansion of trade had direct and far-reaching effects upon religious interests and attitudes, and led to fundamental adjustments in the organization and appeal of religious denominations. The period, indeed, was one of revolution within the churches which produced an almost completely new institutional structure by the time it had run its course. Old religious forms were swept aside, and new denominations arose and were accepted within the Nova Scotian society. These sweeping changes involved issues of control which extended throughout the organization of the provincial society. Efforts of Halifax to strengthen the controls of political and cultural institutions centred in the capital as a means of securing a position of metropolitan dominance were paralleled by efforts to strengthen the controls of the Church of England. The immediate effect of the Revolution was to weaken seriously religious leadership in the out-settlements.

Before the Revolution, Congregationalism had been undergoing changes which greatly limited its spiritual influence. Schisms in New England resulting from the "Great Awakening" had enhanced the conservatism of the orthodox churches with effects evident in the increasing emphasis upon the form rather than upon the substance of religious services. Though the churches in Nova Scotia before 1776 escaped the direct influence of the evangelical movements, they felt the influence of the reactionary tendencies which had set in. Among the various Congregational organizations in the province at the time the Revolution broke out, there was lacking any vigorous spiritual life. So long as there was no threat to the social influences of the churches, this lack was not seriously felt. What was lost in religious fervour was gained in social respectability; status in the community implied membership in the church. With the outbreak of the American Revolution, however, the social supports of the churches were greatly impaired. Many of the Congregational ministers identified themselves with the revolutionary cause and eventually withdrew to the American colonies, and, although the great body of members remained loyal, the churches became suspect in the eyes of colonial officials. As a result of the stigma of disloyalty, they lost the prestige and claim to respectability which had been the chief forces holding them together. Without a sufficient supply of ministers, many of the regularly constituted Congregational organizations found it increasingly difficult to maintain the controls of church government, and a spirit of acrimony tended to replace one of harmony among the general membership.

The effect of the Revolution upon the Methodist societies of the Yorkshire English was almost as unfavourable. The strength of the Methodist societies depended upon the evangelical fervour of the members, and this led to a reliance upon vigorous evangelical leadership. The Revolution cut off a supply of Wesleyan missionaries and new additions to the population from Yorkshire, and, divorced from outside contacts, the evangelical enthusiasm which had been aroused by Wesley's preaching in England steadily cooled under pioneer conditions of life. The other nonconformist religious denominations were also weakened to some extent by the Revolution. The Presbyterians of Truro were cut off from a supply of ministers from the American colonies. The German Lutherans and French and Swiss Calvinists faced even greater official indifference than before 1776 to the problem of supplying them with clergymen of their own faith. The Quakers, at no time influential, increasingly lost their identity as a religious sect when they became divorced from their fellow brethren in the old colonies. The Roman Catholic Church, though maintaining the attachments of the Micmac Indians, the French Acadians, and the Irish from Newfoundland continued to suffer under constitutional disabilities which the Revolution did not tend to ease.

The Church of England, on the other hand, secured new supports as a result of the war. Advantages which the Congregational churches lost with the increasing emphasis upon loyalty the Anglican Church gained. The colonial government vigorously promoted its interests as a means of strengthening the imperial connection. The greater importance of military interests enhanced its favourable position. Finally, the Loyalist migration brought new additions to membership and a considerable number of ministers to extend its constituency throughout a large section of the province. Yet, in spite of these favourable circumstances, the influence of the Church of England was not greatly increased. The new economic ties being forged by Halifax with its hinterland failed to be reinforced by spiritual ties forged by the church. The reason, on the one side, lay in the lack of vigorous leadership within the church itself, and, on the other side, in the stiff cultural resistance of the out-settlements. Though an episcopacy was erected with a resident bishop in charge, the control of missionary activities remained in the hands of the Society for the Propagation of the Gospel and only slowly was there any improvement in the type of clergymen sent to the colony. Opportunities to extend the influence of the church were lost by the reluctance of missionaries to undertake strenuous preaching assignments and by their lack of a sympathetic understanding of the problems of the colonists. The result was that the church gained few if any new recruits from the ranks of those denominations disorganized by the Revolution, while it eventually was to lose a number of its own followers.

The failure of the Church of England to provide effective leadership was emphasized by the success of new religious movements in the out-settlements. The evangelical preaching of Henry Alline among the New England settlers and of William Black among the Yorkshire English represented an effort to revive the religious feeling cooling within the Congregational churches and Methodist societies. The Newlight movement was a direct product of the disintegration of the Congregational churches, while Black's evangelical labours were undertaken to meet needs left unfilled by the Wesleyan Conference in England. But the implications of these movements extended much further. The spread of religious evangelism emphasized the cultural autonomy of the hinterland, and sharpened the divorce between the colonial aristocracy of Halifax identified with official and trading interests and the great mass of the population identified with fishing and farming interests. The conflict of economic interests, evident in the strained relations between the Legislative Assembly and the Council, found expression in the antagonism between the nonconformist churches and the Church of England, and that antagonism was brought into bold relief by the evangelical movements. The problem presented in the out-settlements in maintaining their economic autonomy with the loss of their markets in New England found its counterpart in the problem of maintaining their cultural autonomy with the loss of New England leadership. The relief secured in the economic sphere through smuggling, privateering, and representation in the Legislative Assembly was secured in the cultural sphere through evangelical religious movements. Eventually there emerged powerful Baptist and Methodist churches out of the ferment aroused by Henry Alline and William Black. With the turn of the century, two other religious denominations gained considerable accessions of strength and served to reinforce autonomous tendencies in the hinterland of the province. The shift to Baptist doctrines in the Newlight churches brought about the defection of the more orthodox Congregationalists and their eventual absorption into the Presbyterian Church, and with the Highland Scot migration to Pictou County and Cape Breton, Presbyterianism became firmly established in eastern Nova Scotia. Roman Catholicism likewise grew rapidly in influence as Antigonish County and Cape Breton became populated largely by Highland Scots of that faith.

The organization of these four denominations upon a provincial basis effectively isolated the Church of England in Halifax and Windsor and paved the way to the abandonment of its claim as the established colonial church. From Sydney to Yarmouth, along a line extending through Pictou, Truro, Cornwallis, and Annapolis, and back through Liverpool and Lunenburg, the Anglican Church had been forced to retreat in face of rival religious denominations. The struggle was far from over at the end of the century, and continued particularly around the controversial issue of denominational colleges, but from it the church steadily emerged with fewer special privileges and with greatly reduced influence.

The migration of Highland Scots closed the last frontier in the settlement of Nova Scotia, and later movements of population largely passed by this province. Developments in the Maritime region after 1800 brought into prominence new forms of economic exploitation which shifted attention to New Brunswick. The rapid expansion of the timber trade was the chief note in the economic development of British North America during the early part of the nineteenth century, and the St. John, Miramichi, and Ottawa valleys became areas of dominant importance. In New Brunswick, entrepreneurship from Maine and capital from overseas combined to set in motion the streams of squared timber destined for the overseas market. A shipbuilding industry developed to support the growing trade in timber, and ships as well as timber usually found a ready sale in Brtiain. The growing industrial structure gave rise to an increasing demand for labour, and waves of Irish immigrants populated the new towns and the frontier areas of settlement. Since the soft-timber lands bordered rich river valleys, the expansion of the timber trade was accompanied by the expansion of agriculture, in eastern Nova Scotia and Prince Edward Island as well as in New Brunswick. The economic and social effects of the timber trade were felt throughout New Brunswick and to some extent also in Prince Edward Island and Nova Scotia. Where the industry was dominant, other economic activities were subordinated to its interests, and there was a consequent failure to build up a diversified economy to meet the shocks of a rapidly shrinking market when British trade policy ceased to provide preferential protection for colonial timber.

The farmers and young men engaged in the trade developed habits which unfitted them for the conditions of rural life. The life of the lumbermen resembled in many ways that of the *coureurs de bois*. Neither completely detached from, nor completely a part of, the rural communities, they exerted a disturbing influence upon established social controls while failing to develop new controls adapted to their particular needs. Where there were regular camps there emerged something of a distinctive group life with its distinctive set of social mores, but the habits developed in this environment rendered more difficult the adjustment when the camps broke up and farm work commenced. Only slowly did there appear any sort of occupational demarcation between the lumbering and farming classes. This development awaited the pushing back of the timber frontier out of the reach of the farm communities, and the shift to industrial techniques requiring a full-time labour force. Until such economic specialization occurred, communities in close proximity to the timber trade felt the full force of its disorganizing effects.

The growth of an irregular labour force in the timber trade, and unemployment in the shipbuilding industry in times of depression, gave rise to problems of destitution particularly in such towns as Saint John. Crime emerged along the highways of trade and in the centres of industry, and intemperance increased throughout the rural society and assumed considerable proportions among those engaged in the timber industry. Growing debts, and a greater emphasis upon money values, weakened the moral as well as economic basis of the agricultural communities.

The growth of commercial organization in the timber trade introduced new economic interests and had an unsettling effect upon the class structure, particularly of New Brunswick. The growing body of American and Scottish merchants assumed an increasingly important role in the economic and social life of the province and steadily challenged the pretensions to social superiority of the old landowning and professional aristocracy established after the Loyalist migration. On the other side, the large Irish immigrant group became sharply marked off from the more substantial elements of the population, and tended to become associated on the cultural fringe with the Acadian French. Religious differences, especially between Protestant and Roman Catholic, hardened the social divisions forming along cultural lines. As industrial techniques became more elaborate and day labour more in demand, a social group approaching in character a proletariat made its appearance. These tendencies were most evident within the St. John Valley where capitalistic developments in the timber trade and shipbuilding industry had progressed furthest, but the hardening lines of class conflict extended out into the fringe settlements of New Brunswick. In Prince Edward Island, the system of absentee ownership introduced a different sort of rigidity in cultural organization. Disturbances in religious organization also accompanied the developments taking place in New Brunswick after 1800. The immigration of Americans, English, and Irish, and the intrusion of evangelical movements from outside, destroyed many of the supports which the Church of England had established in the province after the Loyalist migration. Roman Catholicism gained in strength as the Irish immigration brought in great numbers of adherents, and the evangelical work of Baptist and Methodist missionaries, from Nova Scotia and the United States, won the allegiance of the considerable nonconformist population and gained numbers of recruits from the ranks of the Anglicans. The Baptist Church emerged here, as in Nova Scotia, as the chief religious denomination, and the growing influence of the Methodist, Presbyterian, and Roman Catholic bodies emphasized still further the failure of the Church of England to maintain its position of dominance. In Prince Edward Island the predominant Scottish population secured the supremacy of the Presbyterian Church.

With the development of the timber trade the continental pull upon the economy of the Maritime region became marked and this shift in emphasis introduced striking differences between the development of New Brunswick and that of Nova Scotia. The

tightening bonds of American capital, and the increasing dependence upon the American market with the shrinking of the British
market for timber, were powerful forces pulling New Brunswick
into the American orbit. Railway projects designed to strengthen
the links with the United States were only abandoned when Confederation provided a tie with the continental British colonies.
For this reason, the development of New Brunswick was in many
ways more closely related to that of the Canadas than to that of
Nova Scotia. It constituted something of a watershed between
the development of the purely Maritime colony reaching out into
the Atlantic and that of the St. Lawrence–Great Lakes colony
reaching into the continent. By the early part of the nineteenth
century the chief lines of development in Nova Scotia had become
firmly established. The fishing industry and trade gave to the
province its basic social character and not until those economic
activities were severely dislocated by the industrial revolution in
iron and steel was this character materially changed. In New
Brunswick, the frontier phase of development had no more than
set in by 1800. The developments which took place after were of
a kind which involved expansion into the continent, into the
Ottawa Valley and Great Lakes region as into the St. John and
Miramichi valleys.

CHAPTER IV

The Backwoods Society
of Upper Canada*

WITH THE SETTLEMENT of Upper Canada in the early nineteenth century, there emerged the first distinctively agricultural frontier in British North America. The agricultural industry assumed considerable importance in New France and the Maritime colonies, but other interests—the fur trade, fisheries, or timber trade—constituted the main drive of economic exploitation, and it was not until expansionist forces had been spent that agriculture began to assert itself as a primary industry. In Upper Canada a similar dualism appeared in the frontier economy to the extent that agricultural settlement was related to the development of the timber trade in the Ottawa Valley, but the relation was one which did not extend beyond the recruitment of settlers as such. Once settled in the country, the farm population was considerably removed from the area in which the timber industry was being developed and thereby was sheltered from its disturbing influence. The social problems of Upper Canada were almost entirely those of a purely agrarian frontier, and consequently were in striking contrast to those of New France or the Maritime colonies.

Although the opening up of the agricultural resources of Upper Canada really began in the early years of the nineteenth century, some colonization was under way considerably earlier. The conclusion of the American Revolution released a large body of people who had favoured the British cause, and those in the up-country

*From *The Social Development of Canada*, pp. 204–24.

turned to Canada as a field for settlement. The Loyalist migration hastened the organization of the Province of Upper Canada and led to the adoption of a policy encouraging colonization. Simcoe's vigorous programme of road building had in view the closely related needs of defence and settlement, and these early efforts to open up the country did much to divert to the province a part of the great western migration of American peoples which set in after 1790 with the end of the Indian wars. American frontier farmers poured across the St. Lawrence and Niagara, to join the Loyalists about the Bay of Quinte and in the Niagara district and to extend settlement along the whole north shore of Lake Ontario. Scattered overseas colonization ventures, chiefly of Scottish Highlanders, served to push settlement into less accessible areas within the province.

This influx of population, however, was unrelated to the activities of any dominant set of economic interests within the colony. A large part of it represented a spilling over of the American frontier movement of people. The fur-trade merchants located in Montreal thought in terms of a commercial empire reaching into the Northwest, and agricultural settlement played little part in the erection of such an empire; the problems of Upper Canadian pioneer farmers did not enter into the politics of the Beaver Club. Promotion of agricultural settlement in Upper Canada by the state arose largely from the interest in the strategic military value of the area. Transportation facilities were geared to the needs of defence rather than markets, and the limitations of economic self-sufficiency sharply restricted settlement. So long as the population remained small and hugged the lake and river shores no considerable problem of markets arose. The chief concern of the settlers before 1812 was that of clearing the land and establishing homes, and the simple wants of the household could be met by domestic manufacture or through the sale of the readily transportable commodity of potash. The pioneer economy of Upper Canada during this period, as distinguished from the frontier economy which developed after 1814, was one based upon self-sufficiency, and the independence gained therefrom enabled the colony to escape problems associated with the price system.

A similar self-sufficiency obtained very largely with respect to social and cultural needs. The farm communities of Upper Canada before 1812 inherited the simple, primary social institutions of the American frontier. The Loyalist and American settlers, for the most part, were thoroughly adjusted to the conditions of pioneer life.

That is not to say that they accepted a completely orderly and settled mode of life in their new homes. The frontier was the habitat of the impatient and restless, and its very character implied an emancipation from social controls and a reliance upon individual effort and will. The people found in Upper Canada before 1812 were a product of the frontier heritage. However, though many of their habits and ways of life appeared distasteful to cultured observers from overseas, the early pioneer farmers drawn from the American frontier possessed a resourcefulness which enabled them to surmount the difficulties which they faced. The apparent absence of problems of destitution and mental disease might be taken as indicative of the capacity of these settlers to adjust their habits to new needs. Personal disorganization resulting from the sudden emancipation from all social control was avoided by the flexibility of social organization.

Pioneer social institutions were for the most part closely adapted to the simple needs and wants of the population. The family constituted the basic institution in the economy and social structure, while strict codes of honesty and morality rested upon the sanctions of the neighbourhood group, and forms of mutual assistance and relief provided for the wants arising from misfortune. Distinctions of social class found little recognition in the pioneer communities where the demands of neighbourhood association pressed so heavily upon the inhabitants. Even with respect to religion there was no great failure to meet the needs of the population. Itinerant Methodist preachers, already familiar with the pathways leading into the American frontier communities, found their way across the St. Lawrence River to carry the message of the gospel to the Upper Canadian farmers. Many of the Loyalist and American settlers were Methodists, and the highly centralized missionary organization built up by the Methodist Episcopal Church in the United States made possible a ready supply of clergy. Quakers, Moravians, and members of other religious sects who settled in Upper Canada carried with them the simple organizations of their faith.

What colonization from overseas took place in Upper Canada before 1812 did not introduce disturbing influences into the rural society to any considerable extent. Most of the overseas colonists were Higland Scots, and, if they lacked the experience and resourcefulness of the American settlers, they inherited the traditional close group controls of the clan organization. Their tendency to settle together enabled them to resist many of the disorganizing effects of new social conditions. Adjustments of the individual came about with the support of the group, and too radical deviations from traditional mores were strictly checked. This group or clan authoritarianism was reinforced by the authoritarianism of the Roman Catholic priest or Presbyterian minister. Though few clergy were available, the ecclesiastical system of government was preserved as part of the group organization. The inevitable conservatism of such leadership within the Scottish communities had the effect of arresting economic progress and cultural advancement, but during the early years of settlement the strain upon the individual in adjusting himself was considerably eased and any general breakdown of the social organization avoided.

Only in the small towns growing up along the shore of Lake Ontario did the simplicity of pioneer life give way to the greater complexity of a pecuniary civilization. Here the erection of gaols indicated the approach of problems of social welfare which were to bear more heavily upon the society in a later period. The tavern and retail store emerged as the chief centres of contact between the town and the country. The army, church, and, in the capital, governmental services introduced a hierarchy of social classes which became more pronounced as the towns grew in size. The establishment of schools indicated a growing concern for education, and emphasized more sharply still the distinction between this privileged group in the towns and the mass of pioneer farmers without. The inhabitants of the towns tended to be attached to the Church of England, and the colonial government sought to vest this church with the privileges of establishment. The erection of places of worship and rectories in the chief centres of population indicated the church's anxiety to identify itself with official and military interests in the province and provided something of a forecast of its later incapacity to serve the rural communities. For the most part, the towns exerted little influence beyond their immediate surroundings. They were garrison centres of the Empire in Upper Canada, and, if they provided the rural society with little leadership, their contacts with the country were so few that they introduced no disturbing influences.

The society of Upper Canada before the War of 1812, of course, was far from stable, but the absence of serious problems of social organization stands out in striking contrast to the later period. In 1812, the population of Upper Canada was 33,000 after thirty years of settlement; by 1851 it had grown to 952,000. The contrast between the rate of increase of population in these two periods provides in itself sufficient reason to consider the interval 1812–20 as the watershed between two sharply separated phases of development. After the war, a set of forces were unloosed which brought about far-reaching changes in the character of society in Upper Canada.

If the war appeared to re-emphasize the strategic military position of Upper Canada, the developments after asserted her importance as an economic frontier within the British colonial system. Restrictions upon alien landholdings which stopped up the flow of American settlers coincided with a newly awakened fear in Britain of over-population which gave rise to schemes for encouraging emigration to the colonies. The settlement of disbanded soldiers in strategically if not agriculturally favourable areas of the province served the purpose of defence while at the same time relieving the home exchequer. Government- and parish-assisted emigration was undertaken to lessen the burden of poor-rates and to strengthen the loyalty of the colonial population. The real impetus to settlement, however, came from the development of the timber trade. The shift from a reliance upon furs to timber involved the transportation of a bulky rather than compact cargo to the British market and raised the problem of a return cargo. The desire of shipowners to secure a profitable return load for their timber vessels resulted in unloosing upon Upper Canada a swelling tide of immigration. The port of Quebec developed as the poor man's route to Upper Canada, and the large numbers coming in this way were sharply differentiated from the more fortunate arriving by way of New York. Cheap ocean rates and a more liberal policy of granting land made possible the unassisted movement of population to Upper Canada during the twenties and thirties. Settlers pushed into the interior of the province, and backwoods communities separated by many miles from the lake shore came into being. The growth of settlement about Perth, Peterborough, in the heart of the western peninsula, and on Lake Huron marked the widening belt of population stretching across the province.

Economic expansion and the rapid growth of population imposed heavy strains upon the pioneer social organization which had been established before 1812. The opening up of the Ottawa Valley gave rise to a society of unattached male workers who spent the winters in camp and the summers in floating timber down to the market in Quebec City. But the disorganizing effects of this society were little felt by the rural frontier pushing westward into Upper Canada. The Precambrian Shield sharply separated the soft-timber lands of the Ottawa Valley from the hard-timber lands of the Great Lakes region, and those engaged in the timber industry were chiefly recruited in the cities of Montreal and Quebec from the surplus labour force of the mature French Canadian farming community or, later, from the bodies of Irish immigrants. The timber trade, as a result, did not noticeably increase the mobility of the population of the frontier rural areas. It was a metropolitan industry, involving large capital outlays—the timber merchant—and a regular labour force which increasingly became differentiated from the rural population and came to constitute rather a part of an urban proletariat.

Problems of the rural frontier of Upper Canada derived largely from the character of colonists and of settlement in the period after 1814. The great bulk of overseas settlers came in as single individuals or families, and lacked the group supports enjoyed by the Highland Scots. Complete strangers to the conditions of pioneer life, their adjustments were slowly and painfully made. The large number of failures was evidence of the trials they faced. The disbanded soldiers and commuted pensioners were the least able to adapt themselves to the demands of pioneer farm life, and contributed most heavily to the ranks of habitual drunkards and vagrants, but among the whole body of overseas colonists the incidence of failure was high. The considerable number of pauper immigrants added to the difficulties of social adjustment while it increased the strains upon the inadequate social services of the colony. The lack of agencies to provide assistance and advice to recently arrived immigrants shifted heavy burdens upon the local community; an absence of leadership in the location of settlement involved severe personal hardships when a reckless land policy made the individual selection of location an extremely hazardous undertaking. Though the local communities assumed extensive functions of relief and assistance, such agencies proved less effective when settlement tended to become dispersed and needy families were separated by considerable distances from neighbours. The accumulation of distressed persons in the small towns, the result of failure on the land or the lack of capital to begin farming, gave rise to a growing need for such agencies as houses of refuge, hospitals, and mental homes. The establishment of a house of industry in Toronto was a recognition of the new demands pressing upon the social organization. For the most part, where indiscriminate charity failed to provide for the needs of the unfortunate classes, the gaols served as a means of removing them from the local communities.

The increasing mobility of population, and the growing numbers of those drifting into the towns, added to the tasks of law-enforcement authorities. The rural society as such produced no serious problem of crime. The modest equipment of the pioneer farm homes offered little temptation to commit burglary, and the capital of the backwoodsman could not readily be removed or disposed of. Breaches of the criminal law, however, became more prevalent as the simplicity of early pioneer life tended to disappear. The presence in the country of ne'er-do-weels shipped out from respectable English middle-class homes, the influx of Irish workers and female domestics, and the construction of canals in various parts of the province introduced new disturbing influences in the society of Upper Canada which were reflected in the pressure upon gaol accommodation and in the establishment of a provincial penitentiary. The growing problem of classification of penal inmates, and the lack of institutions to care for juvenile offenders, were indicative of the increasing diversity in the character of crime and criminals.

The increasing strains upon social organization were more evident with respect to the primary and cultural institutions of the local pioneer communities. Though the family retained many important economic and social functions, it proved a far less effective social institution among the overseas colonists than among the early Loyalist and American settlers. The long frontier tradition in America had produced a type of family closely adapted to the needs of rural pioneer conditions. The overseas colonists did not share in this tradition, and the individual, accustomed to look outside for the satisfaction of many of those needs which in a pioneer society could be taken care of only within the family, found himself frustrated and dependent upon his own resources. The considerable nervous strain imposed upon overseas farm women in the country as a result of isolation, and the prevalence of drinking habits among the men, were indications of the failure of the family to satisfy such needs as that of companionship when other social supports were absent. Though limitations of the family were not wholly responsible, the personal disorganization of so many overseas colonists revealed, at least in part, the failure of this primary institution to assume functions ordinarily performed in mature societies by secondary organizations.

If human companionship was the want most keenly felt by recent overseas settlers in Upper Canada, the lack of vigorous cultural leadership left marks more deeply impressed upon the rural communities. The poverty, hard work, and deadening routine of pioneer farming discouraged efforts to maintain social or cultural standards. Superior educational attainments, certainly, were of little advantage in wringing a livelihood from the soil, while the preservation of the refinements or impedimenta of "polite society" served only to divert much needed labour or capital from the farm. This ceaseless pressure of the pioneer economy involved sacrifices which in the end impoverished the cultural life of the community. A disregard for precautions with respect to health and physical welfare imposed eventually heavy costs upon both the individual and the society. If the neglect of such things as the teeth and eyesight of children transmitted physical handicaps to the new generation, the neglect of elementary principles of sanitation imperilled the health of whole communities. The pioneer began unable to afford the decencies of life; he often ended by losing an appreciation of their worth.

This was true of educational institutions. The isolation of farm homes, and the urgent requirements for farm labour, made school attendance difficult in the rural districts. Even where country schools were established, the teaching was so bad that little learning was imparted. The emphasis in the frontier upon economic exploitation discouraged entry into service occupations such as teaching, and the scattered teachers in Upper Canada were largely recruited from the ranks of those who had failed in other occupations. These obstacles to the establishment of an effective educational system were largely unavoidable in the early years of pioneer settlement, but they contributed to the growth of an attitude of indifference to education which provided little preparation to meet the more exacting demands of society when pioneer conditions had disappeared. The social costs of some of this negligence tended to be postponed, but the pioneer society did not escape certain immediate effects. Observations made by British travellers in the country were coloured by their class bias, but they do suggest serious shortcomings in the cultural life of the communities of Upper Canada. The influences of the frontier upon a population unequipped to deal with its demands tended to a general lowering rather than raising of standards, and this tendency became more pronounced when standards became increasingly diversified.

The large overseas immigration introduced new ethnic and cultural distinctions between groups in the rural communities of Upper Canada. The lines forming to mark off the Loyalist from the American settlers, largely as a result of prejudices arising out of the War of 1812, were extended when the English colonists held themselves aloof from the Americans. The Scots, Irish, and other ethnic groups, in turn, tended to form cultural islands in the larger community. This ethnic segregation weakened relationships of co-operation and mutual assistance in the pioneer society. On the other hand, to the extent that assimiliation did occur, it tended to take the form of accepting American habits of thought without acquiring the American's pioneer way of life. The doctrine of equality went to the heads of the overseas immigrants, and they exerted their emancipation from traditional controls before they had fully learned the lessons from their new experiences. Assimilation, or Americanization, consequently, had something of a disorganizing effect in destroying the inherited culture of the overseas colonists before they had become a part of the pioneer culture.

The class distinctions among the overseas immigrants served even further to weaken the social organization of the rural communities of Upper Canada. The two ports of entry, Quebec and New York, symbolized the new social division which was transposed from the homeland to the Canadian backwoods. The attempt to maintain this division made more difficult the task of erecting new social controls in communities which could not afford the luxury of segregation. For the most part, the attempt ended eventually in failure. Only in a few instances, such as in that of the settlement north of Peterborough, were members of the socially superior class able to segregate themselves in some degree from the common folk, and then only at a price which was socially painful. Throughout rural Upper Canada class distinctions tended to disappear. Efforts to erect a colonial aristocracy through making large grants of land to favoured individuals failed to produce more than a class of speculators as greater profits could be made by dealing in, than by working, the land. Apart from a few isolated cases, such as Talbot and MacNab, landholders did not seek to secure social position by establishing themselves on large estates. The economic laws which discouraged the growth of a landed gentry operated equally effectively in reducing the farm class to a common social level. The capital, educational attainments, and refined tastes which some of the overseas colonists brought with them were little if any advantage in achieving success in agriculture, and distinctions arising out of inherited wealth disappeared when those who began with the least worldly goods often ended by acquiring the most. Furthermore, the frontier did not produce a labour group which became distinguished from the body of farm employers, and attempts to maintain traditional master–servant relationships soon had to be abandoned. The social demands of the pioneer society reinforced the economic demands, and select social circles disappeared in face of the need among neighbours for mutual help and sympathy. Only in the towns, where governmental and military officials, Anglican clergymen, and well-to-do merchants congregated, did there emerge anything approaching a socially superior class.

This disintegration of class distinctions served to release the expansionist forces of an agrarian frontier. Economic resources were not diverted into wasteful channels to support the vestiges of aristocracy; nor was the development of new techniques and methods of farming retarded by influences of tradition. Whatever course of action appeared to promise the greatest pecuniary returns was followed regardless of standards of respectability or social worth. But, while the economic gains from the disintegration of class distinctions were immediate and direct, some of the social gains were more remote and were offset by immediate cultural losses. Emancipation of the lower-class overseas immigrants from the obligations imposed upon them by the traditional class structure encouraged the display of vulgar pretensions of equality which had little relation to pioneer standards of social worth. On the other hand, the loss by the socially superior class of their hereditary prerogatives discouraged the preservation of values of social leadership accepted within the traditional class structure. A disregard on the part of both classes for standards of respectability and social worth meant, to some extent at least, a disregard for standards of moral decency. Much of the cultural heritage of the overseas immigrants consisted of rules of conduct governing relationships between the privileged and unprivileged, and the breakdown of these relationships weakened considerably the mores. The effects were evident in a general lowering of standards, among the emancipated "gentry" as well as among the common folk. The latter lacked the cultural and moral leadership of a true social élite, the former felt no obligation to provide such leadership.

The sharp division between town and country meant that the leadership lacking in the rural communities was not supplied by the urban centres. Among a considerable section of the population of the towns the chief concern was that of securing political or military preferments, and those with more ambitious prospects sought gain from the speculation in land. The economic welfare of the farmers was of little consequence. Even the retail merchants, who apparently sought a livelihood by trade with the rural inhabitants, were often more interested in acquiring land in payment for debts than in building up a healthy cash business. The pecuniary and cultural interests of the town inhabitants divorced them from the rural communities. The political organization of the colony reinforced the exclusiveness of these groups and accentuated the isolation of the rural communities. The state was closely identified with urban interests in the colony, and responded slowly to the feelings and demands of the farm population. The irresponsibility of the executive, and the lack of popularly organized parties, deprived the common citizens of an avenue of political expression. The failure of the rural inhabitants to secure cultural status combined with their failure to secure political status. Demands for responsible government were closely related to the social needs of the farm communities. Political unrest was symptomatic of disturbances extending through the entire range of the pioneer society of Upper Canada.

The disturbing effects of overseas settlement in Upper Canada after the War of 1812 were as apparent in religious as in cultural and political organization. A large number of the overseas colonists were members of the Church of England, and it was upon this church as a result that the heaviest strain was placed in meeting the needs of rapidly growing rural communities. Before 1812, the church could fairly adequately serve the colony through its establishments in the chief centres of population; its lack of an effective missionary organization occasioned little loss since it was in the towns that most of its supporters resided and those settled in the country were usually sufficiently near the towns to attend services of worship. But the rapid increase after 1820 of rural adherents of the Church of England in Upper Canada, and the pushing of settlement into the inaccessible backwoods, revealed the inadequacies of the church's policies and methods. Attitudes of religious indifference attributed to the inhabitants of Upper Canada by outside observers probably were confined chiefly to those people belonging to the national church. Certainly, evidence of rural inhabitants failing to support religious services was most pronounced in the case of this religious denomination.

It is true that the very character of pioneer society discouraged acts of religious devotion on the part of the population. The isolation and hard work of pioneer farm life made impossible the observance of many religious practices, and this unsettlement of old habits tended to the neglect of even those practices which could have been observed. Profanity appeared an inevitable ingredient in the habits of pioneer farm work, while Sabbath days provided the only occasions for such recreational activities as hunting or fishing. The lack of opportunities of worshipping collectively discouraged, in the end, private worship among individuals. Pioneer rural conditions, furthermore, tended to weaken those habits of thought which supported devout attitudes. Life in the backwoods of Upper Canada emphasized the ruthlessness of materialistic forces, and the struggle to gain a livelihood forced obedience to them. The atmosphere—and neighbours—were uncongenial to the religious mystic as they were to the poet. Yet the reality of the want felt by large numbers of the inhabitants to join in religious worship was made evident by the success achieved by the evangelical sects.

Where the neglect of religious habits occurred among the population, therefore, the reason would seem to lie largely in the failure of the Church of England to adapt itself to the conditions of the pioneer society. The reluctance of hard-working farmers to drive many miles over bad roads to attend a brief devotional service which offered little in the way of emotional stimulation could rarely be overcome by appeals to the feeling of loyalty to the church. With its dependence upon services in regularly appointed places of worship, and its reliance upon a ritual attractive to a sophisticated population, the church found itself unable to maintain the support of rural parishioners scattered over large areas. Its class and political bias served to divorce it even further from the rural communities. The concern to establish exclusive educational institutions, the partiality shown by many of the clergymen for the company of "polite society," and the anxiety of the ecclesiastical authorities to court the favour of a government upon which it depended for its privileged position, won for the church a claim to respectability but only at the price of losing its title to spiritual leadership. The shift of the allegiance of a large number of the rural inhabitants from the church to the more evangelical denominations provided concrete evidence of its weakening influence in the community. Efforts to bring about reforms within the organization of the church and to build up a competent staff of missionaries suited to the type of work required came too late to arrest its decline in leadership.

The other denominations did not wholly escape the disturbing effects of rapid settlement after the War of 1812. The great advantage of Presbyterianism in the early years of settlement lay in its reliance upon congregational principles of church government. To a very considerable extent, the people made the church, and, wherever the people moved, the organization of the church followed. The fact that most of the early Presbyterians in Upper Canada were Scots had simplified the task of organizing the church. Clan and congregational loyalties combined to favour the preservation of habits of religious worship. With the increase in the number of Presbyterian adherents in Upper Canada in the twenties and thirties, however, the strengths of congregational principles became less apparent and the weaknesses of a lack of strong centralized organization more evident. The strict Presbyterian discipline required trained clergymen, and with increasing population a sufficient supply was not readily available. The jealousy with which congregations preserved the right to appoint and dismiss those who served them discouraged ministers from emigrating from Scotland when they were uncertain of obtaining or retaining a position. The trials incurred by the Rev. William Proudfoot in Upper Canada before he received a call to a charge were illustrative of the weaknesses of congregational principles of church government. The development in Scotland of missionary organizations did something to meet the difficulties. Schisms within the church produced liberal denominations more alive to the possibilities of missionary work than was the Church of Scotland. Nevertheless, the supply of clergy remained for some considerable time insufficient to meet the demand.

Other weaknesses in Presbyterianism in a rural frontier became apparent. The obstinacy with which ministers conformed to the Presbyterian discipline tended to confine their influence to the faithful adherents. So long as Presbyterians were settled in compact communities, the refusal of the minister to dispense the sacraments to non-members of the church occasioned no great hardship, but as population became more scattered, and members of other religious denominations became interspersed among Presbyterians, the rigidity of the church's discipline made itself more felt. In sparsely settled communities, where a minister for each denomination was a luxury which could not be afforded, a degree of co-operation between the churches was highly necessary, and the Presbyterian Church failed to avail itself of the opportunities which such co-operation offered.

A shift in the attachments of a number of Presbyterians to the Methodist or Baptist denominations indicated weaknesses in that church as well as the aggressiveness of the evangelical sects. More striking still was the challenge to the Scottish leadership within the church itself and the growing strength of evangelical Presbyterianism. This movement, it is true, derived its support chiefly from the American-born settlers in the border communities where ministers, thoroughly schooled in the religious evangelism of the American West, introduced such practices as the protracted meeting and temperance pledges, but it had the effect of restricting the influence of the Scottish churches to the immigrants from overseas. The stern and uncompromising theological doctrines and scholarly erudition of the Scottish pastors made little appeal to those who had not been reared in a strictly Calvinist society. Evangelical Presbyterianism spread as the demand for a more sympathetic religion made itself felt in the rural settlements of Upper Canada.

For the most part, the developments in Upper Canada served to emphasize the strengths of Methodism as a frontier religious movement, but, even with respect to this denomination, the War of 1812 and its aftermath brought disturbing influences to bear. The cutting off of the supply of Methodist Episcopal preachers during 1812–14, the outburst of ill feeling against the United States, and the immigration after 1814 of Methodists from Great Britain encouraged the intrusion of Wesleyan missionaries into Upper Canada, and the internecine struggle for ecclesiastical sovereignty which ensued darkened the pages of the history of Methodism during the next two decades and embittered relationships within the church particularly in those areas where the rivalry was most keen. The conflict, however, was not wholly disadvantageous to the Methodist cause as the number of missionaries in Upper Canada was actually increased thereby. Moreover, to the extent that the field was successfully divided between the Wesleyans and the Episcopal Methodists, the one group of missionaries tended to maintain the support of the overseas immigrants and the other group the support of the American-born settlers.

In other respects, the organization and practices of the Methodist

Church proved extremely well adapted to the conditions which developed in Upper Canada with the rapid growth of settlement. The retention by the central Methodist conferences of the right of making appointments saved Methodism from the damaging effects of long-drawn-out negotiations between congregations and ministers such as was evident in the case of Presbyterianism. In a community where the population was extremely scattered, the Methodists did not wait until congregations could be formed, but rather relied upon the itinerant preacher who travelled from one settlement to another, and from one household to another, holding devotional services where people could be got together. The division of the province into a number of circuits, and the shift of preachers to different circuits at the end of each year, not only assured that no section would be overlooked but provided the inhabitants with a wide variety of talent. The local preachers in the more settled communities performed those day-by-day tasks of a regular clergy which could not be taken care of by itinerants.

The enterprising character of both the itinerant and local preachers of the Methodist Church was in striking contrast to the more leisurely manners of the clergy of the Church of England. The fact that many of the former possessed scarcely the rudiments of learning was little disadvantage in a community which set no high value upon knowledge. The fervour and earnestness with which they performed their duty, and the highly emotional content of their preaching, appealed to a population which knew few diversions. No intellectual or social chasm separated the Methodist preachers from their followers, and they were able to meet on a common basis of experience and understanding. The development of such techniques as the protracted and camp meetings enabled the Methodists to overcome even more successfully the obstacles to religious services in the backwoods. While the itinerant preacher sought out the household of the pioneer, the camp meeting, in turn, provided the pioneer with sufficient occasion to search out the religious service. It offered an opportunity, in communities where such opportunities occurred only infrequently, for numbers of people to participate in social gatherings. If the distance travelled was considerable the attractions of the week-long camp meeting afforded ample compensation.

The fanaticism loosed by the Methodist evangelical movement proved something of a disturbing force in the society of Upper

Canada. Work and domestic duties were often neglected to attend religious services, and the highly emotional reaction resulting from conversion occasionally led to personal disorganization. In addition, the aggressiveness of the evangelical sects contributed to a growing intolerance of different religious faiths. There was lacking in Methodism the deeply embedded liberal philosophy evident in the secessionist Presbyterianism of such people as Proudfoot. The mass appeal of the Methodist preachers did much to strengthen the popular will but less perhaps to increase public intelligence. There emerged a type of leadership which, as exemplified in Egerton Ryerson, might be described in some respects as "boss" rule; a not wholly satisfactory substitute for the rule of the Family Compact. But these undesirable features of the Methodist movement were largely the inevitable by-products of a far-reaching social revolution taking place in Upper Canadian society. Evangelical Methodism was an expression of social dissatisfactions with an order of privilege; it provided, at a time when secular means of communication were still largely ineffective, a means of outlet for democratic feelings being generated on the frontier. This political appeal of Methodism was closely related to its religious and moral appeals. The spread of a belief in temperance, a quickening of the cultural life of farm communities, and a strengthening of religious sentiments followed in the wake of revivals, and the group rapport developed through such religious association provided a basis for the erection of the democratic party system.

Other religious sects, particularly the Baptists, tended to support the evangelical movement set under way by the Methodists. As the spirit of revival gained force, an increasing number of churches felt to some degree its influence. On the other hand, the unity of the Protestant body was considerably weakened by denominational schisms which resulted in the emergence of a great variety of religious sects. The bitter conflicts between the different branches of the Protestant churches evident during the thirties and forties were symptomatic of the passing of the simplicity and co-operative spirit of pioneer social conditions. Other influences tended to widen and deepen the roots of such conflicts. The immigration of Irish peoples which began in the 1820's and continued throughout the next two decades considerably increased the Roman Catholic population in the province, and the hostile attitudes to the Irish, derived largely from economic and social sources, found expression in movements directed at the Roman Catholic Church. It is true that the earliest formed lodges of the Orange Order, emerging in those sections of the province where the population was predominantly Protestant, performed chiefly social functions; they provided the one means of social intercourse familiar to the early settlers from overseas. A much more aggressive set of lodges, however, were organized in the 1830's, almost wholly within the triangular area formed by the towns of Kingston, Bytown (Ottawa), and Peterborough, and these arose directly in response to the growing threat of the large Irish Catholic population. The bitterness of religious conflict immediately made itself apparent in the local communities, and its effects upon colonial politics became increasingly felt with the union of Lower and Upper Canada and the extension of the democratic process.

The growth of religious conflict was indicative of the emergence of new disturbances in the society of central Canada. The focal points of Protestant-Catholic antagonism were to be found very largely in areas where public works were undertaken and in towns growing rapidly from the influx of workers, and this was true also of sectarian conflict within Protestantism and of more general forms of social conflict. The increase in the number of people dependent upon wages for a livelihood, and the growth of towns, introduced new kinds of tensions in the society. The large Irish immigration, and seasonal unemployment associated with the construction industry, imposed heavy strains upon the inadequate social services of local communities, and still greater burdens had to be assumed during those intervals when the railway "booms" of the forties and fifties collapsed. The business cycle was essentially a new phenomenon in the economy of Upper Canada, and few supports had been erected to relieve the effects of its downward swing. The apprehension resulting from the increase in the numbers of those people who were not satisfactorily provided for within the economic structure found expression in attitudes of hostility, apparent in the bitter feelings towards the Irish Catholics, and in the development of new economic philosophies some of which, as propounded for instance within one or two religious sects, had definite socialistic tendencies. The increase in the number of Irish inmates in the gaols and penitentiary, and the emergence of a problem of prostitution, indicative of the wider social effects of commercial expansion and the growth of towns, reinforced attitudes of hostility which had their basis in fear or dissatisfaction.

Social alignments emerged in terms of new social divisions. The increase in the numbers of the wealthy class paralleled the growth of an urban proletariat, and the segregation which had proved impossible in the rural communities became conspicuous in the urban centres when the rise of real-estate values produced exclusive residential areas. The extension in the influence of select social and cultural institutions was only partly offset by the establishment of organizations serving the needs of the working population—trade unionism awaited the development of industrial capitalism after 1870—and this cultural disfranchisement of a large section of the urban population was accompanied by an increasing divorce between religious leadership and the unfortunate classes. Such disturbances in social organization, if little more than a warning of the kind of social problems which were to be thrown up by the expansion of industrial capitalism in the latter part of the century, had already become apparent in central Canada in the fifties and sixties.

Actually, however, the problems of social organization which emerged after 1850 had little to do with adjustments which had been set under way with the frontier expansion of agriculture after the turn of the century. The growing trade in wheat, and railway building, increased the importance of commercial interests, and it was commercial expansion which produced the town and the resulting problems of social organization. Within the rural communities, by 1850, cultural stability had become established to a very considerable extent. Social welfare institutions had grown up to meet the simple needs of a farm population; the family had become fully adapted to a rural environment; strains within the class structure had been eased by the growing preponderance of second-generation settlers and by the ceaseless pressure of the rural agricultural economy; a provincial system of education had been established; and rural religious sects and denominations were becoming accommodated to one another and satisfactorily meeting the needs of the population. A complete integration of the culture was not accomplished—the rise of the city and opening of the West resulted in new pulls upon the population of the rural communities—but by 1850 the frontier expansionist phase of agriculture in central Canada had run its course, and social reorganization in terms of a mature agricultural economy had proceeded a considerable distance. Later forces of social disorganization emerged outside of rather than within the rural communities of this region.

CHAPTER V

The Gold-Rush Society
of British Columbia and the Yukon*

DEVELOPMENT of placer gold mining on the Pacific Coast
in what was to become the province of British Columbia gave rise
to a type of society very different from any which had grown up in
the eastern regions of Canada. The phenomenal rate of growth,
the character of the population attracted by a gold rush, the high
mobility of those engaged in mining, and the isolation of the area
from the outside world gave to the gold-mining society a distinctive character. The long streams of eager miners reaching into the
interior in search of gold, and the sudden accumulation by the
fortunate few of substantial fortunes, struck the imaginations of
those both within and outside the area in a way that scarcely any
other kind of social phenomenon did. The unsettling effects of the
gold rush reached back into older societies thousands of miles
removed, and forward into a distant interior inhabited by natives
and fur traders.

The development of the Fraser and Cariboo mining regions took
place in terms of "rushes." Placer gold mining made heavy demands
upon labour and provided a field of endeavour in which returns,
occasionally fabulous in size, could be secured without any lengthy
period of outlay or preparation. In spite, therefore, of restrictions
imposed by the Hudson's Bay Company, hostile to the mining
industry, and the lack of adequate transportation facilities, the
movement of population into the two colonies of Vancouver Island

*From *The Social Development of Canada*, pp. 308–26.

and British Columbia from 1858 to 1862 was phenomenal. The influx began in the early spring of 1858. In the four months of April, May, June, and July of that year, something like twenty-five thousand persons arrived in Victoria or found their way overland to the Fraser River. Though the next year the movement abated, and, indeed, many returned to California disappointed with the findings, a steady stream of miners during the years 1860, 1861, and 1862 pushed into the mining areas. In the latter year the influx of population once more assumed the character of a rush, several thousands leaving England, Canada, Australia, and New Zealand to seek their fortunes mining gold.

The extremely rapid growth of population in such a short time imposed strains upon social organization which were intensified by the character of the people who joined in the rush. Before 1860 the lower Fraser constituted a frontier of California and almost the whole of its population was drawn from this older mining area; but as the fame of the Fraser River diggings became more widespread, people poured in from various parts of the world and many of these had had no previous mining experience. If many of the problems of the new society resulted from the undisciplined character of the California miners, others resulted from the inexperience of adventurers from outside. These two layers of population remained sharply distinct during the early years of development, and each set its distinctive imprint upon the society. Other characteristics of the population carried threats to the new social order. The gold rush involved, as scarcely any other movement of population, a complete tearing away from old ties and traditional controls, and this emancipation was more thorough because it extended to such large numbers of people at the same time. Joining the rush to the mining frontier was something in the nature of a "grand spree" for the individual. The engagement in mining was not intended to be of long duration, and this feeling that the return to a settled mode of life was not far off encouraged an attitude of making the most of a brief period of freedom. The seasoned miners looked upon their occupation as of a more permanent character, but even among them the dominant urge was to strike it rich and then get out of the country. The result was that the temptation to enjoy life to the full tended to be overwhelming, and defeated any desire to establish enduring social relationships and institutions for the future.

Finally, the absence of family settlers made for unstable conditions in the mining frontier. The hazards accompanying the journey to the Pacific Coast, and the nature of the mining occupation, discouraged female immigration, and the society became almost wholly made up of men. Only in the towns, more especially Victoria, did anything approaching normal family life appear. Some alliances between the Indians and whites took place within the mining interior, but most of these were between retired Scottish fur traders turned hostel keepers and squaws presumably gifted in the culinary art. The miners had little desire to settle down to home life and particularly in a country in which they intended to stay for only a short time. Little promise of matrimony accordingly was held out to girls immigrating to the colony, and their opportunities for employment were confined to domestic work in Victoria. Some women were sent to the country by charitable organizations in Great Britain, but the movement never assumed more than trifling dimensions.

In addition to the rapid growth and composition of the population, the nature of the mining industry itself made difficult the establishment of stable social organization. A considerable mobility was characteristic of the total population. Exhaustion of the bars on the lower Fraser led to the pushing of miners farther up the river and eventually into the Cariboo country, and this shift of population came about by a series of sudden rushes after the circulation of reports of new findings. New mining camps grew up overnight; old mining towns vanished almost as suddenly. There was little in the mining community which possessed the character of permanency.

The seasonal nature of the mining industry intensified the mobility of the population. Large numbers of miners returned to Victoria to spend the winter, and this influx and exodus of people weakened community organization in the capital as in the mining interior. The summer tended to be a period of feverish activity and the winter a period of complete idleness. The sharp separation of work from leisure meant that when working the miners neglected interests other than the purely economic while during periods of leisure they tended to give themselves up wholly to play. Placer gold mining was fatiguing and was carried on largely in isolation from fellow men, but, when the season came to an end and the miners returned to the city, the rigorous tasks of the summer gave way to the more pleasant pursuits of the winter. Emotional urges long held in restraint through the lack of leisure and human companionship suddenly found release, and, with the proceeds of the year's labour, the miners enjoyed an interval of complete relaxation. It was in the mining towns, accordingly, that some of the most serious problems of the mining society emerged. Here miners returning from the interior joined recent arrivals, and the total population tended to be of a floating character. Problems of destitution, crime, morality, cultural organization, and religion, though extending into the interior, centred very largely in the town of Victoria.

Problems of destitution were associated with the influx of people unsuited to the life of a mining community, the highly speculative character of gold mining, and the long period of idleness during winter months. The familiarity of the Californians with mining techniques, and their willingness to accept the trials and discomforts of mining life, gave them a great advantage over others in making the personal adjustments necessary for success on the new frontier. Failure recorded in terms of destitution or personal disorganization had a much higher incidence among those who lacked experience in mining. They were less prepared to face reverses, hardships, and strenuous toil than those with a disciplined schooling in mining, and consequently their over-optimism when they arrived in the country quickly gave way to despondency and despair when the first efforts to locate gold ended in failure. On the other hand, if they chanced to stumble upon a rich find they seldom considered the possibility of their luck coming to an end. As a result, a large proportion of the destitute and personally disorganized individuals found in Victoria during winter months was made up of those who had entered upon the occupation of mining from other walks of life; even in adversity, many of the panhandlers and casual labourers who frequented the poolrooms and taverns of the town were people who boasted of their family connections and educational attainments. Not all the failures in Victoria, however, were drawn from the ranks of those unsuited to the conditions of mining life. The highly speculative character of mining meant that even some of the most seasoned miners failed to secure returns from their labour and capital. The miner often had to be "staked," and he faced the risk of not being able to pay off his debts or to accumulate sufficient to carry him over the winter months. Even when the season had been a successful one in the way of returns, the miners often spent everything they had during the early part of the winter and were left with nothing to live on for the rest of the year. In gambling, drinking, and other forms of dissipation, men of wealth sometimes became paupers in a single evening.

The mining population, for the most part, treated none too kindly those unprepared to pass the severe tests imposed by the rigours of work and manner of life. Few had time or inclination to show concern for the failure. The claims of friendship operated within small groups, and a helping hand was readily given out to the needy "pal"; but there was no strong sense of community obligation, and collective efforts to provide charity met with the resistance of a stubborn individualism. The lack of alternative occupations accentuated the difficulties of those who had failed in mining. Within Victoria, organizations made up particularly of philanthropic-minded ladies undertook to provide aid to some of those in need; the unfortunate miner, however, was likely to be too proud to accept assistance proffered in this way. A form of begging grew up as a regularized system of taking care of those without means. For those with Oxford degrees or with other attributes which secured the favourable attention of colonial officials, employment by the government provided a welcome shelter from the harsh penalties imposed upon the unsuccessful by the frontier mining society.

The influx, into Victoria and the mining interior, of criminal elements from California, the isolation of the colony from the outside world, and the considerable mobility of the population gave rise to immediate and pressing problems of law and order. The danger of disastrous clashes between the American miners and the Indians was only narrowly averted by decisive action on the part of the authorities, and the gangster rule which such leaders as Ned McGowan sought to establish threatened to remove policing powers entirely out of the hands of the government. Though no complete breakdown occurred in the administration of justice, the limitations of the policing power were evident in the failure to prevent criminals from escaping across the border or evading arrest in the interior. Even after criminals had been arrested it proved difficult to bring them to a place of trial and to keep them under confinement. The frequent escape of prisoners on the way to trial or after they had been sentenced to gaol discouraged arrest on the part of the police, and, if punitive measures could not be immediately applied, the offenders were often permitted to remain at large. Instances of miners taking the law into their own hands were not absent in the distant interior, and these efforts to secure justice probably met with little disapproval from the few police on patrol. Even more difficult in many ways was the task of maintaining order in the rapidly growing town of Victoria. Here, particularly during winter months, large numbers of professional crooks, gamblers, and confidence men mingled with the miners recently returned from the summer's toil and with the local inhabitants. Petty crimes, street and dance-hall brawls and bar-room fights were frequent occurrences in the town.

In addition, the highly lucrative but illegitimate trade in whisky with the Indians constituted a serious threat to order. The proximity to Victoria of the demoralized tribes of Songish Indians increased very considerably the tasks of policing and law enforcement. The apprehension of the whisky traders was extremely difficult because of the lack of reliable witnesses willing to testify and the corruption of police officials, while the sale of liquor to the Indians introduced new problems of order when fights broke out between the intoxicated natives or between them and the white men. The increase in the penalties imposed upon conviction was offset by the high profits from the trade and the comparative immunity from arrest. The trade continued to flourish in spite of efforts to suppress it, and its demoralizing effects upon the white community were as great as upon the native.

To meet the problem of crime, agencies of law enforcement were created and improved. The administrative officials in Victoria profited by their long experience in the service of the Hudson's Bay Company, and to the tradition of law and order secured through the Company was added the prestige and power of the British Empire. A contingent of Royal Engineers was dispatched to the colonies, and it combined policing functions with such other duties as that of building roads. The number of regular police was increased, gaols were established in Victoria and New Westminster, and a system of law courts was erected for the whole area. As a result of such measures, an uncontrolled frontier dependent entirely upon vigilante committees for the maintenance of law and order never emerged in British Columbia. The presence of a large number of Californians in the area constituted a serious threat to the formal institutions of law. With the experiences of the 1849's still fresh in their minds, the Californians placed little reliance upon the police and courts of law to preserve order, and, while this suspicion of state institutions gave to the informal organization of the mining frontier a flexibility which enabled it to withstand the social strains of the early stages of the mining rush, the failure to admit the supremacy of the formal law carried ultimate threats to the whole system of justice. As the society became more complex, direct action in the maintenance of law would have become increasingly ineffectual and would eventually have taken on the character of gangster as opposed to collective rule. But this development was successfully checked by the colonial authorities supported by British elements in the population. That is not to say that problems of crime were not of a serious character within the mining frontier of British Columbia. But the existence of such problems did not lead to a breakdown of the authority of law. The tradition of British justice secured respect for the institutions of judicial administration even when those institutions failed to maintain complete order.

In the wider sphere of morality, the major problems of the mining society were drinking, gambling, and prostitution. These problems were largely confined to the towns and particularly to Victoria. Drinking was prevalent within the mining camps as within the towns, but in the mining camps liquor constituted more an item of diet than a means of dissipation. The same was true, though to a lesser extent, of the liquor served by the hostels along the road reaching into the interior. Here drinking was heavy but it took place among miners who lingered only long enough to secure food and rest before continuing their journey. In the towns, however, drinking became associated with idleness, and during the winter the numerous taverns of Victoria were thronged with miners returned from the interior. The sale of liquor constituted one of the chief business interests of the capital, and heavy drinking in the town contributed to rowdyism, petty crime, and personal demoralization.

Gambling was likewise common in the mining society and particularly in the mining towns. The playing of cards or the participation in other gambling games provided a means of passing the time and satisfied the needs of the miners for human companionship. The very nature of the mining occupation favoured a gambling spirit. Chance played a great part in the finding of gold, and considerable risks were taken with the uncertain prospects of high returns. Broke on one day and rich on the next was a familiar experience of many miners, and there was a tendency as a result to assume a careless and, at the same time, sporting attitude to the making of money. Gambling during the winter in the towns was little more than a continuation of the gambling carried on during the summer in the search for gold. Confined to the miners themselves, the recreation of gambling, though at times involving high stakes, was generally harmless, but professional gamblers quickly took up positions at strategic points and much of the fruits of the miners' toil was drained into these parasitic channels. Almost every poolroom, bar, and barber shop in Victoria combined gambling with its legitimate function, and, wherever any concentration of miners took place, small knots of earnest gamblers were to be found.

Prostitution emerged inevitably out of a situation in which the population was predominantly male and was engaged in an occupation which brought in ready cash. The inaccessibility of the area to prostitutes from outside was offset by the proximity to Victoria of a large demoralized Indian population, and a regular trade grew up between the town and the native encampments. Squaws plied the streets of Victoria, and brothels, under the management of white men, were established in the town and along the road leading to the Indian villages. The survival of practices of slavery among the Indians promoted prostitution as girls were virtually sold to white managers. The traffic in Indian females became closely linked with the liquor traffic, and the trade in the one promoted the trade in the other. Prostitutes served as go-betweens in the sale of whisky to the Indians, and the demoralization resulting from the drinking of whisky increased reliance upon prostitution. At the height of the mining boom, the traffic assumed considerable proportions. As the community became older, and links with the outside world closer, professional prostitutes began to replace those secured from the Indian tribes.

Within the community, movements emerged to raise moral standards. The small but substantial group of respectable heads of families in Victoria became increasingly alarmed as the widespread immorality of the society began to threaten their own security. Efforts to establish healthy recreational facilities and to promote reforms such as temperance were indicative of the growing moral consciousness of the community, and more stringent police regulations were secured to support these informal controls. But such measures of reform were more in the way of guarding against the moral contamination of contacts with the mining masses than in the way of raising the moral standards of the miners themselves. The temperance reformers and youth leaders played heavily upon their claims to respectability, and their usefulness was confined very largely to those who belonged to the exclusive circles of Victoria society. Moral reform among the mining population awaited leadership which relied upon appeals to their distinctive interests, and such leadership developed slowly without the aid of the family group.

Like problems of morality, those of cultural organization revealed in striking fashion the effects of the rapid growth and instability of the mining society. The population was made up of a great number of nationalities suddenly thrown together in a community where no sort of segregation was possible. Canadians, Americans, Australians, New Zealanders, English, Irish, Scots, and various national groups from Europe jostled together along the trails into the mining interior or within the mining towns. To some extent the English, and particularly those who boasted university degrees or aristocratic ancestry, kept themselves apart from the rest of the population, but such distinctions tended to be artificial and aroused no recognition on the part of the general population. The cultural heritages of the various groups were largely lost in the general mixture of nationalities. Social divisions did appear along economic or political lines, but they tended to emphasize the lack of distinctive features within the mining population. The older inhabitants in the colony had been traders in the Hudson's Bay Company, and, identified with government employment, they considered themselves something of an aristocracy apart from the great mass of miners. The struggle for responsible government hardened the lines marking off this privileged group, and the prerogatives of class superiority became caught up in political issues. The acrimonious relations between newspapers in the colony reflected underlying animosities between economic and cultural groups.

Other social divisions quickly developed in the colony along racial lines. The inherited antagonism of the Americans to Negroes came to the fore when large numbers of the dark race, many of them escaped slaves, found their way into Victoria and some of the smaller mining towns. Displays of racial tolerance on the part

of the British peoples served only to aggravate the strained relationships by giving the Negroes an undue sense of their importance
and thereby irritating even more the American populace. Riots in
the theatre of Victoria and bitter controversies over the issue of
attendance of Negroes at religious worship were indicative of the
intensity of the racial conflict. Besides the Negroes, the Chinese
constituted something of a despised race in the mining society,
though their general inoffensiveness provided little occasion for
acts of vituperation. The Chinese worked the diggings abandoned
by the whites, and, so long as apparently inexhaustible supplies of
gold were to be found further inland, their presence aroused little
resentment by the miners. It was when the supplies began to be
exhausted, and opportunities for employment scarce, that feelings
of racial antagonism towards the Chinese became widespread
among the population. Economic recession and eventual industrialization finally crystallized the extremely bitter issue of Oriental
immigration.

Institutions developed to provide cultural leadership, but little
support was secured from the great mass of gold-hungry miners.
Newspapers played the chief role in arousing opinion about public
issues and in developing a community consciousness. The reform
editor who boldly challenged the vested privileges of party, class,
and church won a position of influence equal to that attained by
the evangelical religious leaders in the older Canadian colonies.
But the newspapers of the time, and particularly those appealing
to a somewhat crude and preoccupied mining population, set no
high standards of propriety in manners of expression or questions of
discussion, and accordingly took no conspicuous lead in the raising
of the cultural level of the mining community. Fraternal societies
and clubs made their appearance in Victoria and New Westminster
where there was a concentration of persons of wealth and leisure,
and libraries were established to serve the needs of the reading
public, but few of the large body of miners profited from these
cultural agencies. Similarly, education remained an insignificant
cultural force, though institutions grew up under the direction
largely of the church or private individuals to provide instruction
to children found in the larger centres. The absence of the family
accounted for much of the weakness of cultural organization, as
the effects of its absence extended into every sphere of social life.
Cultural values were forgotten in the mad search for gold. The
character of the mining society emphasized the present at the

expense of the past and future. The community inherited no rich cultural life and it built up no tradition to be passed on to new generations.

Concentration upon the present became still more conspicuous in the weakness of religious organization. If the miners gave little attention to the future, they were likely to prepare even less for life in the hereafter. The nature of their occupation discouraged attitudes of devoutness, and carelessness towards matters of religion was enhanced by the absence of female companionship. There is little evidence that the miners, cut off from any sort of religious service, felt the lack of means of worship as, for instance, did many of the pioneers of Upper Canada. Some of them, it is true, carried with them to the mining frontier habits of devoutness which persisted within the highly materialistic social milieu. But most of them quite cheerfully accepted a state in which the minister of the gospel did not enter to disturb the customary disregard of the Sabbath or the indulgence in playful vices.

Vigorous efforts were made by the various churches to propagate the faith on the mining frontier, and some success was achieved by the more enterprising of the missionaries. Roman Catholic, Church of England, Congregational, Presbyterian, and Wesleyan denominations were represented, and the first two quickly became organized into bishoprics. Proselytization among the native populations gave to the churches a vast constituency in which to work, and, for the most part, the same missionary organization was employed in serving the mining communities. The Roman Catholic Church had become most deeply entrenched in the work with the Indians, but the Church of England secured the advantages of official recognition and enjoyed a privileged position. The bitterly controversial issues in the politics of the colony were closely identified with the issue of Church of England supremacy, and attacks upon the governing clique were indistinguishable from attacks upon the hierarchy of the church. Much of the attention directed towards religious matters in the colony, as a result, was concerned with questions of privilege rather than with those of spiritual leadership. The Church of England, as so often in colonial possessions, sacrificed the goodwill of the great mass of the people in return for the uncertain advantage of securing official favour. The bitter attacks made upon it in the press and on the platform lowered the tone of political life and served to bring religion into discredit.

These controversies, of course, were largely confined to Victoria and New Westminster. Within the mining interior the various missionaries carried on their work with less regard to matters of politics or denominational rivalry. The highly mobile character of the mining population made the task of holding religious services an extremely difficult one. Towns or mining camps suddenly grew up and then as suddenly disappeared, and efforts, particularly of the Church of England, to build places of worship were largely wasted when depopulation left church buildings without congregations. Even itinerant missionary activities proved largely ineffectual as miners were often isolated in groups of two or three and few of them showed any inclination to go long distances to a religious service on the only day in the week in which they could rest and attend to such menial tasks as cooking and mending. In a frontier mining community such as British Columbia there was no great concentration of miners settled in village communities with their wives and families, and opportunities of evangelization like those seized by Wesley among the miners in England did not occur. Religious evangelism made no conspicuous headway among the population. The highly individualistic character of placer gold mining may have been in part responsible, but even more the absence of a female population left religion without its chief support. Social reorganization on any sort of permanent foundation awaited the establishment of the family, and the slowness with which this basic institution was introduced checked reorganizing movements such as religious evangelism.

In a sense, the reorganization of the mining society never became complete. As the community became older, and the rapid influx of population into the area came to an end, the institutional structure was able to embrace a greater number of the needs of the population. The administration of government underwent improvement, systems of police and courts of law were extended and made more effective, charitable organizations and recreational facilities developed, the moral sense of the community became more alive to the dangers of intemperance and vice, the basis of a system of elementary public schools was laid, and churches gained prestige with the erection of permanent and imposing places of worship.

But these gains were being made at the very time when exhaustion of gold was bringing near to collapse the whole economic structure erected upon the foundation of mining. In British Columbia there was no easy transition from a frontier to a diversified economy. In many respects, the mining society was swept aside before a new society could be erected. Other industries, such as farming and lumbering, grew up around mining and eventually came to supplant it in large part, but the labour force and capital structure fostered by the mining boom could not be supported by these secondary economic activities, and adjustment involved the painful processes of depopulation and economic recession. To some extent development after 1870 took place upon the economic wreckage left behind with the passing of the mining period. Eventually the potentialities of the area were sufficiently attractive to promote new economic activities and the erection of a society upon a more secure basis. By the latter part of the century the sweep of industrial-capitalist forces generated in eastern Canada was wide enough to embrace the Pacific region. Economic growth took place in terms of the links forged by the Canadian Pacific Railway, and British Columbia became now a frontier of industrialism.

The opening up and exploitation of the mining resources of the Kootenay were part of the process of industrialization which included the development of the lumbering industry, the fisheries, fruit growing and canning. While industrialism in British Columbia, however, led to an increasing emphasis upon capital in mining as in other activities, a new frontier emerged in the Yukon where individual miners once more took the lead. The Yukon inherited many of the economic techniques of the Fraser River and Cariboo mining areas, and developments during the period 1897–1905 resembled in many respects those which had taken place in British Columbia forty years earlier. The undoubted richness in gold of the Klondike River bed, and the subsidiary streams of the Yukon, quickly attracted a large body of experienced prospectors and miners once the first discoveries had been made. But very soon fabulous stories of enormous wealth spread, and there followed a mad rush into the area of people from all walks of life. Reports of the hardships of the trip, and lurid descriptions of society in the mining camps, served only to fire the imagination of those seeking release from the boredom of life in settled communities. Something like 40,000 people found their way into the area during the period of the rush; the police estimated the population on January 10, 1899, as 28,018.

Of these the great majority were people who lacked any previous experience in mining. The Yukon made an appeal which attracted an overwhelming number of raw recruits who were only painfully

organized into a disciplined army of miners. It was this body of
gold seekers, composed of men of all ages and of a great variety of
occupations and social backgrounds, who proved so difficult to
absorb during the period of rapid development from 1898 to 1902.
In contrast, the seasoned American and Australian miners, like the
Californians in British Columbia, readily adapted themselves to life
in the diggings. On the other hand, the Americans and Australians,
by the very fact that they had previous experience in mining,
carried with them habits of thought which clashed with inherited
British cultural values, and this conflict of authority was to prove
a seriously disturbing factor in the political and social life of the
Yukon. Problems of law enforcement, morality, cultural organization, and religion reflected the pull of these two opposing systems
of thought, and, if the stubborn individualism of the seasoned
miners checked the establishment of order through constituted
authority, the intolerance of the Canadian official class prevented
the easy working of the informal controls of the miners' code.
These problems were complicated by the influx along with Americans and Australians of numerous other ethnic and racial groups.
The diversified cultural heritages of the Yukon population made
difficult the establishment of any set of social values either through
constituted authority or voluntary association.

The large number of professional criminals, gamblers, whisky
runners, and prostitutes who arrived in Dawson during the period
of the rush added to the problem of erecting a stable social organization. In many respects, the activities of these parasitical groups
were subject to the control of the code of the seasoned miners and
suitable sanctions had evolved, but such activities were not recognized, except within the criminal code, in the system of Canadian
cultural values which had been imported from without. The
formal machinery of the state proved highly effective in dealing with
the depredations of the criminal, but efforts to treat the activities
of gamblers and prostitutes as crimes resulted in releasing such
people from the more effective controls of the informal community.
Though unrecognized by authority, the gamblers and prostitutes in
Dawson City constituted an unavoidable element within the population. The predominance of men in the mining population enhanced the disorganizing influence of parasitical social groups.
Some women came in with, or later joined, their husbands, but
the female population for the most part consisted of public
entertainers, dance-hall girls, and prostitutes. The free flow of gold

in the community encouraged such occupations, while other occupations were lacking to attract more respectable women. Dawson
with its mining hinterland was a male society, and it was the needs
of the men which determined very largely the kind of services and
social institutions found in the community.

The nature of placer gold mining in the Yukon added to the
difficulty of erecting stable social institutions. Even more speculative in character than that in the Fraser and Cariboo had been,
gold mining in the Yukon led to a population which was kept
continually on the alert, waiting to hear of new finds richer than
anything which had already been discovered. Dawson City was
something of a nerve centre of the whole area, and here newcomers
and returned miners congregated, ready to dash off at the first
whisperings of a strike. Rumour came to play a dominant part in
setting in motion the springs of collective action, and sudden
rushes punctuated the constant milling around of the aimless mass
of gold seekers. The tempo of the society of Dawson as a result was
kept at fever pitch. While one part of the population was anxiously
waiting opportunities to stake profitable claims, another part was
recklessly spending the returns from previous operations. The
seasonal nature of the mining occupation intensified the unsettled
character of society in Dawson. While the long days of the Arctic
summer led to a period of strenuous activity in the diggings, the
long nights of the Arctic winter led to a period of relative inactivity
in Dawson. There was little time during the summer for such menial
tasks as the cooking of proper foods; there was a great deal of time
in winter for loafing and dissipation. Dance halls and saloons
thrived in a climate where warmth and cheerful illumination were
not easy to find.

The geography of the Yukon basin tended to concentrate the
population in and about Dawson. The richest of the creeks were
not far distant, and all the creeks upon which mining took place
were tributaries of the Yukon or Klondike rivers which joined at
the site of the town. Other mining centres—Circle City, Rampart,
Nome, Sunrise, and Fairbanks—grew up in the Alaska territory,
but the Yukon developed largely in isolation from these areas.
There was not, as in British Columbia, a string of mining towns
or camps reaching far into the interior, each serving the more
immediate needs of the population though depending upon larger
centres to supply a number of secondary services. Centralization
within the one town of Dawson intensified very considerably the

problem of community organization. Here the task was faced of converting a huge mining camp into a stable community. A complete lack of sewerage facilities, sidewalks, and zoning restrictions was an inevitable accompaniment of conditions where the first residents simply pitched tents or built rude shacks preparatory to engaging in prospecting and mining operations. The cabins of the mining creeks reached back into the town, and there was virtually no distinction between the mining population and town residents.

Other factors enhanced the dominance of the mining population within the town of Dawson itself. Unlike Victoria, which had grown up as a fur-trading post and which continued to support a local aristocracy of officials sharply divorced from mining interests, Dawson lacked any tradition of past greatness and contained no population identified with rival interests to mining. The erection of the miners' tents or shacks marked the beginnings of the town's history, and the few government officials who later came in never became socially differentiated from the great mass of inhabitants. Business and social services emphasized the absence of needs other than those of a mining population. Dawson was completely exposed to the influences of the frontier which surrounded it on all sides. Within the town as a result the disorganizing features of the mining society were sharply focused.

The disorganization of the society was more complete because of the short time within which the gold rush took place. Though miners had come into the Yukon in the early 1890's and there were many new arrivals after 1900, the mass movement of goldseekers occupied little more than eighteen months. The influx of population did not occur in terms of a number of waves between which there were periods of adjustment but rather took place in terms of one mighty wave which was only checked through the lack of winter transportation facilities. The whole community was populated by newcomers at the same time, and the result was an almost complete absence of experience within the community upon which to erect stable social institutions. Few societies of comparable population were ever so completely unorganized as that of the Yukon in the early summer of 1898. Orderly social relationships and social controls were almost entirely lacking where all the members of the community had been suddenly brought together for the first time.

Yet the very factors which accentuated the early disorganization of the mining society promoted the establishment of a new social order. The growth of a community consciousness and the erection of a network of social institutions and controls proceeded rapidly in an environment where all the people had equally few ties with the past, experienced much the same kind of problems of livelihood, and were engaged in the same occupation of gold mining. The completeness of the break with the society of the outside world and the concentration upon a single economic interest meant that new adjustments came about readily and tended to proceed at the same rate among all the members of the group. Cultural conflict as a result did not seriously delay the creation of a new social order. It is true that the old miners disliked the newcomers and that bitter controversies raged about issues of government and the regulation of mining, but these conflicts were not a reflection of deeply embedded interests which set up barriers between social groups and made effective collective action difficult. The absence of privilege and vested interest as means of establishing authority in the Yukon allowed freer expression to the natural impulses of the population, and, if those impulses tended immediately to an unrestrained licence, they favoured eventually the establishment of orderly conditions in the community.

Outside aids, of course, were of considerable importance in establishing a stable organization. The chief of such agencies was the North West Mounted Police which quickly took up strategic positions in the Yukon territory and not only succeeded in maintaining a state of law and order but, by means of checking the supplies people had before setting out on the inland journey to Dawson and by constant patrols along the routes of travel and the mining creeks, served as something of a social welfare institution. Behind the Mounted Police rested the authority of the Canadian government, and, although many of the local officials were accused of corruption and the officials in Ottawa were often ignorant of conditions in the mining frontier, the introduction of British traditions and practices of justice arrested the development of popular methods of law enforcement such as those secured within miners' meetings and associations. Fraternal societies and lodges, and even to some extent trade-union organizations, reached out from older communities to assist in establishing institutions within the distant mining frontier. Finally, religious denominations vigorously promoted the spiritual and social interests of the mining population. Among the older denominations, the Roman Catholic, Anglican, Presbyterian, and Methodist churches were most active.

Of evangelical religious organizations, the work of the Salvation Army was conspicuously successful, and here, as in the rapidly growing urban communities, the methods employed by the Army were closely adapted to the needs of the population.

Institutional controls derived from outside, however, were effective only as a result of the development of an underlying social consciousness favourable to the establishment of order within the community. This was true even of the work performed by the Mounted Police. That is to say that processes of social reorganization were generated from within rather than from outside the society. Lacking external aids the establishment of social order would have come about more slowly as the experience of mining communities in Alaska amply demonstrates, but these aids in themselves provided no solid basis upon which to erect a stable society. Collective efforts were canalized and provided a more permanent goal of achievement; they sprang, however, from the urge of the people themselves to better their conditions.

New accommodations and the establishment of order did not proceed unhampered by forces of disturbance within the society. Institutional rivalries particularly between religious denominations, increasing racial bitterness with the growth of feelings of self-consciousness on the part of certain groups, and problems of capital and labour as the operation of mining passed into the hands of large corporations and the miners found themselves becoming day labourers, gave rise to new points of conflict within the community. For the most part, however, these disturbances were associated with the developments of a society which had already passed beyond the frontier stage. Like British Columbia, the Yukon very soon faced problems of economic recession and de-population when exhaustion of resources began to take place. The development of secondary economic activities, and the shift to machine methods of production and large capital organization in mining, were indicative of the passing of the earlier frontier of individual enterprise. The Yukon became caught up, if somewhat remotely, in the wider structure of industrial capitalism in Canada. But these new adjustments came about very largely after the boom society of 1898–1902 had disappeared. Within this four-year period the development of the Yukon passed through the full cycle of social disorganization and reorganization; for study of these social processes, few social laboratories could be more revealing.

CHAPTER VI

The Prairie Wheat-Farming Frontier and the New Industrial City*

THE CONSTRUCTION of the Canadian Pacific Railway, the exploitation of the mineral resources of the Kootenay, and the gold rush to the Yukon paved the way for the rapid economic expansion in Canada after 1900. Manufacturing industries which had survived the long depression of the seventies and eighties by means of protection secured through the National Policy and by combination and price control responded quickly to new developments taking place after the turn of the century. The enormous demands made by gold mining in the Yukon for capital and consumers' goods promoted industrial expansion and the establishment of new manufacturing plants, while the considerable movement of population into the Northwest resulting from the gold rush contributed to the settlement of the prairies, and the expansion of wheat farming in turn led to still greater demands for manufactured commodities. The building of two new transcontinental railways reflected the buoyant prospects of manufacturing and wheat farming, and metal mining in Northern Ontario developed largely as a by-product of these railway undertakings. The emergence of the pulp and paper industry emphasized the importance of the new northern frontier, while the daily newspaper which this industry made possible increased the extent of urban concentration and metropolitan control. Expansion into new frontiers in Canada after 1900 took place through the leadership of dominant industrial

*From *The Social Development of Canada*, pp. 380–94.

and financial centres, particularly Montreal and Toronto. The enlarged scope of financial organizations, improved techniques of transportation and production, and new sources of power made possible a diversity in the nature of economic activities and in the kind of resources brought under exploitation. The great number of new frontiers—manufacturing, agricultural, mining, lumbering, pulp and paper, and fishing—which emerged after the turn of the century was indicative of the wide sweep of industrial-capitalist expansion. Problems of social organization in various Canadian communities were evidence of the disturbing effects of such expansion.

To the extent that these problems were associated with the development of industrial manufacturing and the rise of cities they were not strikingly different from those found in such older industrialized countries as Great Britain, Germany, and the United States. Canada shared in technological improvements in the use of iron and steel which led to far-reaching changes in processes of production and in methods of transportation, and the effects of such developments upon social organization tended to be much the same throughout the western world. The fact that industrial entrepreneurship and organization extended into Canada from Britain and the United States gave her the advantage of the experiences of these countries. A considerable familiarity with the nature of the problems of industrialism was secured even before these problems had appeared in Canadian communities.

But if Canada profited some from the experiences of her neighbours, vested interests operated as an effectual check to the easy diffusion of ideas from outside. The claim, as made for instance by manufacturers with respect to problems of labour, that conditions were different in Canada retarded the acceptance of social policies successful elsewhere. The result was that problems even when not distinctive to Canada required solutions which could only be fashioned out of the raw materials of Canadian experience. However, the most crucial problems were distinctive to Canada in that the particular character they assumed resulted from a great variety of economic developments rather than from the development of industrial manufacturing by itself. The opening of the West and the exploitation of the pulp and mineral resources of the Precambrian Shield accompanied the growth of manufacturing in the central provinces, and it was this combination of economic developments which gave to the industrial-capitalist society of Canada its distinctive character. A purely urban society did not emerge in central Canada; nor did a purely agricultural society grow up in western Canada. Metropolitanism became a dominant feature of Canadian community organization, but it was a metropolitanism in terms not of one economic interest but of a great variety of such interests, and the way in which these interests were related to one another determined the distinctive pattern of social development.

It was this fact, furthermore, which sharply set off developments in Canada after the turn of the century from developments which had taken place before. Urbanization as such was not something which began at any particular time; Montreal, Quebec, Halifax, and Toronto grew into substantial cities during the nineteenth century, and, if Montreal and Toronto (together with Hamilton and Winnipeg) forged ahead more rapidly after 1900, the growth of the twentieth century was a continuation of that of the nineteenth. Similarly manufacturing had grown up throughout the whole of the nineteenth century, and by 1870 many of the towns along the Grand Trunk Railway from Montreal to Sarnia had become important industrial centres. But it was not until the end of the century that urbanization and industrialization joined forces, and industrial concentration—and industrial cities—became a dominant feature of Canadian life. This development was made possible by the sudden opening up of new resources of industrial capitalism—in the West and the North—which called for large-scale organization and mass production in manufacturing. The new industrial-capitalist society was one associated with the extension of metropolitan organization into fields of economic exploitation stretching across the whole of Canada. Thus the problems of Canadian communities after 1900 were not simply the problems of the preceding century on a grander scale. New forces combined to give rise to distinctively new social developments, in urban and rural communities alike; an examination of problems of social welfare, crime, morality, cultural organization, and religion serves to emphasize this fact.

Immigration in large numbers from overseas, expansion of manufacturing enterprises, and the rapid growth of urban communities after 1900 resulted in new problems of social welfare associated with the slum, overcrowding, and poverty. The opening up of new farming, mining, and lumbering frontiers made possible the absorption of that surplus labour which possessed the character of mobility, but within the recesses of the cities there accumulated a growing number of people who possessed neither the desire nor the ability to move. The city selected the failures out of the streams of overseas immigrants and out of the armies of industrial workers recruited by, and often ill paid within, the factory. Even the extractive frontier industries, though absorbing increasing numbers of workers, contributed to social dependency, over-crowding, and the development of slums when seasonal unemployment resulted in the drifting of unattached and homeless men to the city to spend the winter. The rural background of a large section of the urban population, and the exaggerated view of the potentialities of western expansion, led to a failure to appreciate the nature and extent of the social effects of industrialization and urban growth. It is true that the period before 1913 was one of unbounded prosperity, and the demands made upon social welfare agencies were not overwhelming, but the feeling of security to which these buoyant prospects gave rise accounted for the failure to do anything about those very real problems which emerged independently of, and in some cases conditiond by, prosperity. Straitened financial resources, a reliance upon obsolete techniques of charity, and an almost complete lack of trained workers were characteristics of institutions of social welfare before the First World War.

Similar factors gave rise to new forms of crime and explain the failure of law enforcement agencies to deal adequately with this problem. Crime inevitably accompanied the process of assimilation of immigrant groups and infractions of the criminal code were particularly evident among second-generation immigrants where social and personal disorganization extended furthest. It was within the community structure, however, that the chief factors determining the extent and nature of crime were to be found. In some respects, Canadian institutions of law and order escaped disorganizing forces evident in the United States. The influence of the West in regard to crime was very different in the two countries. Though an interval of general disorder occurred between the passing of the control of the Hudson's Bay Company in 1871 and the organization of the North West Mounted Police in 1874, and immigration and railway building provided points of disturbance throughout the period of development before 1914, the vigilance of the Mounted Police and the predominantly British background of the population checked the growth of crime in the Canadian

West, and the habit of carrying fire-arms evident in many western American communities never developed; here neither the Indian nor the desperado was a continual threat to the life of the settler.

Again, the larger Canadian cities were more sheltered than were the American cities from any undesirable influence the West might have exerted; the Great Lakes and Precambrian Shield provided an effective barrier to close and constant intercourse. The result was that organized crime in Canada emerged almost wholly out of conditions within local urban communities and from the influence of the larger American cities. If this meant a slower growth of the more elaborate forms of crime, the development of improved techniques of dealing with the criminal was similarly retarded. Though the British heritage, and the dominantly rural background of the population in the cities, had the effect of making law-enforcement agencies highly effective in the apprehension and conviction of criminal offenders, the nature of the problem of urban crime required new tools of reformation and, in the forging of these, judicial agencies in Canada lagged behind those of other countries. The necessity of paying greater attention to the character of the criminal and less attention to the nature of the crime, and of devising   improved methods of treating criminal offenders, was only slowly realized by Canadian judicial authorities.

The effects of this lag were evident with respect to crime in general, but they were most seriously felt with respect to the particular problem of juvenile delinquency. Juvenile delinquency was almost wholly peculiar to the city. Conditions of urban life greatly restricted the scope of parental controls while increasing immensely the variety of activities indulged in by children, and only slowly did there arise agencies to meet the needs of the juvenile population and new methods of treatment in dealing with juvenile criminal offenders. To the extent that public recreational facilities failed to be developed to offset the loss of those means of recreation which had been provided within the rural environment, the child was forced to place dependence upon street play-groups and gangs. On the other side, to the extent that there was a failure to distinguish between juvenile delinquents and adult criminals, within the police court and penal institutions, the child was subjected to the demoralizing influence of traditional methods in the treatment of crime. The establishment of reformatory institutions after 1860 was a recognition of the desirability of classifying prisoners, but such institutions did little in the way of improving methods of punishing or reforming juvenile offenders. The distinction between juveniles and adults in methods of determining guilt and of reformation came only with the establishment of juvenile courts and with legislation dealing with juvenile delinquency; the next logical step of abandoning the distinction between socially dependent and delinquent children, though increasingly made within social welfare institutions, was retarded by the constitutional rigidities of a federal system where social dependency was a provincial and crime a Dominion matter. In the field of prevention, reform efforts consisted largely of the public-playground movement and the establishment of juvenile and youth organizations chiefly under church leadership. Distinct advances were made in both directions, but vested interests, particularly of old established institutions, and public indifference checked the introduction of fundamental changes. Ultimately, attacks upon methods of dealing with juvenile delinquency involved an attack upon methods of dealing with crime in general, and here traditional interests offered more determined resistance. Though the work of voluntary associations such as the Salvation Army, and the appointment of royal commissions to inquire into penal methods, were indicative of the growing appreciation of the nature of the problem among certain sections of the community, eventual reform awaited more widespread changes in public attitudes.

Developments in Canada after 1900 provided new points of disturbance to the moral order. As in most rural frontiers, no serious problems of morality emerged in the rapidly expanding wheat-growing communities of western Canada, but in other areas which came into prominence after the turn of the century such problems tended to become widespread. Extractive industries grew up along the Precambrian Shield or within the mountain valleys of British Columbia, and here the predominance of men led to a weakening of mores associated with family life. The disintegration of moral standards which resulted from adjustments of such a large, purely male, population was not confined to these frontier communities. The chief centres of mining, lumbering, or of the pulp and paper industry were to be found in areas which skirted the thickly populated communities of central Canada or which reached back from the urban communities on the Pacific Coast. The presence of these male-populated centres within short railway distance of Montreal, Toronto, Winnipeg, or Vancouver constituted one of the most distinctive features of urban society in Canada and accounted in large part for the particular character of moral problems. Workers engaged in the outlying industries found their way readily into one of the cities, particularly during winter months; professional prostitutes serving the needs of a purely male population passed backwards and forwards between cities and centres in the hinterland. Vice suppression in the cities intensified the moral problems of the hinterland, while suppression in the hinterland intensified the problems of the cities. In addition to such influences, moral standards in Canadian cities were subject to the various disorganizing effects of rapid urban growth. The strains upon family organization, particularly of immigrant groups, resulting from the new conditions of life, the greater opportunities for sexual licence made possible by the breakdown of neighbourhood controls, and the demoralizing effects of starvation wages in marginal industries and service occupations, were evident in the increase of desertion, illegitimacy, and prostitution.

The predominantly rural background of the Canadian urban population checked effective movements of reform. Most of the immigration to Canada after 1900 came from European peasant districts, and, by segregation, the immigrants who settled in the city clung tenaciously to the strict mores which they brought with them. The rural–urban movement of population within Canada resulted in a similar transference of mores from an environment to which they were adapted to one to which they were not. The recruitment by Canadian cities of a peasant or rural population secured strong supports for traditional moral standards, but it retarded the adjustment of those standards to the new conditions of urban life. Puritanical moral controls within the family and community involved the heavy price of failing to meet some of the most crucial social problems of urban society. Prostitution, venereal disease, and illegitimacy taxed the resources of welfare and medical agencies so long as the first was treated as a crime and the other two as just punishments for sin. Reliance upon police controls and social ostracism served only to drive prostitution underground and to shroud the whole subject of sex under a veil of ignorance; commercialized vice, venereal disease, and illegitimacy rapidly increased in situations where even the discussion of sexual problems was strictly tabooed. These particular forms of social disorganization were part of the much larger problem of adjustment of moral standards in the urban community. The law, custom, and formal

organization of Canadian cities were only slowly adapted to meet
the new demands of urban life upon the individual and family
group.

The development of industrial capitalism, urban growth, and
the appearance of new outlying frontiers imposed heavy strains
upon cultural organization. A Canadian proletariat grew rapidly as
manufacturing extended throughout central Canada, and for a considerable interval agencies such as trade-union organizations were
lacking to secure the social status of this class in the community.
Conflicts of interest between employers and workers were typical
of strains in cultural organization resulting from social divisions
along economic, regional, ethnic, or religious lines. The increase in
value of real-estate property in certain sections of the city, and
building restrictions secured by property owners jealous of the
advantages of exclusiveness, made possible a segregation of social
classes which had been impossible in rural communities. The settlement of immigrant peoples in isolated groups accentuated the
tendency for a number of cultural islands to develop in the city
sharply separated from one another. Natural areas emerged in terms
of processes of urban growth, and the boundaries of these areas
coincided with cultural boundaries imposing strict limitations upon
social intercourse. Consciousness of community lagged behind the
erection of the urban physical structure, and community services
rested upon no solid basis of collective sentiment. Efforts of those
institutions which sought to develop a realization of common
interests were offset by the activities of those institutions which
emphasized cultural differences within the population. Even those
institutions which presumably existed to serve the total community
—churches, fraternal societies, and certain welfare organizations—
recognized the reality of social divisions, and, indeed, tended to
maintain such divisions, by organizing along class or ethnic lines.
Cultural conflicts secured accommodation within the institutional
structure, but these conflicts made impossible any sort of real integration in the total social organization of the urban community.

Cultural strains resulting from metropolitan expansion and urban
growth extended into the rural hinterland of central and eastern
Canada. The movement of population from the country to the city
presented rural districts with problems of depopulation and a
serious lack of leadership. There was no longer felt the invigorating
influence of new population elements, and in some marginal farm
communities isolation led to a degree of inbreeding dangerous to

the physical and cultural welfare of the inhabitants. To some extent, closer contacts with the city, made possible by improved means of transportation and agencies of communication, served to offset the effects of the drain of the city upon the rural population. Rural organizations developed to capitalize upon the advantages of increased communication with the outside world and, at the same time, to assert the distinctiveness of the rural way of life. There was implied in the rise of such movements a realization of the threat of metropolitan expansion (in the form, for instance, of the tourist trade) to the rural culture. In areas where vigorous leadership was lacking, the rural culture suffered either through isolation or through the dominance of the nearby urban centres.

In the northern and western frontier areas of development, problems of cultural organization were very different. The absence of family life, and a concentration upon a single economic interest, had the effect of weakening cultural interests in the mining, pulp and paper, and lumbering communities of northern Quebec, Ontario, and the interior of British Columbia. Trade-union organizations made little headway, and the most active form of cultural association was to be found in nationalist groups. Fraternal societies, libraries, and educational institutions were erected only with the establishment of family life. In western Canada, the rapid growth of population, the settlement of large blocks of land by immigrants unacquainted with the English language and Canadian customs, and the concentration of people upon the task of making a living from wheat growing made difficult the creation of cultural institutions adequate to serve the needs of the community. The segregation of ethnic groups, in particular, limited social intercourse and weakened organizations depending upon the active participation of the members of the whole community. Social clubs, libraries, and other cultural institutions grew up slowly in the prairie towns and rural districts.

More serious still was the problem of providing elementary education to the large school-age population. The scattered nature of settlement, the lack of trained teachers, and the indifference to education of the foreign and of some of the English-speaking settlers were obstacles to the establishment of educational institutions. The considerable use of cash, however, in an agricultural region where wheat was the chief staple made possible the rapid accumulation of financial resources to support public schools, and an increasing number of trained teachers were recruited from eastern Canada as large salaries made teaching an attractive profession. Problems of education, and of cultural leadership generally, persisted in those areas where poor soil made farming a marginal industry or where foreign groups remained isolated from the English-speaking community. Throughout the prairies, the occurrence of drought seasons or sharp declines in the price of wheat resulted in placing heavy strains upon cultural institutions.

Other cultural problems evident in Canada after the First World War had already become apparent before 1914. The shift of the flow of the surplus labour force of rural Quebec from industrial centres in the United States to industrial centres within the province itself involved far-reaching adjustments in the cultural institutions of French Canada and raised new problems of conflict in the relationship of French and English peoples. The growing importance of the northern mining and pulp and paper frontiers in the economy and politics of central Canada hardened tendencies of regionalism in Canadian national life. The development of manufacturing in western Canadian cities, and rural–urban migration, had effects upon the older settled rural prairie districts, particularly Manitoba, similar to those which had become pronounced in central and eastern Canada. These and other problems were evidence of the continual emergence of new points of disturbance in Canadian cultural life. On the other hand, much had been accomplished by 1914 in the way of adjustment to conditions thrown up by industrial-capitalist expansion after the turn of the century. Trade-union movements in central Canada and farm movements in western Canada were typical of the sort of solutions being attained on the cultural level. More significantly still, the strengthening of national sentiment was indicative of far-reaching adjustments to the metropolitan organization of industrial capitalism. The nation emerged as something of a cultural focus in Canadian community life; national associations with headquarters in one of the larger cities and regional offices across the country provided a type of leadership in keeping with the demands of the new metropolitan economy.

Industrialization and expansion into the West and North widened the field of religious institutions and called for the development of radically new methods of organization and of new sorts of appeals. Churches organized on a national basis had grown up by the turn of the century and were much better equipped as a result than the earlier colonial denominations to meet the needs of rapidly growing and distant communities. The establishment of mission stations in western Canada was evidence of efforts to extend the field of religious ministrations. By 1900 leaders of most of the religious denominations had been thoroughly schooled in the needs of a rural society, and lessons learnt from experiences in older agricultural communities proved useful when the church moved into the western rural frontier. Yet many shortcomings in religious organization and appeal quickly became apparent in efforts to serve the scattered prairie settlements devoted to the raising of wheat. Denominational rivalry prevented effective co-operation, and centres of population were provided with far more churches than they required while isolated areas were left without regular services of any sort. Dominance by eastern interests in the councils of the churches, moreover, checked the development of an aggressive policy of championing the interests of western farmers. Unlike the evangelical sects of earlier Canadian rural frontiers which owed no close allegiance to any outside body and which could therefore crystallize in their religious appeal the political dissatisfactions of the population, the churches in western Canada found it necessary to avoid any close identification with economic or political interests. The failure to associate with powerful farm movements involved an immediate loss of influence in the western prairie communities and, in some instances, ultimately led to the emergence of new religious movements which combined their religious appeal with an appeal to economic and political dissatisfactions.

The failure of the church to align itself with new occupational interests and marginal social groups was even more conspicuous in the growing Canadian cities and their industrial hinterlands. The fact that urban communities in Canada inherited a culture largely agrarian in its origin enabled the churches to maintain an appearance of strength. But many of their most faithful followers were people who had moved from rural areas, and participation in religious activities represented a survival of habits of an older culture. Problems of an essentially urban or industrial-capitalist society lay largely outside the province of interest of the churches. The failure to develop a social philosophy offering any solution to the pressing problems of industrial workers—in the factory or in mining communities—had the effect of lessening the dependence of this section of the population upon religion. Successful business people tended to dominate in church politics, and the middle and upper classes came to form the chief body of church supporters, while skilled workers and the industrial proletariat turned increasingly to other agencies for leadership. When the church took the side of employers on issues such as strikes, as it sometimes did in the early years of the century, the loss of goodwill among the labouring population became still more pronounced, but even efforts to assume a neutral position did not keep the support of workers who felt the need of a positive policy on the part of the church. Among some of the leaders of the church, even before the First World War, there was a realization of the necessity of developing a more sympathetic and understanding approach to the problems of labour, but the defections from the church among working-class people indicated that such adjustments were not sufficiently extensive to maintain unimpaired the influence of religion.

The churches failed even more to meet the needs of that large section of the population upon the cultural fringe of the urban community: slum dwellers, transient workers, petty crooks, prostitutes, and others. These "outcasts" of polite society found no recognition within religious denominations. Respectability was a condition of membership in the church, and respectability was maintained by ignoring undesirable members of the population. Charitable contributions to the poor and sermons denouncing vice were means of preserving the isolation of these contaminating elements within the urban community. The psychological and philosophical assumptions of most of the leaders of the church, and the orthodox techniques of evangelization, made almost impossible the adoption of effective methods of dealing with problems such as the slum, crime, and prostitution. Some of the more enterprising of the churches undertook programmes of an experimental character, but early activities for the most part were confined to pious declarations from the pulpit.

Religious leadership among such marginal groups in the urban community came from new evangelical sects, particularly the Salvation Army. The rapid growth of this movement in Canada, with the immigration from Britain in the 1890's, paralleled the successes of the Methodist and Baptist revivalist sects in the early part of the century. The Army was a product of the industrial revolution, and its organization, techniques of preaching, and appeal were thoroughly adapted to the conditions of the urban environment. By 1900, it had made considerable inroads into the followings of the established denominations, and, if the rate of its growth fell off after 1914, it was because the traditional churches learnt valuable lessons from its experience. The securer establishment of the foundations of religion in urban society came with the recognition of the possibilities of evangelism among the newer sections of the population. In the pushing of religious influences into these frontier urban areas, the Salvation Army played a highly important role.

The First World War marked something of a transition in developments in Canada after the turn of the century. Social problems which had arisen in the period before the war had by no means secured complete solution, and new social problems emerged, but in many respects there was established some sort of equilibrium in social structure. Industrial-urban communities by 1914 had attained some degree of maturity, and most sections of the western prairies and the older established centres of the pulp and paper industry and of mining in the North had passed out of the raw frontier stage. If new areas still were being opened up, as in the Peace River district, and if industrialization was being extended beyond its former limits (into Quebec and the West), these developments did not become the dominant note in Canadian social life. Financial concentration, rather than the concentration of industrial plants, was the most marked economic tendency after the First World War. Social problems associated with industrial urbanism and metropolitan expansion in the 1920's were not essentially different from those social problems which had emerged during the early years of the century, and developments in the early period consequently provided a wealth of experience to meet the needs which arose in the later period. The elaboration of social welfare agencies, the growth of a familiarity with improved techniques in dealing with problems of crime and juvenile delinquency, the rise of a more realistic attitude to questions of morality, the establishment of organizations providing more vigorous cultural and educational leadership, and the broadening of religious programmes were an indication that reorganization had advanced considerably in the chief social institutions of the community. Much remained to be done it is true, but the most critical problems of Canadian communities after 1918 were no longer associated with the development of new economic enterprise and the opening up of new areas of economic exploitation.

War and depression imposed new and heavy strains upon institutions of social life, and adjustment to the conditions which arose from these developments became the chief problem of social organization. The sudden collapse after the inflationary boom in 1919 and the much more prolonged depression which followed the stock-market boom of 1929 were accompanied by widespread unemployment and acute economic dislocations in exposed areas. To some extent the problems of Canada were problems of the western world resulting from the First World War and national policies of economic autarchy. To a very considerable extent, however, the Canadian depressions represented the backwash of forces of frontier economic expansion which had run their course. Depletion of resources and loss of markets for staples were not something new in Canadian experience. Earlier frontier economic enterprises —the fur trade, fisheries, timber trade, wheat growing in central Canada, and gold mining in British Columbia—eventually encountered either or both of these limitations to expansion. But the decline of one frontier economic enterprise led quickly to the promotion of another. Expansion in new directions made possible the avoidance of general economic depression resulting from the economic recession of older industries. After 1920 until the Second World War no conspicuous new development took place to offset the depletion of the resources or the drying up of the markets of those frontier enterprises which had expanded rapidly in the early years of the century. The exhaustion of gold in the Yukon, the emergence of a dry belt in the western prairies, the disappearance of timber stands in northern lumber communities, the increasing overhead costs of and declining returns from the coal industry in Nova Scotia were problems of exposed areas which reached back into the whole Canadian economy. The social maladjustments resulting directly or indirectly from these economic dislocations became the major note in the social development of Canada in the years after 1920. They were an indication of the passing of the frontier stage of economic expansion; on the other hand, they gave emphasis to the importance of such expansion in the building of the Canadian community structure.

PART II

Religious Organization in the
Development of the Canadian Community

CHAPTER VII

Religious Organization
and the Rise of the
Canadian Nation, 1850–85*

I N   1824 the Canada Conference of the Methodist Episcopal
Church was formed. In 1925 the United Church of Canada came
into being. The story of Methodist development in Canada within
this hundred-year period appears at first glance to be very largely
a story of successful efforts to bring about the independence of the
church of outside controls, and the union within one body of the
different Methodist groups in the country. That was particularly
true of developments within the period from 1850 to 1885. In 1850
there were five distinct Methodist churches in Canada and only a
few less in the Maritime Provinces, most of them owing some
attachment to outside ecclesiastical bodies. By 1885 these various
churches had become united within one self-governing religious
denomination—the Methodist Church of Canada.

Developments within the other leading Protestant denominations
were not unlike those which took place within Methodism. With
them, also, the movement seems to have been one of increasing
union within the national community, and, again, this was particularly true of the period from 1850 to 1885. Though the Church of
England faced no problem of disunity, except as related to the

*From *The Report of the Annual Meeting of the Canadian Historical Associa-
tion*, 1944, pp. 86–96. With permission of the publisher.

conflict between high church and evangelical elements, the need of identifying itself more closely with the Canadian national community led first to the organization of synods within the various dioceses, beginning in 1857, then to the organization of provincial synods, beginning in 1861, and eventually to the organization of a general synod for Canada in 1893. By means of these constitutional adjustments, the Church of England in Canada emerged in fact as well as in name. The achievements of Presbyterianism in the same period were even more spectacular. In 1844 there were eleven separate Presbyterian churches in Canada and the Maritime Provinces, many of them closely tied up with mother churches in Scotland. By 1875 these eleven churches had given way to the one self-governing national church—the Presbyterian Church in Canada. The development of the other Protestant denominations followed very much the same pattern. Lutherans, Baptists, and Disciples of Christ, to mention only the more important, moved steadily in the direction of a closer identification with the Canadian national community during the years from 1850 to 1885.

The conclusion, therefore, would seem to be that the period from 1850 to 1885 was one characterized by a growing national consciousness within all the churches in Canada, not excepting, indeed, the Roman Catholic Church. Religious bodies which had grown up in the country without any close relation to the community in which they operated had come increasingly to identify themselves with that community in the form of the Canadian nation. The striking coincidences, within this period, in the development of religious, political, and economic organization appeared particularly to support the thesis that the movement in the direction of unity and national autonomy was a movement characteristic of all forms of association, including churches. Efforts of religious bodies to strengthen denominational organization and means of self-government derived support from, and in turn provided support to, such efforts in the political and economic field.

The history of the larger denominations after 1885 seems to confirm the view that the development of religious organization has been closely related to the development of a united autonomous nation. The union of the Methodist, Presbyterian, and Congregational churches in 1925 might well be considered as simply another step in the direction of a complete uniting of religious forces—or, at least, of Protestant religious forces—within the national community. Strengthening of means of denominational co-operation has been accompanied by a weakening of doctrinal differences. The increasing social consciousness of the churches has led not only to a closer identification with the national community but to an increasing awareness of the fact that the differences within their teachings were of little significance in relation to their common interest in promoting the cause of Christianity. It is not very easy to determine today, from the character of the religious service, the denominational affiliation of the particular Protestant church one may find himself in. War and depression have emphasized the singleness of purpose of religious organization.

These facts have been well recognized, and their significance is not questioned here. The movement towards closer union within the national community has certainly been one of the striking characteristics of recent developments in religious organization in other countries as well as in Canada. It may be questioned, however, whether this movement has proceeded in as unqualified a fashion as many church historians have assumed. The church historian has almost invariably been a historian associated with one of the large denominations; only such denominations can support schools of theology on a sufficiently high academic level to promote research in church history. The result is that a biased view of religious development has tended to prevail. Church history has been written very largely in terms of the history of those denominations which have attained a position of respectability in the community; only passing notice has been given to the role of religious movements operating on the social fringe of the community. This has been particularly true of church history in Canada. Developments of the past have been viewed in relation to the position of the larger denominations of today; an evolutionary conception of growth has been accepted. The result, it is submitted, is a distorted picture. It would be no more unjustifiable to view religious developments in Canada as culminating in the rise of the Jehovah's Witnesses than it is to view such developments as culminating in the formation of the United Church of Canada. When religious developments in Canada are viewed as a whole, rather than as something relating simply to the larger denominations, a very different picture emerges. It becomes evident then that the movement within religious organization in the direction of a closer union within the community has almost invariably been accompanied by a movement in the opposite direction of division and separation from the community.

This was true of religious developments within Nova Scotia after

1760 with the growth of Protestant settlement and the establishment in the country of Protestant churches. Congregationalism, which was carried over from New England as a part of the social structure of the village community, shortly broke up into a number of divided churches in Nova Scotia as a result of the religious revival promoted by Henry Alline. The Newlight movement involved a disintegration of the ties of church and village and the organization of religion free of any entanglements with the community; the worldliness of the church gave way to the other-wordliness of the sect. Similarly, efforts of the Church of England to secure its position as the established church of the province received a sharp check with the rise of the Methodist movement under William Black which, like the Newlight movement, disavowed temporal ties of any sort. Newlightism and Methodism represented a break away from a traditional order of political patronage and social status and a reassertion of the purely religious message of individual salvation. It was no accident that these movements grew up during the period of the American War of Independence and the migration of United Empire Loyalists. Revolution and migration imposed heavy strains upon both the political ties of Empire and the social ties of the local village. To a population cut off from the traditional controls of a secular society, the religious message of the evangelical sect provided a new basis for fellowship and belief.

By the end of the century, the Newlight and Methodist movements had become the dominant forces in the religious life of Nova Scotia and also of New Brunswick. Striking changes, however, by then had become apparent in the character of these movements. With the shift of the Newlights to a Baptist position and the organization of a Baptist Association in 1800, and with the break of the Methodists from American sectarianism and their tie with the English Wesleyan Conference in the same year, there emerged out of the earlier Newlight and Methodist evangelical sects the Baptist and Wesleyan Methodist churches closely associated with the political-social order of the community which they served. These developments are the sort seized upon by the church historian in support of the view that a movement towards union and autonomy has characterized the growth of churches in the country. The important fact is overlooked that the establishment of Baptist and Methodist denominational organization in 1800 was followed by the emergence of new evangelical sects—the Newlights as a religious group separate from the Baptists, the Freewill Baptists, the Scotch

Baptists, Bible Christians, Primitive Methodists, Methodist Protestants, Campbellites, and others.

Efforts of the Baptist and Methodist churches to identify their interests more closely with the interests of the community—evident, for instance, in the support given to the establishment of educational institutions and to temperance reform—led to a strengthening of their social position, but at the price of weakening their position of religious leadership among those masses of the population standing on the social fringe of the community. The growth of the timber trade and of trade with the West Indies, and the rise of the ship-building industry, brought new wealth to the Maritime Provinces and supported tendencies towards a sharpening of class divisions within the colonial society, but these developments also promoted increased mobility of population and the extension of settlement into areas of the country hitherto populated only by Indians and Acadian French. It was within these areas of change of population that the newer evangelical sects gained their chief support. The Freewill Baptist movement grew very rapidly in western Nova Scotia and in New Brunswick, the Scotch Baptists and Bible Christians exerted their greatest influence in Prince Edward Island, while such sects as the Primitive Methodists were most active in the rapidly growing town of Saint John. The principle of the sect, of separation of the religious body from the community, persisted in the religious organization of the Maritime Provinces at least until well past the end of the first half of the nineteenth century. The reason is to be found in the persistence during this period of a condition where the opening up of new areas of social life offered challenges to a traditional order of social status in the community.

If attention is directed to Upper Canada, much the same pattern is evident in the development of religious organization. The spread of Methodist and Baptist movements from the United States into Upper Canada followed the rapid settlement of the country with the conclusion of the American War of Independence in 1783 and the Indian War in the West in 1795. The early Methodist and Baptist preachers, notwithstanding charges by spokesmen of the traditional churches that they were foreign agitators intent on promoting republican ideas of government, were interested in only one thing— the salvation of individual souls. They interpreted their function as one which had nothing to do with the jurisdiction of states or philosophies of political parties. Thus they challenged the political privileges and claims of the Church of England and the Church of

Scotland, not by attacking these churches, but by withdrawing themselves from the community and promoting the establishment of an order of society on a purely spiritual basis. This character of the early Methodist movement needs to be emphasized in particular because of the tendency to associate the name of the political-minded Egerton Ryerson so closely with its development, overlooking the fact that the movement had existed for over a quarter of a century in the country before the Ryerson brothers joined its ranks. During that earlier period of Methodist growth, the movement assumed very much the character of a religious sect.

The pamphlet written by Egerton Ryerson attacking the position taken by the Rev. John Strachan in promoting the cause of the Church of England represented a fundamental shift in the Methodist viewpoint. The Methodist and Baptist movements had grown out of the social situation of the backwoods community. With overseas immigration, particularly of people with wealth, and the growth of towns, strains within the organization of these evangelical sects became evident, and adjustment involved a strengthening of ties with the community. Union of the Canadian Methodists and English Wesleyans in 1832, which gave rise to the Wesleyan Methodist Church of Canada, involved an almost complete abandonment of the sect principle of separation from the secular world. The growing importance of the Methodist religious journal—the *Christian Guardian*—and the increasing participation of Methodist leaders in politics, brought new sources of strength to the Methodist denomination in the political and social order of the colony. Likewise, the tie of the Canadian Baptists with the English Baptists in 1837, and the organization of the Canada Baptist Union in 1843, resulted in a considerable weakening of the sect principle of other-worldliness and in a strengthening of the social supports of the Baptist denomination. It is not insignificant that the work of the Rev. Egerton Ryerson, the most prominent of the leaders within the Wesleyan Methodist Church, was largely associated with the towns of Toronto and Kingston, while the work of the Rev. John Gilmour, equally prominent within the Canada Baptist Union, was largely associated with the towns of Montreal and Peterborough. The Methodist and Baptist churches oriented themselves increasingly about the new centres of social and political influence.

As in the Maritime Provinces, however, such tendencies towards a greater integration within the colonial structure were offset by tendencies towards religious division and withdrawal from the secular world. The union of Canadian Methodism and English Wesleyanism in 1832 was followed almost immediately by a break of a number of local preachers from the Canadian Conference and the organization of the Methodist Episcopal Church of Canada. At the same time, new Methodist sects entered the country—the Primitive Methodists in 1830, the Bible Christians in 1831, and the Methodist New Connexion in 1837. The Baptists were also faced with a problem of religious division and conflict. Organization of the Canada Baptist Union in 1843 led to schisms within a large number of the local churches and in the organization of the Regular Baptist Union of Canada in 1848 with membership confined to strict Baptist churches. The separation of the close communionists from the open communionists represented a break in Baptist ranks which reached much deeper than doctrinal differences; the intolerance of the close communionists was an intolerance of a religious sect which set itself solidly against the more worldly attitude of their open communion brethren. The multiplication in the number of Methodist and Baptist groups after 1830 was accompanied by the spread of new religious movements into the country. The Christian Church, Disciples of Christ, Irvingites, Mormons, Millerites, and Davidites were some of the religious sects which came to exert a considerable influence in Canada in the years from 1830 to 1850. The shift in religious organization back to the principle of the sect indicated very clearly that the conditions which had promoted the rise of the Methodist and Baptist movements in the first place had not disappeared. The extension of backwoods settlement, and the growth of public works, had the effect of throwing up new "social masses" made up of people who lacked status within the established social order of the community. Status was attained by such people within the religious order in the separation of the "elect" from the unsaved of the world, and in the substitution of spiritual for secular standards of social worth. Thus the movement within religious organization in the direction of a closer identification with the values of the outside world could be carried only so far. The sect principle in religious organization continued with the persistence of conditions of social disequilibrium.

After 1850, again, in spite of achievements in the way of church union, tendencies towards religious division were not completely absent. The Plymouth Brethren, Christadelphians, and a number of other sects made their appearance in Canada within the period 1850–85. Nevertheless, the view that the development of religious

organization in this period was characterized by an increasing movement towards unity and autonomy is substantially correct. The
explanation of such a movement, however, was not to be found in
any general principle of evolution but rather in conditions which
were peculiar to the social situation at that time. The kind of
church unity which became established was the kind associated with
a social system which had no further means of expansion. After
1850 Canada was left without any real frontier; population movement was largely into the United States—to the rapidly growing
industrial cities of the East and to the rapidly settling prairies of the
West. What frontier areas Canada possessed—in her pioneer industrial towns along the Grand Trunk Railway and in her government-
sponsored agricultural settlements in Muskoka—had a population
too small to support any significant movement of social or religious
reorganization. Within the new mining towns of British Columbia,
movements growing out of a condition of social unrest were not
lacking, but the population of these mining towns was largely a
male population which sought other than religious means of social
expression. The emphasis in religious organization in Canada, as a
result, was upon consolidation; upon efforts to control the home
market. Church union, like confederation or associations of economic
groups, was a protective device. Religious enterprise could no more
afford the wastes of competition than economic enterprise. Both
found support in the strengthening of ties with the state. Sabbath
observance laws, in the same way as tariffs, were means of enlist-
ing the support of the state in meeting what was considered unfair
competition. This alliance of the churches with the secular community in promoting the interests of a moral order was one which
met with little challenge from religious bodies disavowing any
connection with the secular community because of the absence of
conditions disturbing to an established order of social status.
The sect gave way almost entirely to the church, and the cause
of national solidarity was furthered by the close identification
of religious organization with the organization of the national
community.

   That condition came to an abrupt halt about 1885. Almost the
very year which witnessed the union of the Methodist churches in
Canada witnessed also the rise of the Holiness Church and the
Salvation Army. During the thirty years from 1885 to 1914, new
evangelical movements grew very rapidly in the country; abandoned

Salvation Army temples in a great many small towns in Ontario today afford an idea of the strength of this religious body about 1900. In some of the larger cities, evangelical mission churches, without any denominational connection, made their appearance, and the size of their Sunday as well as week-day congregations attested to the declining influence of the traditional religious denominations. Efforts on the part of the older churches to forestall the growth of the new evangelical sects were not lacking, in the establishment, for instance, of city missions, but these efforts for the most part were ineffectual. Among very large sections of the Canadian population after 1885—in the new and isolated prairie settlements and in the transitional areas of the growing cities—the evangelical sect crowded out the traditional church.

The instabilities of religious organization were closely related to the instabilities of the Canadian community structure after 1885. The opening of the West, the discovery of gold in the Yukon, and industrial growth in central Canada led to new movements of population and to the emergence of social conditions unfavourable to an established order of social status. The rise of the Holiness Church and the Salvation Army coincided with the completion of the Canadian Pacific Railway. The organization of mission churches and the spread of the Pentecostal movement into Canada took place during the years which witnessed the promotion of amalgamations in Canadian industry, industrial concentration in strategic urban centres, and the construction of two new transcontinental railways. The evangelical preaching of the Rev. P. W. Philpott in Hamilton in the early years of the present century was a social phenomenon not unrelated to the establishment by American manufacturing enterprises of branch plants in the country. Growth of population and increasing population mobility reflected the expansion of economic life, and, in turn, were reflected in the growth in variety of religious sects. The "closed frontier" of 1850–85 which restricted the development of new religious movements gave way to the "open frontier" of 1885–1914 which promoted the breakdown of the established religious order and the emergence of new religious divisions.

Developments in religious organization since 1914 have taken place too near in time to be clearly discerned, but certain tendencies seem evident. Those evangelical religious movements which took their rise within the period 1885–1914 have moved steadily in the

direction of a greater accommodation with the community in which
they operate. That tendency is very obvious in the case of the Salvation Army. In spite of control from headquarters, the Army in
Canada has become very much a Canadian Army, while, at the
same time, social pressures have led to a shift away from the position of the religious sect; the Army has assumed increasingly the
character of a social service agency. Such a development has not
been unrelated to developments taking place within the older
religious denominations; the increasing emphasis upon social service
activities among them also has been evident in the emergence of the
institutional church with its imposing buildings housing swimming
pools, gymnasia, and facilities for club meetings, and with its elaborate administrative organization. The humble origin of the Salvation Army may still be reflected in the social standing of the majority of its following, but an increasing number of wealthy patrons
indicates a move in the direction of increased respectability. The
other evangelical sects which took their rise before 1914 have been
faced with much the same sort of problems of adjustment though
social accommodation has not gone quite as far as in the case of the
Salvation Army. The organization in 1919 of the Pentecostal Assemblies of Canada is significant as indicating an effort to relate
the Pentecostal movement more closely to the Canadian national
community. Change in the form of organization of the movement
was accompanied by fundamental changes in its social basis.

Yet a glance at developments in religious organization in
Canada after 1919 is sufficient to dispel any notion that there was
an uninterrupted movement towards religious union and closer
identification with the national community. Organization of the
Pentecostal Assemblies of Canada was followed by religious
schisms which gave rise to a number of new Pentecostal sects under
different names. Union of the Methodist, Presbyterian, and Congregational churches not only left in its wake a continuing Presbyterian Church more fundamentalist than the old, but a great
number of unused church buildings which were taken up by various
evangelical sects or by free-lance evangelical preachers. In Alberta,
union was followed by the almost complete breakdown of denominationalism with the rise of the Social Credit movement. It is not
sufficient to answer that these new religious movements were mere
ripples in the religious current which did not affect the direction
of flow of the main stream; the break of Luther from the Church

of Rome or of Wesley from the Church of England might likewise have been viewed by contemporaries as a mere ripple in the religious current. The new evangelical sects in Canada after 1919 grew out of social disturbances related to new developments in the community. The strength of these sects in northern Alberta and Saskatchewan, in the mining towns of northern Ontario, and in the newer industrial communities of central Canada and the West in the 1920's and 1930's suggests the close relation between their rise and the emergence of new "social masses" on the fringe of the social order.

From this it would seem apparent that developments in religious organization in Canada in the years after the First World War were following along lines very similar to those which had been followed earlier. Throughout, a movement towards a strengthening of the ties of church and community was accompanied by a movement in the opposite direction of a separation of the religious from the secular order. Such a development was inevitable in the very nature of the religious institution. The religious sect, the moment it was organized, came to be made up of people holding office, and the prestige attached to such office was determined very largely by the social position of the religious body in the community. Salaries could be paid, and large church edifices constructed, only if financial contributions could be secured from the wealthy or, at least, from the well-to-do. Thus, inevitably, the religious sect came increasingly to accommodate itself to the secular order. Secular values permeated its teachings; the energies of its leaders were directed into channels of community endeavour. The result was, in the end, that the status system of the religious order came to coincide with the status system of the social order. The religious sect passed from being a sect to become a church.

In doing so, it did not cease to perform its religious function, but it did cease to perform the social function of providing leadership to those foot-loose elements of the population which had no recognized place within the established social order. The person, for instance, of rural background who found himself in the rapidly growing city was essentially a person cut adrift from society. His integration into the new society could be brought about only through a redefinition of standards of social worth. Such a redefinition could be secured in the fellowship of the saloon where worth was measured in terms of the tippler's capacity to consume.

It was secured very effectively in the fellowship of the religious sect where worth was associated with the convert's degree of spirituality. The insistence on the part of the sect that it was not of the temporal world derived not from any peculiarity of religious doctrine but simply from its peculiar social function. It separated itself from the traditional social order in erecting a new social order in which status was given a spiritual basis. Thus the other-worldliness of the sect sprang from social pressures which were as insistent as the pressures which determined the worldliness of the church.

The effect of social influences tending towards sectarianism has been strikingly evident in the development of Protestantism in Canada. Whether it has been equally evident in the development of Roman Catholicism is a question not considered in this paper. It may be suggested, however, that the differences in the development of Protestantism and Roman Catholicism are more apparent than real. In French Canada after 1760, the Roman Catholic Church developed within a closed social system, and there were as a result few pressures of a kind which threatened the close tie between church and community. Where those pressures have arisen, the church has sought adjustment through an extension of its system of religious orders; the new religious order assumed very much the character of the new religious sect. Thus within Roman Catholicism, as within Protestantism, there has been a shifting away from, as well as a shifting towards, a worldly position in the community, the only difference being that in the case of Roman Catholicism it has usually taken place within the framework of the Church. That, however, has not invariably been the case. There have not been lacking in Canada reformation movements not greatly different from the Protestant Reformation in Europe in the fifteenth and sixteenth centuries. It is only necessary here to call attention to the recent schism within the Ukrainian Catholic Church in Canada. Other less spectacular, but no less significant, examples could be found. Furthermore, there has probably been a greater shift of Roman Catholics to Protestant religious sects than is generally realized.

One difference has to be recognized between the development of Roman Catholicism and Protestantism. The Roman Catholic Church has been able to a greater degree to check or control movements of its adherents into new areas of development, and in Roman Catholic communities there has been less as a result of that un-restricted type of development associated with frontier movements of population. This fact, however, provides no reason for qualifying the thesis set forth in this paper. To the extent that a closed social system obtained, regardless of the nature of the forces which promoted such a condition, the full identification of religious organization with the community was possible. Consequently, where a church was able to control effectively a social system in the way of preventing any development unfavourable to its position, conditions were established which stifled the free operation of processes of social expansion.

This is simply another way of saying that religious systems are dynamic only so long as social systems are. There is no intention in this paper to suggest that tendencies towards division and sectarianism are at all times characteristic of religious development. Such tendencies obviously are not characteristic of religious development in isolated primitive societies nor were they of religious development under feudalism. In a primitive society the conditions of a closed social system are maintained through the heavy weight of what Bagehot called the "cake of custom," and in feudal society they were maintained through the authoritarian controls of a rigid institutional order. Furthermore, for very much the same reasons, a tendency towards division and sectarianism has been less evident in the religious development of Canada than of the United States. Forces of expansion in American national life have been a great deal stronger than such forces in Canadian national life; the American frontier developed unchecked by political and cultural influences of traditional authority which operated so powerfully within the Canadian frontier. The result has been that established religious systems have found even less support within the social order. Union of churches and their identification with the national community have proceeded much more slowly than in Canada; division and separation of religious organization from the community have assumed a great deal more prominence. Religious sectarianism, indeed, had its principles written into the formal constitution of the Republic!

These considerations suggest that the sectarian religious movements with which we are familiar have been movements closely related to the commercial and industrial expansion of the western world during the past three or four centuries. It is true, of course, that very similar movements emerged much earlier in the development of Christianity and were particularly evident during the eleventh and twelfth centuries, but there was a period in between, associated with the high-water mark in feudal development, when a condition of stability in religious organization tended to prevail. It was with the breakdown of the feudal order that there were unleashed forces of expansion in economic and social life which resulted in an upsetting of established religious systems. The conflict which emerged, centred about the issue of church and state, was very largely a conflict between the church and sect ideas of religious organization, and, as such, it was not essentially different from the conflict in religious organization in more recent times, even though what has been known as the state church has ceased to exist. The long struggle of the Baptists, for instance, to free religion from the control of the state was simply an expression of the sect principle that the spiritual and temporal belonged to separate worlds. The struggle in this instance took the form of challenging vested interests of land and office because the church which was attacked was a church which clung to feudal types of relations within the community. When attention is directed to the efforts of Pentecostal sects in Canada to purify religious teachings, the point of attack is not greatly different; it is the relation of the church to the community which is challenged. That relation, over the years, has changed somewhat in character—financial contributions from wealthy citizens (many of them, in fact, not belonging to the church to which they contribute), and propaganda and lobbying, have taken the place of grants of public land and prerogatives of public office—but it still rests upon a body of vested interests in the community.

With the rise of nationalism in the western world, the identification of the church with the community has come very largely to be an identification with that particular form of community which is known as the nation. One of the fullest expressions of such identification is to be found in one of our own churches, the United Church of Canada, but this tendency has been characteristic of the development of religious organization generally. Even churches which have claimed to be universal have found it necessary to exploit national sentiment in the interests of solidarity. It is not without reason, therefore, that considerable emphasis has been placed by church historians upon the close relation between religious and nationalist movements. What is so often overlooked, however, is the fact that nation building, like empire building, involved a very considerable upsetting of traditional social relations; nationalism was closely associated with rapid economic expansion in terms of metropolitan centres and free enterprise, and the folk cultures of the local community disintegrated in face of the intrusion of the pecuniary conventions of the national community. Thus tendencies in religious organization towards a closer identification with the national community resulting from the rise of nationalism have been offset by tendencies towards religious division growing out of conditions of social disequilibrium produced by economic expansion through free enterprise. National unity in the past has depended upon the operation of forces making for disunity as well as unity in the social structure of the community.

It may be that movements of sectarianism will be much less evident in the future development of religious organization. Nationalism in recent years has come increasingly to depend upon the control of economic enterprise, and the nation state, like the earlier feudal state, may very well succeed as a result in erecting about itself a closed social system. The almost complete identification of religious organization with the nation under such circumstances would be inevitable. Economic forces which check any easy rise in the individual's social position in the community lend support to a movement in the direction of a rigid organization of religious life. Thus, while many Methodists and Baptists in Canada in the nineteenth century became rich and the change in their social status carried with it changes in the social position of the churches to which they belonged, the Jehovah's Witnesses and Four Square Gospellers of today may remain forever poor with the result that the religious sect of today may be the religious sect of tomorrow. If that should be the case the stratifications within the religious structure would assume much more of a feudal character. Present religious divisions would be perpetuated, and the historic role of the religious sect in forcing adjustment within religious organization would be brought to an end.

The very existence, indeed, of the religious sect would be jeopardized in face of the powerful combination of church and state. The legal ban placed upon the Jehovah's Witnesses in Canada during the Second World War could be considered an act justified in terms of the military crisis, but it had a significance which reached far beyond the problem growing out of the situation produced by war. There was much in the character of the Jehovah's Witnesses which was a painful reminder of the Anabaptist sects in Europe at the time of the Protestant Reformation. Religious sects by their very nature are at war with society, but where conditions are such that eventual accommodation is possible, this act of war assumes the form of a withdrawal into a spiritual world. Where, however, eventual accommodation is denied, the sect's reaction may be one of militant aggressiveness in an effort to make over society to its liking. Thus a strengthening of the ties of church and community through the support of the state results almost inevitably in forcing deviant religious movements into a revolutionary position, and the acceptance of such a position brings about in the end their extinction through the action of the state. Out of such a development state and church would emerge as one.

CHAPTER VIII

The Religious Sect in
Canadian Politics*

THIS PAPER IS CONCERNED with the part played by evangelistic religious movements in Canadian politics and, more particularly, with their influence upon the development of liberal political thought in the country. It has been assumed by most students of Canadian church history that the evangelistic religious movements, through the support of radical programmes of political reform, have made substantial contributions to liberal thought. This paper contends that such a view has been based upon a superficial examination of the facts. While it is true that the evangelical churches have at times lent support to the cause of political radicalism, it is questionable whether such support has been nearly as significant as supposed in revealing their political thinking. It is argued here that the political activities of the evangelical churches have not grown out of a deeply embedded political philosophy and that the real contribution to the development of liberal principles of government must be sought not in their activities but rather in the peculiar role of the religious sect out of which the evangelical churches had developed. Discussion of the part played by evangelistic religious movements in politics compels consideration of the political influence of the sect as well as the church.

For the purposes of this paper, it seems best to confine the discussion to three evangelical groups which have played an important role in Canadian politics: the Baptists in Nova Scotia, the

*From the *American Journal of Sociology*, LI, no. 3, Nov., 1945, pp. 207–16. With permission of the publisher.

Methodists in Upper Canada, and the followers of William Aberhart in Alberta. The contribution of these groups to the cause of
political radicalism has been well recognized.

In Nova Scotia the Baptists constituted a distinctive revolutionary
force in religious and social life toward the close of the eighteenth
century, and early movements of political reform owed much to
their indirect and direct support. Similarly, in Upper Canada, the
Methodists, in the two decades of political turmoil after the war of
1812–14, strongly supported radical political movements in the
country in opposition to the Family Compact; and the close
working alliance which grew up between Egerton Ryerson, the
acknowledged leader of the Methodist Church, and William Lyon
Mackenzie, the leader of the Reform party, was indicative of the increasing active participation of Methodists in politics. The radical
political implications of the religious movement in Alberta founded
by William Aberhart are obvious: the Social Credit party, with its
sweeping programme of monetary reform, grew directly out of
Aberhart's Prophetic Bible Institute. Here, very definitely, political
revolt was born out of a movement which had grown up on a
religious foundation.

A combination of forces led to this alignment of the evangelical
churches with radical movements in the country. In the first place,
vested interests of denominationalism tended to produce such an
alignment. The evangelical churches found themselves opposed by
the old, traditional churches closely associated with the state or
with ruling parties in the state. The Baptists in Nova Scotia and the
Methodists in Upper Canada were compelled to fight church establishment to secure the rights to which they felt themselves entitled
as religious denominations, and, in fighting church establishment,
they inevitably found themselves fighting all the forces of special
privilege and reaction in the country. Somewhat similarly, William
Aberhart, in attacking the claims of the powerful and wealthy
churches represented in Alberta, many of them with strong creditor
interests in the province, found himself launching out in an attack
upon those business and political interests which largely supported,
and in turn were supported by, these churches. The evangelical
church, the moment it became denominationally conscious, very
naturally championed the cause of religious freedom in one form
or another, and such championship threw it on the side of political
radicalism in the country.

Strong social forces as well, however, tended to an identification of the evangelical churches with the cause of political radicalism. Of these, regional-economic interests were by far the most important. Their effect was to strengthen greatly the tendencies deriving from denominational interests.

The political affiliations of the evangelical churches were determined by the kind of area from which they drew their support. The established or traditional churches were the churches of the metropolis. Their most imposing houses of worship were located in the better residential sections of the larger centres of population; their most successful ministers occupied city pulpits. Within governmental centres, in particular, their influence tended to be dominant. They gave expression to the interests of Empire or nation. The evangelical churches, on the other hand, grew up as religious sects on the social fringes of the community. Their emergence as new sects represented efforts of scattered or downtrodden folk, neglected by the traditional churches, to develop a form of religious fellowship on their own. It was in outlying areas of the country, or within working-class sections of the city, that sectarian activity flourished.

Thus the separatism of the sect, its efforts to separate itself from the worldly society, became, within the evangelical church, closely related to political separatist movements in the hinterland or in marginal urban areas. The political reaction against the control of the metropolis—the struggle to secure a greater measure of local political autonomy—found support in, and in turn supported, the isolationism of the religious sect. Rebellion in the backlands expressed itself usually in religious as well as in political form; few movements of political independence in history have been unrelated to movements of religious schism. The attempt of Brigham Young in Utah to bring into being a theocratic state largely independent of the federal authority provides possibly the best example on this continent of the combination of sectarian religious and frontier political separatism, but similar forces in Canada led to like forms of political and religious expression.

The struggle of the Baptists in Nova Scotia in the late eighteenth century to secure an independent religious life was simply a part of the much larger struggle of the Nova Scotian out-settlements to resist the domination of Halifax and to free themselves from the restrictions of the British colonial system. The collapse of Congregationalism had followed upon the break of Nova Scotia from New England with the American Revolution, and the rise of the New-light Baptist movement represented an effort to strengthen the position of the out-settlements which had lost the support of the tie with New England. The aggressive separatism of the new religious sect was not unrelated to the efforts of the town meeting to control local village affairs, to the refusal of local magistrates to convict for offences against unpopular colonial laws, and, during the Revolution, to smuggling and tax evasion, and, after the Revolution, to the conflict between the Assembly and the Council and the growing demand for responsible government.

Similarly, the struggle of Methodism in Upper Canada became closely tied up with efforts of the backwoods farm communities to free themselves from the controls of centralized land-granting, taxing, and road-building authorities. The chief strength of the traditional churches, and especially of the Church of England and Church of Scotland, was in the larger towns and the provincial capital. These churches represented the official classes of the community—the classes which had a stake in the imperial connection —but made no effective effort to serve the outlying backwoods farm population. Political dissatisfactions of people who, because of their isolation, had little voice in government, found expression in religious separatism. Methodism grew rapidly in outlying sections of the country and supported efforts to secure a greater measure of local independence and colonial autonomy.

The close relation between frontier political and religious sectarian separatism can be seen even more clearly in Alberta in the religious-political movement led by Aberhart. Aberhart's break with the traditional organization of religion forced him into an isolationist position. The dominance of the national churches became closely associated in his eyes, and in the eyes of his followers, with the dominance of the large eastern cities and of the federal authority. On the other hand, the religious separatism of Aberhart's new sect—its attempt to stand apart from the worldly society—became closely associated with the political separatism of such a frontier area as Alberta. It was not difficult for Aberhart to translate the religious exclusiveness of the Prophetic Bible Institute into a political exclusiveness, once he became leader of the Social Credit party. The society of the elect found expression now in political terms. It was not without significance that some of the more prominent members of the Social Credit Government belonged to the Mormon church in southern Alberta. The religious-political experiment in Alberta resembled very closely that tried much earlier in Utah; in both cases, religious separatism sought support in political separatism, and encroachments of the federal authority were viewed as encroachments of the worldly society.

Regional interests which found expression in movements of religious and political separatism were closely related to economic interests. The society of the backlands or of the urban working-class area was a debtor society. The religious sect attracted the support not only of the isolated but of the economically dis-possessed. It provided a cheap religion in that it did not make heavy financial demands for the support of elaborate places of worship and highly educated clergymen. Furthermore, it provided, in the way of preaching appointments, occupational opportunities for young men (and, in some cases, young women) who did not have the means of securing the training necessary for a professional career. It was the poor fishermen and farmers of Nova Scotia who largely comprised the early following of the Baptist Church. The debt-ridden farmers of the Upper Canadian backwoods communi-ties rallied about the banner of the Methodist itinerant preachers. Aberhart secured his greatest support, both as a religious evangelist and as a political campaigner, in that area of Alberta stretching northeast from Calgary to the Saskatchewan border, the approxi-mate centre of which is the town of Hanna. It was here that the drought was most fully felt.

The message of the religious evangelist as a result became easily translated into economic panaceas of various sorts. Magical remedies were seized upon to solve problems of the economic system just as patent medicines and the prescriptions of the quack are seized upon to deal with bodily ills. Monetary experiments, in particular, have tended to be closely related to religious experiments in the means of salvation. Resort to the use of scrip or to the estab-lishment of special banks served the purpose of strengthening the isolation of the religious group and, at the same time, of offering a solution to the problem of debt. The close relation between sec-tarian techniques of religious control and monetary techniques of economic and political control has been most evident, of course, in the Social Credit experiment in Alberta; here the Mormon members of the Government in particular had a perfectly good historic example in the use of scrip and the carrying-on of banking operations by the Mormons in Utah. Awareness of monetary solu-tions of economic problems was less fully developed among the earlier evangelical religious groups in Canada, but the pressures of a rigid credit system in the hands of the merchant class in Nova

Scotia and Upper Canada, and the shortage of money, led to economic dissatisfactions which found expression among Baptists and Methodists in demands for economic reforms not unlike those of Social Credit.

The denominational, regional, and economic interests of the evangelical churches were probably most responsible for their support of radical political movements in the community. To some extent, as well, the nature of the evangelical religious appeal in itself may have contributed to a fostering of an attitude of political radicalism. Such an appeal involved a sharp break from traditional theological systems; theological trappings, and an elaborate ritualistic system, were cut through to emphasize the elementary problem of man's relation to his God. At the same time, conversion involved an equally sharp break with his past for the individual. The effect of this was to encourage an untraditional approach to problems of life in general. It was for this reason that followers of new religious sects often became the most active in promoting novel types of economic activity. Something of the experimental attitude was carried over into politics as well.

These considerations suggest the nature of some of the more important factors favouring the alignment of the evangelical churches with radical political forces in the community. It would be a mistake to conclude from this, however, that these churches have invariably lent support to the cause of radicalism. If the political activities of the Baptists in Nova Scotia, the Methodists in Upper Canada, and the followers of William Aberhart in Alberta are examined further, it will be found that these groups, while at times supporting radical political movements, have at other times constituted a distinctive conservative influence in the community. Indeed, in the decisive tests of strength between opposing political forces in the country, they have more often thrown their weight on the side of conservatism. This fact has to be recognized before any conclusion can be drawn respecting the relation of the evangelical churches to political thought.

In Nova Scotia, in the second quarter of the nineteenth century, opposition to the non-sectarian educational policy of Joseph Howe, the leader of the Reform party, led the Baptists to shift to the Conservatives in the province. It was a prominent Baptist—J. W. Johnson—who became the leader of the Conservative party, and the votes of the Baptist population were decisive in bringing about the defeat of the Reformers in the election of 1843. Likewise, in

Upper Canada, the early alliance between the Methodists and Reformers was sharply broken in 1833, when Egerton Ryerson came out in opposition to William Lyon Mackenzie; and in the election of 1836, and again in the election of 1844, the Methodist vote was at least in part responsible for the Tory victories. Even moderate reform leaders, like the Baldwins, were unable to rely upon Methodist support. In Alberta similar tendencies were evident within the combination erected by Aberhart out of religious and political materials. Aberhart himself never really ceased to be a conservative in political outlook, and the political party which he founded moved steadily in a conservative direction. The radicalism which persisted within the party came very largely from elements which became a part of the political movement after 1935 but which were quite unrelated to the religious movement led by Aberhart. Frontier agrarianism continued to force the party into a radical position, but radical tendencies were sharply checked by the strength of sectarian religious influences.

Factors which at one time favoured the alignment of the evangelical churches with political reform in the community favoured their alignment with conservative forces at another. Denominational vested interests changed in character as the evangelical church became less concerned about the privileges enjoyed by the older, established churches in the community and more concerned about protecting privileges which it itself had secured. The sect grew into the church and, in doing so, found its interests more closely identified with the interests of the traditional churches. Promotion of such objects as education, temperance, and Sabbath observance forced the evangelical church into opposition to religious movements more evangelistically aggressive, and secular movements which threatened the teachings of religion. Baptist Church leaders in Nova Scotia and Methodist Church leaders in Upper Canada increasingly directed their fire against the new religious sects which sprang up in the community, while by 1935 Aberhart in Alberta was feeling very keenly the competition of rival radio evangelists in Calgary. Subsequently his churches in the country were steadily crowded out by churches organized by the new sects. The threat of the loss of some of its members to other religious bodies weakened in the evangelical church an interest in the cause of religious freedom, and only in those churches, such as the Quakers and some of the smaller Baptist groups, where the spirit of the sect remained strong, have liberal principles been adhered to consistently. Denominationalism tended to make the more prosperous evangelical churches increasingly dependent upon the state and the community at large.

At the same time the evangelical churches, in gradually with-drawing from sectarianism, became much more a part of the metropolitan structure. With the migration of their followers, they established themselves in the larger centres of population, and their leaders became much more sympathetic to the views of city resi-dents. Their houses of worship began to rival in elegance those of the older churches, and most of their leading ministers came to occupy city pulpits. Country stations were increasingly neglected, and methods of organization such as itinerancy and street preach-ing, which had been developed to make possible the serving of people in the country or in working-class districts of the city who could not be reached within regular places of worship, were aban-doned. The evangelical churches came to draw most of their financial support from the cities, and from the better residential sections and, consequently, to identify their interests with the interests of the metropolitan population. They became churches of Empire or nation rather than the churches of the social fringe.

Such a development was clearly evident with respect to the Baptists in Nova Scotia and the Methodists in Upper Canada. The considerable influence exerted within the Baptist denomination by the Granville Street Church in Halifax, after its break in 1827 from the Church of England, and the shift of denominational leader-ship from preachers and laymen attached to churches in the out-settlements to preachers and laymen attached to the church in the capital, were indicative of fundamental changes in the position of the Baptist group. The leadership of Dr. E. A. Crawley in Baptist educational endeavours reflected the greater dependence upon the resources of the metropolis. Likewise, with the Methodists in Upper Canada, the increasing importance of Toronto as a Methodist centre, and the union in 1832 with the English Wesleyan Confer-ence, reflected the closer identification with the political interests of the capital and with the British imperial system. New Methodist leaders emerged with much stronger urban ties, and new tech-niques, such as the religious journal, developed which strengthened the influence of churches in the larger centres. The change in the character of the Methodist camp meeting from a religious gather-ing held in the backwoods to a religious gathering held in summer resorts and attracting city people was suggestive of the new Metho-dist appeal.

At first glance it might seem that the religious-political movement founded by Aberhart in Alberta escaped developments leading to a closer identification with metropolitan interests, but in actual fact it did not. The increasing competition of radio evangelists led Aberhart and his fellow preachers to place less emphasis upon the appeal to country people and to think more in terms of the work of the large city churches in Calgary and Edmonton, while, at the same time, the political party which grew out of the religious movement steadily ceased to be a frontier party and became more interested in building up a national following or, at least, in securing acceptance within the nation at large. Efforts in various parts of the country to secure the election to Parliament of Social Credit members was an indication of the extent of the shift away from the early position of sectarian and provincial separatism.

The change in the position of the evangelical churches in the cities was accompanied by a change in their relation to the wealthier economic classes. Substantial men of business, though not necessarily changing their religious affiliations, began to make financial contributions to these churches on the theory that their teachings made for good citizens and for well-disciplined workers. At the same time, many of the adherents of the evangelical church became rich themselves. The asceticism cultivated within the religious sect tended to success in business enterprise, and religious nonconformists were likely to find their way into mercantile pursuits in particular. Commercialism favoured the sort of qualities developed within the sect, while, on the other hand, members of the more traditional churches were likely to avoid commerce as something not becoming their social position.

Commercial prosperity thus inevitably resulted in considerable changes in the economic status of the membership of the evangelical churches as over against the membership of the traditional churches. The evangelical churches ceased to be churches of the poor as an increasing number of their members became substantial citizens, and such a shift in social status led to a shift in political attachments. An anxiety to establish a claim to a position of respectability led these churches to repudiate their earlier connections with the socially humble and politically radical. The increasing conservatism of the Baptists in Nova Scotia and the Methodists in Upper Canada can be explained at least in part on these grounds. By the middle of the nineteenth century these churches had many wealthy members. In Alberta the same sort of thing happened, but it was more evident within the Social Credit party than within the Prophetic Bible Institute. In the election of 1944 many prominent Alberta business men—and, there is reason to believe, a number of large business firms outside—lent their active support to the party which nine years earlier had advocated a radical programme of monetary reform.

In the end the evangelistic religious appeal also tended to the development of attitudes of conservatism among the followers of the evangelical churches. While such an appeal did promote, on the one hand, a more rationalist approach to the problems of life, it promoted, on the other hand, a narrow intolerance which increasingly found expression in anti-liberal forms of behaviour. Religious sectarianism involved a shift to a more fundamentalist, elementary conception of religion; it represented a reversion to a simpler form of Christianity. Its appeal, therefore, was essentially reactionary in character. New movements within theological thought were strongly resisted by the religious sect, and it was almost inevitable that something of this theological illiberalism would be carried over and become identified with political illiberalism. The feeling developed by the evangelistic religious sect that it possessed the only true means of salvation led to a type of bigotry which found expression in politics as well as in religion. Reliance upon special revelation ruled out discussion as a way of arriving at decisions, and the religious evangelist was likely to prove highly impatient when caught within the checks and balances of democratic political processes.

Consideration of the influences which tended to force the evangelical churches into a conservative position in politics, as over against those influences which tended to force them into a radical position, suggests that the nature of their political alignments at most can only in part be explained in terms of a fundamental political philosophy. Evangelical church leaders displayed considerable capacity to change their minds, and the minds of their followers, to suit circumstances; and it was never possible to predict what political programme they would support at any particular time. They developed no consistent body of political principles.

The explanation for this would seem to lie in the sectarian origin of the evangelical church. Religious sectarianism as such tended to foster an attitude of political indifference. The whole attention of the individual was directed to the state of his (and of his neighbour's) soul. So long as the sect remained truly evangelical in character, it avoided any connection whatsoever with secular groups or associations, remaining wholly other-worldly. This was true of the Baptists in Nova Scotia, of the Methodists in Upper Canada, and of the religious movement led by Aberhart in Alberta, as it has been true of all other sects.

Although the preaching career of Henry Alline, the founder of the Newlight Baptist Church in Nova Scotia, coincided almost exactly with the period of the American Revolutionary War, he referred to it only twice in his journal, and then quite incidentally. The Newlight movement grew out of the unrest created by the Revolution, but the Newlights carefully avoided any identification with political interests. Their strength as a religious sect largely derived from such non-involvement in politics. Similarly, the Methodists in Upper Canada made their greatest gains just before and after the War of 1812–14, but few Methodist preachers expressed any interest in the controversies growing out of the war or in the subsequent fierce political conflicts. Methodist preachers and Methodist converts subordinated political allegiances to what they considered the much more important allegiance to their God. Likewise, during the period in which Aberhart gained his greatest influence as a religious leader in Alberta, he had no interest whatsoever in politics, and his followers tended to be people who engaged very little in political activities and who were little informed respecting political issues.

The effect of the sectarian religious appeal thus was virtually to disfranchise a considerable section of the population. The religious sectarian in many cases did not vote; if he did vote, he very often took no other interest in public questions. His political allegiances were of a tenuous sort; he made a poor party member because he was seldom prepared to accept the obligations of party loyalty. His religious conscience too often served to justify an attitude of non-co-operation. This resulted in fostering a state of political illiteracy. For the most part, the membership of religious sects was drawn from the least-educated sections of the population, and no attempt was made, within religious teachings, to correct this initial disadvantage in exercising the privileges of citizenship. Rather, ignorance of political matters was considered a virtue of the evangelical-minded person; it was indicative of his complete break from the fellowship of the ungodly and his full participation in the fellowship of the elect. Thus political illiteracy was deliberately promoted by discouraging contact with people outside the group and by discouraging the reading of non-religious publications. Theological commentaries and religious journals, as well as the evangelical sermon, served to weaken efforts of the secular press to build up party loyalties and a political consciousness.

Political indifference gave way to an interest in public issues only when the position of the religious sect was threatened by public policy. It was the leaders who were most alive to the effects of public policy and who, therefore, were most likely to initiate political action to protect the interests of the sect. Indeed, the followers of the religious sect tended to be little more concerned about its interests as a religious denomination than they were about the interests of any secular institution; sectarianism encouraged an attitude of non-denominationalism. The truly saved were members of the spiritual elect, and the preservation of that connection depended upon no formal institutional organization, a common experience of faith being sufficient bond of attachment. The leaders, however—those whose livelihood or prestige depended upon the continued existence of the sect as a religious denomination—became increasingly jealous of its rights and privileges. They built it into a church because their security depended upon the security of denominational attachments. Efforts to strengthen the social position of the church led to the promotion of activities, such as education and temperance, which brought it more closely into contact with other groups. Challenges to such activities compelled the leaders to mobilize their following for collective political action.

It was such vested interests of office which led to the active political participation of the followers of religious sects. Baptist leaders in Nova Scotia, after the turn of the nineteenth century, could not afford to adhere to the position of political neutrality taken earlier by Henry Alline. Attacks upon denominational enterprises which they promoted, in particular a Baptist college, compelled them to interest themselves in matters of politics. If effective political pressure was to be exerted, they had, in addition, to arouse a strong political interest in their followers. Similarly, Methodist leaders in Upper Canada after 1828, in contrast with the earlier Methodist itinerants, found themselves becoming involved in political controversies in support of their denominational claims. Attacks upon Methodist undertakings were in the nature of attacks upon the vested interests of leadership; a denominational college, Sabbath observance, and the cause of temperance were issues which continued to force Methodist leaders into politics in the provincial and municipal as well as the federal field. Aberhart's sudden break into politics can be explained likewise. Increasing competition from rival radio evangelists led him to search for something new in his appeal, and he seized upon the message of Social Credit. Attacks upon his political teachings forced him into politics in their defence. What he did was to convert a religious crusade into a political crusade; political allegiances were forged to take the place of weakening religious allegiances. None of this, of course, was done with a clear consciousness of the effect. Leadership very seldom appreciated the nature of the forces which drove it into certain lines of action, and in no case, perhaps, was this more evident than in the emergence of the Social Credit movement out of the evangelical preaching of Mr. Aberhart.

It was, indeed, one of the paradoxes in the role of the sectarian leader that his evangelical message should lead him, in the end, into political controversy. To arouse concern in the cause of religious salvation—that is to say, to win converts—the evangelical preacher had to resort to the spectacular, and, as the spectacular in religion ceased to be effective in meeting the competition of more aggressive evangelists or of more highly organized religious institutions, the spectacular in politics was sometimes turned to. It was not in any way remarkable that the Rev. T. T. Shields of Toronto, who broke from the main Baptist body on religious fundamentalist grounds, should have sought to maintain the support of his following by discussing in the pulpit highly controversial political issues. Violent attacks upon public men, like the noise of a brass band, create something of a sensation and provide effective advertising. Such attacks, in the end, can only be sustained by pulling the whole following of the church into politics in support of certain lines of action.

The way in which the evangelical church was drawn into the field of politics explains its failure to develop any consistent programme of political action. Lacking any clearly defined political principles, opportunism was the most natural determinant of political action on the part of leaders and followers alike. The nature of the evangelistic religious appeal placed the leaders in a particularly powerful position in mobilizing the support of the followers for political action.

The religious evangelist escaped the checks upon leadership secured through an elaborate denominational organization and an accepted ritual. His relationship to the convert was a purely personal one; it was he rather than any formal church which offered the means of salvation. The result was that the religious evangelist came to assume a very considerable dominance over those whom he converted. The democratization of the institution of religion made possible the concentration of authority in one who enjoyed the privilege of divine revelation. When the religious evangelist moved into the political field, he lost little of his charismatic influence. His strong personal authority made it possible to carry his followers with him no matter what political line he might take. No Roman Catholic bishop could, in fact, ever hope to exert the personal influence over his following as was exerted by Joseph Smith, the founder of the Mormon Church, or by Brigham Young, his successor.

Although Ryerson in Upper Canada was never able to command the support of the whole membership of the Wesleyan Methodist Church, he nevertheless achieved striking success in swinging the Methodist body behind whatever political party he favoured. The Methodists became a powerful pressure group in Canadian politics about the middle of the nineteenth century simply because expediency determined to a considerable extent their actions; they tended to vote in terms of the interests of their denomination without regard to wider public issues, and political solidarity was maintained by effective leadership, at any rate during the period of ascendancy of Egerton Ryerson. Similarly, Aberhart in Alberta could mobilize his following in support of a personally sponsored political programme because of the peculiar type of influence which he had built up as a religious evangelist. It was his boast that he was completely ignorant of economics before his advocacy of Social Credit ideas, but his economic pronouncements were readily accepted because of the claim to divine revelation which he had established as a religious evangelist.

It would be an exaggeration to conclude from this that the influence of the evangelical churches in Canadian political life has been to produce a citizen body politically illiterate or unprincipled, but such a conclusion would contain an element of truth. An indifference to politics which religious sectarianism engendered has checked the growth of political thought, and the weakness of political thought, in turn, in contributing to a political opportunism on the part of evangelical church leaders, has checked the growth of political statesmanship. It is significant that leadership in politics from the Protestant group in the country has come very largely from people with a Scottish Presbyterian or Scottish Baptist background. Denominationalism and religious fundamentalism have exerted too strong a hold upon members of the evangelical churches for them to go far in a career of politics. Much of their energy has been dissipated in support of programmes of moral reform sponsored by religious groups. They have as a result tended to be more successful in municipal or provincial politics, where party organization has been weak and where voting blocs have exerted a much greater influence, than in federal politics. The repeated failure, in Canada as well as in the United States, to build a national party around the prohibition issue was an indication of the limitations of evangelistic religious thinking in politics.

It is questionable, however, whether the political influence exerted by the evangelical church reveals the real contribution of the religious sect to the development of political thought. That is to say, the contribution of the sect should not be sought in the political activities of the evangelical church, whether those activities were in the way of supporting radical or conservative political movements in the community, but rather it should be sought in the religious influence of the sect as such, before it developed into the evangelical church. Its political contribution lay in its very emphasis upon the separation of the religious from the political. The indifference of the religious sect to politics provided a healthy corrective to tendencies within the church to become greatly occupied with political matters and so entrenched in the political interests of the state. It was in the teachings of religious sectarianism that the threat to liberal principles through the alliance of church and state was most effectively met. The religious sect, by concentrating upon the purely religious message of salvation, escaped the demands of nationalism so evident in times of war. Moreover, by placing the emphasis upon spiritual values in the making of preaching appointments, the sect was freed from social pressures making for the development of a denominational bureaucracy which sought support in the bureaucracy of big business and the state. In Canada the maintenance of a successful federal system in particular has depended upon the strength of forces of decentralization, secured, within religious organization, through the influence of new religious sects.

As the sect has grown into the church, new sects have grown out of the church. Thus the effect of the increasing participation of evangelical church leaders in politics has been offset by secession and the emergence of new sects which have withdrawn completely from political activity. In Nova Scotia the rapid growth of the Free-will Baptist movement after 1820 emphasized the weaknesses of the Baptist Church as a result of its shift away from an evangelical position. The entry of the Methodists in Upper Canada into politics under the leadership of Egerton Ryerson was followed almost immediately by the break of the local preachers and the organization of the Methodist Episcopal Church. In Alberta, likewise, the participation of Aberhart in politics led very quickly to the weakening of his religious influence and to the shift of evangelical leadership to new religious sects. It is this persistence of the sectarian spirit in religious organization which has given religion its dynamic force in society. It has exerted a decisive influence upon determining the relation of the church to the state and thereby upon determining the contribution of religion to political thought.

CHAPTER IX

The Religious Sect in
Canadian Economic Development*

THERE IS PROBABLY NO OTHER FORM of organized
group life in the Canadian community which has been more
unstable than the organization of religion. The history of Protestantism in the country is very largely a history of church unions and
sectarian divisions. If account were taken of the activities of the
Jesuit Order in New France, of the defection at various times of
many Roman Catholics to Protestant religious sects, and of recent
anti-clerical movements in the province of Quebec and among the
Roman Catholic immigrant population in western Canada, the
same would be found to be true in a general way of Roman Catholic
development in the country.

The dream of the universal church, of the church which would
unite all nations and all classes, has never been fully realized, in
Canada as elsewhere in the western world. Efforts to accomplish
such an object by the establishment of a state church, by the union
of separate religious bodies, or by the initiation of a new religious
movement which would transcend all other religious groups have
invariably failed in face of the expression of strong separatist forces
in religious organization. Out of every such effort to create an
all-embracing religious body in the community have come new
movements of religious protest—the religious sects.

On the other hand, the sect form of religious organization has

*From the *Canadian Journal of Economics and Political Science*, vol. XII,
no. 4, Nov., 1946, pp. 439–53. With permission of the publisher.

proved equally unstable. The pure sect, the religious group organized exclusively in terms of the other-worldly or spiritual interests of its members, has never been more than an idealistic conception of religious organization finding expression in movements of religious reform at various times. The necessity of existing in a worldly society has led religious sects from the very beginning to accept to some extent a worldly outlook. Where they have not succeeded in developing into churches, or at any rate into types of religious organization accommodated to the secular community, they have perished. Almost from the moment of their inception they have been forced to make such a choice between social accommodation or extinction.

The explanation of these various movements, of church union and sectarian schism, must be sought within the particular situations out of which they developed. A wide variety of different sorts of factors operated to bring about changes in forms of religious organization and in religious thinking. No attempt can be made here to set forth the underlying conditions of religious development. All that can be attempted is to suggest in general terms the way in which religious developments were related to other developments in the community.

The instability of religious organization, characteristic of so much of the religious development of Canada, as of the western world generally during the past nineteen centuries, may be considered in part a reflection of the underlying instability of western economic society. That would appear particularly true of Canada where the economic factor has been so important. Canada grew out of the expansion of western capitalism (the Canadian frontier from the beginning has been an area of capitalistic exploitation) and the demands of capitalism may be expected as a result to have made their effects felt upon the organization of religion as, on the other side, the demands of religion have made their effects felt upon the organization of capitalism. The institutions of religion and the institutions of capitalism have grown out of much the same social situation in the Canadian community. To some extent at least, as a consequence, the instability of religious organization and the instability of capitalism find a similar explanation.

It was out of the social conditions which produced new capitalist enterprise that the religious sect developed, while it was in face of social demands related to the development of large-scale capitalist organization that the religious sect was forced to give way to church forms of religious fellowship. The frontier of capitalism—the area, that is, of new capitalist enterprise—was a breeding ground of the religious sect. The metropolitan society, the society of large-scale capitalist organization, tended to produce the church, or formally organized religious denomination.

Thus, in Canada, the great revivals of religion, the new movements of sectarian religious protest, have been closely related, chronologically and geographically, to the development of new staple or secondary industries in various parts of the country, while the recessions of waves of religious revival, the growth of conditions favourable to the church form of religious organization, have been closely related to the passing of the pioneer stage of capitalist expansion and the emergence of large-scale capitalist organization. The expansion of the fur trade in New France, trade and the fishing industry in Nova Scotia, agriculture and the timber trade in New Brunswick, Prince Edward Island, and Upper Canada, mining on the Pacific Coast and Precambrian Shield, wheat farming on the western prairies and manufacturing in the St. Lawrence–Great Lakes area grew out of conditions which favoured the break from ecclesiastical forms of religious control evident in the rise of the Jesuits, Newlight Baptists, Methodists, Disciples of Christ, Plymouth Brethren, Salvation Army, Pentecostals, Jehovah's Witnesses, and other sects. On the other hand, the development of mature forms of economic organization in the fur trade, fishing industry, timber trade, commerce, agriculture, mining, and manufacturing grew out of conditions which favoured the shift away from religious sectarianism and the strengthening of ecclesiastical forms of organization within the Roman Catholic, Anglican, Presbyterian, Congregational, Baptist, Methodist, and Disciples of Christ churches and within some of the more recently organized religious bodies.

The breakdown of religious denominationalism and the rise of new religious sects on the frontier of capitalism could be accounted for to some extent in terms of elementary economic factors. The primary problem of capitalist growth was the mobilization of capital and labour for economic production. Thus an effort was made to avoid the demands of any elaborate system of social services. It was for this reason that frontier capitalist societies were unfavourable to the strengthening of the organization of the state; extension of state services involved draining off capital and labour into unproductive channels. For the same reason, such societies were unfavourable to the building up of an elaborate ecclesiastical organization.

Church buildings had to be provided and manpower released for the carrying on of religious instruction. Insistence on maintaining certain prescribed standards in the character of places of worship and in the qualifications of the ministry raised costs in the way of building materials, wages, and salaries. The break from religion of frontier populations was a break from a religion which was expensive.[1] Taxation by ecclesiastical authorities was resisted as strongly as taxation by state authorities. The dominant drive of the capitalist frontier was that of economic exploitation.

In contrast, the services of the religious sect were provided virtually free of cost. Few demands were made either in the way of buildings or labour. Much of the preaching of the sectaries was carried on in open fields, barns, private homes, or on the streets, and, where houses of worship were required, they were simply built from local materials and through co-operative labour during slack seasons of the year. The sectarian preachers, likewise, imposed no great economic burden upon the new capitalist society. Many of them were employed on a part-time basis, working during the week and preaching in the evenings and on Sunday, but even when they were employed on a full-time basis they made little demand in the way of salary. They were men without professional training, and, having developed none of the tastes of the social élite, they were prepared to live simply in the manner of the people they served. The contrast in this regard, for instance, between the Methodist saddle-bag preacher and the Church of England clergyman in Upper Canada was striking. No less striking is the contrast today between the Jehovah's Witness worker and the college-trained minister of the United Church of Canada.

It is true that as religious revivalist movements grew, a very great number of men (and, in some cases, women) were drawn into preaching employments with a resulting drain of labour from more productive forms of work, but it is doubtful if this involved any great economic loss to the frontier society. Generally, those people who turned evangelical preachers were the economic misfits of the

---

[1]"All commercial communities," Brooks Adams wrote, "have rebelled against paying for miracles, and it was the spread of a scepticism already well developed in the thirteenth century among the manufacturing towns which caused the Reformation of the sixteenth." *The Law of Civilization and Decay: An Essay on History* (London, 1895), p. 129. Of developments after about 1400, Adams wrote: "Year by year, as society consolidated, the economic type was propagated; and as the pressure of a contracting currency stimulated these men to action, the demand for cheap religion grew fierce." *Ibid.*, p. 157.

community who had no great contribution to make to economic enterprise. Thus Henry Alline, the Newlight preacher of Nova Scotia, dying of tuberculosis, probably would have had to be supported by his family if he had not been supported by the community at large through voluntary contributions. The same was true of at least some of the others who, during the early period of sectarian development, joined the preaching ranks of the Newlights, or of the Baptists, Methodists, Campbellites, Plymouth Brethren, Salvation Army, Pentecostals, and Jehovah's Witnesses. Possessed of few skills and of little education, such people were denied the means of entering other professions, while in temperament or physique they were unsuited to manual labour. If they had not become evangelical preachers, they might well have become pedlars, horse traders, medical quacks, or unemployed village philosophers.

An accounting of the total costs of providing religious services would reveal a very considerable difference between the church and the sect, and in terms of the development of capitalist enterprise this difference has been very important. Shift of support to new sectarian movements resulted in a real economic saving at a time when the community had few reserves in the way of capital or labour. The effect of this saving was evident in the impetus given to the growth of economic enterprise in areas where religious sectarianism developed strongly, as for instance in the Annapolis Valley in Nova Scotia, while the effect of the drain upon economic resources in support of an elaborate ecclesiastical system was equally evident in the weakness of economic enterprise where church forms of religious organization continued strongly, as for instance in Quebec or along the north shore of Cape Breton.

In a more positive way as well, the religious sect contributed to meeting the problem of mobilizing capital and labour in frontier areas and thus in encouraging the development of new economic enterprise. The sect became an important economic group by virtue of the cohesiveness which it developed as a religious group. The economic solidarity of the sect offered a means of offsetting the limitations of individual economic enterprise. Members came to one another's assistance, through co-operative labour, buying and selling, borrowing and lending. Fortunes were kept within the group through restrictions upon marrying outside.[2] The collective

---

[2]"Religion," H. A. Innis wrote, "has been vitally related to the mysteries of life and death and to the family. The decline of the Church in Europe reflected the impact of birth control on the confessional. . . . Religious sects have fostered the

feeling of responsibility for the business reputation of the individual member increased the capacity to borrow. In a larger way, the religious sect developed many of the economic strengths of the closely knit family group; it could operate as a collective body in the labour, commercial, and financial market. Where corporate forms of economic organization were lacking, such an informal corporate organization became of considerable economic importance. The strong position of the Scottish and English Baptists in the business life of Toronto about the middle of the nineteenth century affords an illustration of the economic strengths deriving from the close group controls of the religious sect.

The relation of religious sectarian movements to the development of capitalism, however, was more far-reaching than that suggested in any contribution which such movements may have made to meeting the problem of mobilizing capital and labour. The development of capitalist enterprise required more than simply a reserve force of capital and labour. It required in general terms what has been called the spirit of capitalism. More particularly, it required a population disciplined to the economic demands of capitalistic exploitation. It was in providing such a discipline that religious sectarianism made its most distinctive contribution to the development of capitalist enterprise.

Frontier areas, that is, areas of new economic enterprise, tended to attract a socially undisciplined population; it was the restless, adventurous, and, often, the thriftless and irresponsible who sought their fortune in new lands or in new forms of economic activity. Conditions of life in such areas accentuated the break away from a disciplined routine and from accepted principles of conduct. The sudden break from past associations and the experience of many things which were new and unfamiliar had unsettling effects which were economically as well as socially disorganizing. The importance of chance in determining economic fortune encouraged a

---

accumulation of wealth over long periods by intermarriage of families. Whereas the Church in its fight for sacerdotal celibacy as a means of preventing the dispersion of wealth left itself open to the looting of its monasteries, the Jews and other sects have been persecuted because of the building up of large fortunes. . . .

"In the United States the importance of religion to the growth of trade is shown in the large numbers of denominational periodicals and their promising returns to advertisers in a national market. Significantly, among the first advertisers who were alert to these possibilities were those large-scale dealers in human credulity, the patent-medicine firms." H. A. Innis, "On the Economic Significance of Culture" in *The Tasks of Economic History*, Supplement IV to the *Journal of Economic History*, Dec., 1944, p. 89.

reckless speculative spirit, while disappointment as a result of the failure to achieve immediate riches led to an attitude of irresponsibility and despondency. An unreliability with respect to work, the payment of debts, or the quality of goods offered for sale was an inevitable consequence of the unrestricted exploitation of human and material resources on the frontier of capitalism. To a considerable extent, the most elementary economic virtues such as business honesty, frugality, and industry were lacking among a frontier population.

Indirectly, the social costs of conditions of life in new areas of economic development imposed as well a heavy toll upon economic enterprise. Drinking and gambling, prevalent vices of frontiersmen, cut heavily into savings and greatly reduced the efficiency of labour. Family disorganization weakened one of the important group supports of economic life. Mental breakdowns, suicides, and an increase generally in emotional instability, reduced the number of the steady and reliable among the working population. Economic failure and personal demoralization were closely related in an area which made heavy economic and social demands upon the population. The frontier capitalist society tended to become a society of economic and social misfits.

It was just in its role of converting the economic and social misfits of such a society into useful members that the religious sect gained its enormous importance in the development of new economic enterprise. Religion was made a powerful economic as well as social reorganizing influence by virtue of the very fact that it was made to appeal to those people who were the economically unadjusted within society. It offered a new standard of social conduct, and, in the end, a new economic discipline.

This was true even though the immediate effect of religious sectarianism may actually have accentuated the economic and social disorganization of the community. The difficulties of adjusting to new economic and social demands accounted to some extent for the resort in the first place to a religious interpretation of the problems of life. Religion offered a means of rationalizing failure. The religious convert as a result tended to view with indifference worldly values of economic and social success. The conception of the spiritual elect offered a means of achieving a sense of worth through the experience of religious faith. The saved, though unsuccessful in material terms, could look down with contempt upon those who were successful but were among the unsaved. Thus to some extent worldly standards of industry, frugality, and even, indeed, of moral righteousness were abandoned for standards of spiritual perfection. In extreme cases, complete personal demoralization resulted from participation in religious sectarian activity.

The fanaticism culitvated by the religious sect tended to weaken, in particular, habits of work and saving. All those people who disliked work or who were disinclined to save found a means of escape from such obligations by becoming caught up in religious activities. This was very much true of those people who became preachers, exhorters, or who, in some other capacity, assumed the role of religious teachers, but it was also true in a general way of all those who came to feel that salvation was the only problem of importance to mankind. Attendance, sometimes day after day for weeks at a time, at revivalist, protracted or camp meetings during busy seasons of the year interfered seriously with work, while constant concern with religious matters led to a neglect of family responsibilities in the way of caring for the home and providing some sort of economic security. During 1842, the year of the Millerite craze, for instance, great numbers of farmers and small-town folk in Canada and the Maritime Provinces abandoned work, and not a few of the more ardent sold or gave away their farms or businesses in preparation for the day of the Second Coming. Though in somewhat less spectacular form, the Newlight revivals in Nova Scotia and New Brunswick, the Methodist revivals in Upper Canada, the Salvation Army revivals towards the close of the nineteenth century, and more recent revivals—of Pentecostals, Jehovah's Witnesses, and others—have had similar effects. The economic costs of religious fanatacism at times could be high; there have been instances where whole communities were impoverished through unrestrained participation of the population in religious activity.

There would also seem good reason to believe that fanatical religious movements at times led to a serious weakening of moral standards. The doctrine of salvation by faith when taken literally, as for instance among many of the Newlights in Nova Scotia, gave rise to the view that good works in the way of strict moral conduct or, indeed, of conduct which conformed to accepted standards of decency and honesty were of no account; if a man believed, he was saved regardless of what might be his outward behaviour. An undue emphasis upon spiritual values led almost inevitably to a dulling of people's conceptions of what was right and wrong and, in cases of extreme religious fanaticism, to a complete distortion of moral values. This was particularly true during periods of religious revival when the frenzied religious excitement produced psychological conditions of intimate association favourable to the reckless abandonment of all social taboos and conventions. Sudden increases in illegitimacy rates have been found, on occasion, to have a close relation to outbursts of religious feelings, as for instance in the Onslow Baptist Church in Nova Scotia in 1818. In a general way, those people who were most religious have been found often to be the least reliable with respect to fair dealing and the payment of debts, with consequent economic losses to the community as a whole.

Finally, fanatical religious movements have very often had the effect of increasing personal disorganization in the community, evident in mental breakdown, suicide, and alcoholism. The experience of a sense of sinfulness, as a result of evangelical religious preaching, was intended to be terrifying; the whole complex of reactions to the highly emotional religious appeal was mentally disturbing. When the appeal was made to people who were emotionally unstable to begin with, the results were very often disastrous. Those who were unable to gain the experience of faith in their saviour were driven to the lowest depths of despair, but even those who experienced successful conversion were not always emotionally secure, as the large number of evangelical preachers who suffered mental breakdowns would suggest. The effort to maintain faith involved almost as great a mental strain as the effort to gain faith, and not a few broke under the strain. The view of the Superintendent of the Toronto Lunatic Asylum in 1860 that religious fanaticism was responsible for the mental breakdown of many of the inmates probably had some basis in fact. Outbreaks of religious hysteria were never clearly distinguishable from other manifestations of mass psychic disturbances.

If religious sectarian movements had had no other effect than that of resulting in fanatical expressions of religious feelings, their contribution to the development of economic enterprise would have been limited. The effect of religious fanaticism in weakening habits of work and saving and moral standards and in accentuating the emotional instability of the population certainly was to delay the economic reorganization of frontier society. Among certain sections of the population, religious sectarianism did result in indefinitely retarding economic progress.

Among other sections of the population, however, the disorganizing effects of sectarian religious teachings tended in time to be more than offset by the disciplined effects of sectarian religious controls. The religious sects were compelled to bring the fanaticism resulting from their teachings under control if it were not to develop to the point where it completely discredited religion. Thus the enthusiasm aroused by the religious revival came increasingly to be directed along channels to the advantage of the religious group. The exclusive emphasis upon spiritual values persisted but such values found interpretation within the collective religious body. Authority shifted from the individual to the sect as such, and it was the complete and absolute authority which it came to possess which constituted its distinctive strength as a disciplining social agency.

To develop a body of steady followers out of the sort of people it attracted into its fold, the religious sect was compelled to culti- vate an ascetic outlook on life. The sectarian was the kind of person who could not afford to conform to the conventions of polite society; his break from many of the norms of social behaviour, which found expression in forms of fanatical religious activity, was a reflection of his failure to fit into a traditional economic and social order. What, in effect, the religious sect did was to develop, and rigorously enforce, its own distinctive standards of conduct. It was in this way that its influence gained such importance in the growth of new economic enterprise.

In a general way, this shift within the religious sect from a free and unrestrained expression of religious feelings to the exercise of close group controls over religious conduct was closely related to the shift from a state of economic depression to a state of economic prosperity in new areas of development. The pioneer stage of frontier development tended to be characterized by inefficiency in methods of production, shortage of money, and lack of markets, and the consequent discouragement of the population led to a frantic search for means of escape in religion and in economic and political panaceas of various sorts. With improvements in methods of production, the increase in the supply of money, and the opening up of outside markets, economic conditions generally improved, and the growing importance of the economic motive discouraged a too great emphasis upon purely spiritual values. The unrestrained display of emotional feelings of the religious convert gave way to the carefully controlled religious feelings of the sectarian. The ascetic outlook gained importance as a condition of economic success.

Once cultivated as a means of securing the solidarity of the religious group, asceticism inevitably exerted a considerable in- fluence upon economic and social conduct. Its effect in cultivating habits of saving and thus encouraging the accumulation of capital was particularly important, but hardly less important was its effect in promoting temperate drinking habits and checking gambling and thereby contributing to the creation of a disciplined labour force. Religious asceticism was hostile to the conventional dissipations of the gentleman and to the slothful vices of the poor. Industry, frugality, and moral uprightness became the attributes of those belonging to the spiritual elect. It was through the cultivation of such virtues that economic success was determined in new areas of development. If the ascetic outlook on life developed persons who were dull, narrow, and intolerant, such persons were people of great drive and forceful character. It was out of such stuff that capitalist society was built.

The rise of the Baptists and Methodists to positions of importance in the business life of Canada during the latter half of the nineteenth century offers an illustration of the close relation between the development of religious asceticism and the growth of capitalism. On the other hand, the weakness of a spirit of economic enterprise in areas where traditional forms of religious organization persisted strong, as for instance in areas where religious life centred about the Church of England or the Roman Catholic Church, suggests that where religious asceticism did not develop conditions were unfavourable to capitalist growth. The traditional church, the religious denomination made up of people with social status, was not faced like the religious sect with the problem of creating out of the economic and social misfits of society a body of steady religious followers. The traditional church enjoyed the support of people who already had their own standards of conduct and who, like gentlemen of means for instance, could afford to indulge in such conventional forms of dissipation as drinking and gambling or, indeed, of failing to pay their debts. Class controls defined the limits of permissible behaviour, and the threat of disgrace secured conformity to generally accepted standards.[3] Thus, unlike the

[3]"A man of rank and fortune," Adam Smith wrote, "is by his very station the distinguished member of a great society, who attend to every part of his conduct, and who thereby oblige him to attend to every part of it himself. His authority and consideration depend very much upon the respect which this society bears to him. He dare not do anything which would disgrace or discredit him in it, and he is obliged to a very strict observation of that species of morals, whether liberal or austere, which the general consent of this society prescribes to persons of his rank and fortune. A man of low condition, on the contrary, is far from being a distinguished member of any great society. While he remains in a country village his conduct may be attended to, and he may be obliged to attend to it himself. In this situation, and in this situation only, he may have what is called a character to

religious sect, the church had no need of interfering with the private lives of its members; indeed, the condition of continuing to enjoy their support was the refraining from such interference. For this reason, the church was able to exert little moral influence upon those members of society who had broken away from conventional habits of behaviour. The development out of a frontier population of an enterprising business class and a sober, steady, working class could not come through an emphasis upon traditional values of decorum and moral decency. It required the sort of rigid discipline provided by religious asceticism.

That was true so long as the problem of capitalist growth was one of accumulating capital, recruiting labour, and developing new techniques of production. As capitalist enterprise continued to grow, however, conditions increasingly developed which came to weaken the religious sectarian spirit and to favour the more formal type of religious organization characteristic of the church. Indeed, the very influence of the religious sect furthered the development of those conditions which made its survival impossible. With the expansion of capitalism, wealth accumulated and large-scale economic organization developed. Many of those people who began life in new areas of economic development as failures and who became caught up in sectarian religious movements became the successful of the new capitalist society; their participation in sectarian religious activity was an important condition of their success. Thus the religious sect, in the beginning a religious movement of the economically dispossessed of the community, came increasingly to draw its support from the substantial economic classes of capitalist society, and the conflict of the sectarian outlook with the outlook of the economically successful forced a modification in the character of the sect if it were to avoid extinction.

The ascetic way of life favoured the accumulation of wealth,

---

lose. But as soon as he comes into a great city, he is sunk into obscurity and darkness. His conduct is observed and attended to by nobody, and he is therefore very likely to neglect it himself, and to abandon himself to every sort of low profligacy and vice. He never emerges so effectually from this obscurity, his conduct never excites so much the attention of any respectable society, as by his becoming the member of a small religious sect. He from that moment acquires a degree of consideration which he never had before. All his brother sectaries are, for the credit of the sect, interested to observe his conduct, and if he gives occasion to any scandal, if he deviates very much from those austere morals which they almost always require of one another, to punish him by what is always a very severe punishment, even where no civil effects attend it, expulsion or excommunication from the sect." *The Wealth of Nations* (Oxford, 1880), vol. II, p. 380.

but wealth in itself seriously weakened the values of asceticism. The successful man could afford to indulge in the comforts and dissipations of the gentleman, and became impatient of restraints which denied him the means of such conspicuous forms of consumption. More than this, the ascetic way of life came to act as a positive brake upon the development of economic enterprise. Where emphasis shifted from production to salesmanship, economic expansion demanded the continual increase of consumer wants and consequently an abandonment of the austere values cultivated by the religious sect. The luxury trade became of considerable importance in the development of a mature capitalist economy.

At the same time, religious sectarianism as a disciplining force lost its importance with the increasing emphasis upon pecuniary values and the development of various forms of economic association. Profits or wages served as driving influences in maintaining habits of industry and a spirit of enterprise; economic associations, of farmers, workers, or manufacturers, for instance, established standards of economic conduct through the formulation of codes and through the development of a class consciousness. Such secular forms of control grew up almost entirely outside the province of religious controls and were able therefore to exist in complete independence of religious values. Thus they inevitably came in conflict with sectarian controls based on the view that the only values of life were those of a spiritual character.

If the conditions of capitalist expansion became increasingly unfavourable to the survival of religious sectarianism, they became increasingly favourable to the growth of religious denominationalism. The growth of wealth made possible the support of religious institutions making heavy demands in the way of expensive church structures, denominational colleges, religious newspapers, and highly paid ministers, while the economic and social demands of the capitalist society made virtually necessary the development of such religious institutions. The expensive religious service became an important form of conspicuous consumption; distinctions arising from attendance in exclusive places of worship served as a strong support of a system of class stratification. The religious teachings of the church, with their emphasis upon the virtues of the successful, offered a rationalization of forms of economic behaviour leading to the concentration of wealth and power. At the same time, the good works in which the church was engaged served to cultivate among the poor the sort of virtues necessary to successful capitalist enterprise. The church, in contrast with the sect, recognized different standards of morality for different classes of society. Thus the temperance movement, as over against the sect prohibition on drinking among all its members, tended to represent an effort on the part of the capitalist middle class to control the drinking habits of the working lower class. In various other ways as well, the church became an important support of large-scale capitalist enterprise. The increasing dependence of capitalism upon collective social controls and propaganda was evident in the close relation of big business to the church and to the state. The bureaucracy of business combined with the bureaucracies of church and state in maintaining the controls of the new capitalist society.

So long as capitalism continued to expand, however, such tendencies towards the concentration of power and control in society were checked through the development of new forms of individual economic enterprise and through the consequent emergence of conditions unfavourable to the maintenance of centralized economic and cultural controls. The big business of the metropolis gave way to the individually owned small business of the frontier, and religious denominationalism weakened in the face of social pressures favouring the assertion of the sectarian spirit in religious organization. It was in this way that the expansion of capitalism made for a persistent state of instability in religious organization, in the recurrent conflict between the sect and church form of religious fellowship. Where capitalist development implied the growth, at one and the same time, of new economic enterprise and of large-scale economic organization, there operated in society forces tending to make impossible the stabilization of forms of religious organization either in terms of the principles of the sect or of the church. If sects were no sooner organized than they developed into churches, churches no sooner became denominationally powerful than they lost much of their support to new sects.

Yet the stability of the Roman Catholic Church in the province of Quebec throughout almost the whole of the nineteenth century, and of a number of religious sects in various isolated parts of the country in the past and at the present day, would suggest that there have been certain areas in the Canadian community, social pockets so to speak, in which religious organization has stood largely outside the sphere of influence of capitalist expansion. Within such areas the controls of the local society have been so strong that the population has tended to remain completely divorced from the economic and social order of capitalism. Lack of social mobility has meant little change in the social status of people, and a rigid status system has supported, and in turn been supported by, a sort of ecclesiastical or sectarian theocracy all-embracing in so far as the local society was concerned. Thus in nineteenth-century Quebec religion was organized in terms of a hierarchy of social classes which had little relation to the much more fluid class system of capitalism, and sharp separation from the outside capitalist world was maintained through an emphasis upon ethnic and religious differences and through geographical isolation. Similarly, within the ethnic-religious colony, such as that of the Mennonites, Doukhobors, or Hutterites, the secular influences of capitalism have been resisted with some success, and religious organization has tended to remain stable.

As a result of somewhat similar influences, slum areas whether urban or rural likewise have stood largely outside the range of influence of capitalist expansion, and here also as a result, religion has tended to become organized in terms of a rigid status system. The material and human resources of slum areas are so limited as to make impossible any real participation in capitalist enterprise. People in the slum do not move, either out of the area or upwards in the social scale. Lack of mobility has meant that the status of such people has been fixed, within the slum itself and within the society at large. The result has been an absence of those influences which make for change in forms of religious association. It is not the slum population which affords support to new sectarian movements; the religious sect is a movement of the restless, the insecure, of the people who have lost status and are striving to regain it. The slum population is a population which enjoys social status, accepted by itself and by the outside society; its forms of religious organization, typified by the church mission and "queer" sect, give expression to such a social state.

It is true that to a considerable extent such areas have only succeeded in sheltering themselves from the effects of capitalist expansion on a sort of sufferance. The breaking down of the old French Canadian Roman Catholic society in Quebec in the years since the First World War suggests the failure of efforts to maintain a position of isolation through an emphasis upon ethnic and religious differences in face of irresistible forces of industrialization. Similarly, the increasing secularization of Mennonite society in Manitoba is indicative of the difficulty of maintaining the conditions of a closed social system by a reliance upon religious controls once geographical separation ceases. Where a society stands directly in the path of capitalist expansion it is placed in an extremely insecure position. Even the population of slum areas has been drawn into the productive forces of capitalism when fully exposed to its economic and social demands.

Still, it is easy to exaggerate the strength of capitalist influences in breaking down traditional forms of social and religious control. There is a certain incalculable toughness in society in resisting that which is upsetting or disturbing. Such a toughness is evident within the traditional Roman Catholic society such as that of Quebec and also within such an ethnic-religious society as that of the Hutterites in Alberta and Manitoba. Influences of the capitalist secular society may not be kept out entirely but complete absorption is avoided by some sort of limited accommodation.

In a general way, what is true of such isolated groups in the community has been true to some extent of the Canadian community as a whole in relation to the outside capitalist world. Conditions of Canadian political and cultural development have set sharp limitations upon the uncontrolled expansion of individual capitalist enterprise in the country. The peculiar vulnerability of the Canadian frontier in face of the rapid expansion of the American community to the south has forced a considerable degree of political and cultural control over economic development. The Canadian nation has been produced out of the forces of counter-revolution. Thus the collapse of the old régime in French Canada reflected the growing strength of New England commercialism, but maintenance of the British tie after 1763 compelled the isolation of the Canadian and Maritime colonies from the influence of economic and cultural forces developing strongly within the revolutionary colonies along the Atlantic seaboard. Similarly, the weakening of the British imperial tie evident for instance in the growth of radical political movements in the colonies after 1800 was a reflection of the strength of the new American capitalism with western expansion, but the threat of political encroachment in 1812–14, 1837–40, and again in the early 1860's was met by efforts to isolate the Canadian society from American economic and cultural influences, evident in restrictions after 1814 on Americans settling in the country, the Act of Union in 1840, and Confederation in 1867. Since 1867, the struggle to preserve the political independence of the Canadian community has continued to force a considerable

degree of economic and cultural independence. Although the
pioneers of new developments in Canada, in mining, wheat farming,
and manufacturing for instance, have come very largely from the
United States, American economic and cultural dominance has
been stiffly resisted by resort to such political weapons of control
as tariffs, prohibitions upon the circulation of literature, and imperial preferences. In a sense, because of its political insecurity,
the Canadian community has not been able to risk any break with
its colonial tradition. Throughout, the state has been forced to
intervene, in the opening up of the frontier and in the later development of the more mature economic society. The effects have been
evident in the limitations upon individual economic enterprise with
consequent limitations upon social experimentation.

With respect to religious organization, the struggle to maintain
political independence has meant placing a check upon developments leading to any too great a break from traditional religious
authority. Economic and cultural isolation has given support to a
sort of ecclesiastical or sectarian theocracy within the Canadian
community as a whole. The strength of traditional authority in
religious organization has been evident not only in the position of
the Roman Catholic Church in the province of Quebec and in the
early privileges enjoyed by the Church of England and the Church
of Scotland, but in the tendency of such evangelical religious bodies
as Wesleyan Methodism and the Salvation Army to identify their
interests with the imperial connection and of such present-day denominations as the United Church of Canada to identify their
interests with Canadian nationalism. Canada has proved hostile,
on the one side, to the influences of extreme forms of religious sectarianism as they developed on the American frontier, and, on the
other side, to liberal religious influences as they developed in the
larger American centres and in western Europe. The collective
influence of the community has been exerted to maintain traditional authority in religion. The strength of religious denominationalism and religious fundamentalism in Canadian society today
would suggest that this influence has been exerted with considerable
effectiveness.

There would seem some reason to believe that such rigidity in
forms of religious organization has become even more characteristic of present-day Canadian society as a result of recent tendencies
towards an economic and political collectivism. New technological
developments and new techniques of business organization and

finance have provided large-scale capitalist enterprise with enormous advantages in production and marketing, while the importance of the economic factor in national prestige and defence has forced the even closer control of the state over economic life. Government soil surveys afford an illustration of more careful planning through state direction of agricultural settlement, while the factory town exemplifies the sort of controlled direction of industrial development secured through large-scale private enterprise. The new frontier of capitalism is to some extent an area of planned economic development. It has become as a consequence an area of planned social development as well. The provision of educational institutions, recreational facilities, health services, and, even housing is a responsibility now often assumed by large-scale capitalist enterprise and the state, and the assumption of responsibility carries with it the exercise of a considerable measure of control. The implications with respect to religious organization are particularly far-reaching.

Where the support of large-scale capitalist enterprise and the state is secured, the church is able to entrench itself so deeply in the community that new religious movements have little opportunity to develop. Thus in recently settled areas of Quebec, the direction and control exercised by the state has secured as one of its objectives the preferred position of the church. Similarly, within the factory town, as for instance in Arvida, the financial support of large-scale capitalist organization has provided those churches which meet with favour with overwhelming advantages in competing with rival religious bodies. Economic and political collectivism makes inevitably for a religious collectivism. The centralization of economic and political life favours the centralization of religious life; the claim of patriotism in itself has come to constitute a powerful force in securing conformity to church establishment. The wartime legal ban on the activities of the Jehovah's Witnesses is suggestive in this regard.

If tendencies towards a centralization of control within the state and business have led to a strengthening of the position of the churches in relation to new religious movements in the community, on the other side, tendencies towards a greater rigidity in the social class structure of capitalism have checked the growth of already established religious sects into churches or formally organized religious denominations. In modern capitalist society it is no longer easy to rise rapidly in the social scale; the wealthy have devised effective means of perpetuating their command of wealth while the working masses face the prospect of becoming permanently proletarianized. As a result, the religious sect has tended to become much more, as for instance in the case of the Salvation Army or Jehovah's Witnesses, a form of religious organization serving people of fixed social status in the community, and as a consequence social pressures forcing it to abandon its sectarian character and to seek a fuller accommodation to the secular community have somewhat weakened.

Where social stratification in religious organization has developed to the point where the religious sect and the church have come to serve two distinctly different population groups in the community, the historic role of the sect as a liberalizing influence in society may be considered to have come to an end. The sect operated as a liberal influence because it was composed of people on the make. The striving of sectarian leaders, and of sectarian members generally, for social position meant that the collective influence of the sect was exerted to break the dominance of privileged institutions and groups in society. Sectarianism served as an effective check upon any too great concentration of religious authority in the community or upon any close alliance of the church, the state, and big business. Where the sect, however, has come to be made up of people who accept their position in society, it no longer seriously challenges the vested interests of the established social system. Instead, it secures the patronage of wealthy business men, politicians, and other well-meaning citizens who feel that its teachings, though unacceptable to them, are beneficial to the sort of people it serves. In its relation to the church, it assumes something of the character of the mission or religious order, appealing to that section of the population which the more respectable religious denominations prefer to have nothing to do with. The real conflict tends to become one with secular movements of a political or social revolutionary character which seek the support of the same sort of people the sect seeks. In time to come it will probably be recognized that, from the point of view of maintaining the political, economic, and social status quo, the legal ban during the Second World War on the activities of the Jehovah's Witnesses was a blunder on the part of the Canadian government.

It would be foolhardy to speculate here as to future developments in religious organization. In terms of present-day tendencies towards totalitarianism, an increasingly close alliance of economic, political, and religious forces would seem likely. We are not so far now from having a state religion; much nearer, perhaps, than from having a state church. It is possible that an identification of religious interests with the interests of the nation and big business will become very much more complete in the not too distant future. On the other hand, it is equally possible that the deeply rooted urge within society for the free expression of religious feelings and beliefs will arrest the trend toward such an identification. It is only necessary to recall, and stress, the importance of the role played by religious sectarian movements in sixteenth-century Germany and England in weakening centralized authority within the church and the state, and in economic organization.

CHAPTER X

The Religious Influence in
Canadian Society*

CANADA HAS SUFFERED THROUGHOUT HER HISTORY
by the comparison of her rate of progress with that of the United
States. Almost every traveller to this continent during the past two
or more centuries has found occasion to comment on the apparent
difference in the degree of economic prosperity on the two sides
of the border. Lord Durham was compelled to recognize this difference as one of the underlying causes of political disaffection in the
country. Local observers joined in deploring the failure of Canada
to keep pace economically with the United States. Haliburton, ex-
pressing his views through his fictitious Yankee clockmaker, was
scathing in his denunciation of the lack of industry and business
imagination among his fellow Nova Scotians. Canadians today,
with a similarly critical insight into the economic state of their
country, are but little less inclined to point out the unfavourable
comparison it makes with the neighbour to the south. The belief
persists that the really enterprising Canadian must cross the border
if he is to realize his fullest ambitions.

To some extent this comparison of the rate of economic growth
of the two countries to the disadvantage of Canada has been based
on a failure to see any of the favourable aspects in the development
of the one country and any of the unfavourable aspects in the development of the other. The comparison has seldom, for instance, taken

*From *The Tasks of Economic History*, a supplement of the *Journal of
Economic History*, 1947, pp. 89–103. With permission of the publisher. The
original title read: "The Religious Factor in Canadian Economic Development."

into account the lack of economic progressiveness of the southern
United States. But when due allowance is made for distortions of
the facts, it remains true that there has been absent in Canada to
some extent that spirit of economic enterprise, that drive to secure
the fullest exploitation of natural resources, which has been so
characteristic of the development of the United States. The growth
of capitalism has come about in a slower and more halting fashion.

As a new country with unexploited natural resources, and no
elaborate and costly structure of social services to begin with,
Canada has offered almost as strong inducements to the development of new forms of economic enterprise as the United States.
In Canada, however, in a way that has not been as true of the
United States, various influences of a political, cultural, and
religious character have served to check the free play of economic
forces and as a result to limit economic growth. Rigidities have
entered into the development of the Canadian community which
have had the effect of diverting the resources of the country and the
energies of the people into channels of advantage to non-economic
interests. It would be difficult to say which of such influences, the
political, cultural, or religious, has assumed greatest importance in
establishing such rigidities; all three have been closely related. The
political influence perhaps has been of chief significance in that the
building of a Canadian society has been essentially a political
problem. But if the cultural and religious influences have derived
much of their support from the political, they have served to act,
in turn, as powerful forces in its support. This has been especially
true of the religious influence.

In few countries in the western world has religion exerted as great
an influence upon the development of the community as it has in
Canada. There have been areas, the southern states of the United
States for instance, where it perhaps has been a more powerful force
in local social life, but the influence of such areas in the larger
national community has been offset by that of other areas where it
has had little strength. The so-called Bible Belt might be thought of
as extending not only through the southern but through the northern
sections of the North American Continent to include almost the
whole of Canada within its range. The peculiar political and cultural insecurity of the country in the face of, first, the rapid expansion of the neighbour to the south and, second, the deeply embedded
and often bitter ethnic and regional dissensions among the population has led to a considerable dependence upon religion as a force

in maintaining community solidarity. At no time has religion assumed an insignificant role in the life of the Canadian community. On occasion, it has been a force of dominant importance.

New France began almost as an experiment in theocratic-ecclesiastical control. Not only were Huguenots excluded from the colony but an effort was made to restrict immigration to those who in the eyes of the Jesuit priests could be considered good Catholics. The precarious position of the colony within the American continental system led to the maintenance of strong religious controls as a means of preserving the connection with France. When political collapse did come to the French Empire in America, religion assumed even greater importance as a force resisting absorption into the larger American society. In Acadia, it is true, the militant efforts of anti-British missionaries to isolate their Roman Catholic following led to the complete destruction of the French society, but in Quebec conflict between English governmental, military, and trading interests served to strengthen the position of the church and to make its influence more effective as a barrier to communication between the French and Anglo-Saxon populations. The colony escaped the influence of strong anti-religious movements of thought growing up in revolutionary France through severance of the political tie by the British conquest, and it escaped the influence of similar movements of thought gaining strength in English-speaking America through isolation from the English colonies by the Revolution. As re-established by the Quebec Act, the church of French Canada found new support in the close alliance with the state. Its character was shaped and its strong position determined by forces of counter-revolution.

In the Maritime colonies religion was little less important as a force maintaining political control. Although freedom of worship was granted the early New England settlers, the Church of England was established by law, and efforts of the church to minister to the religious wants of the population secured the full support of colonial authorities. Attendance upon religious services took on the character of a civic duty; indeed, in Halifax, it was made a legal obligation. The effect of the American Revolution was to reinforce these strong religious influences in the cultural life of the community. The large New England population offered a natural channel of communication for the spread into the Maritimes of revolutionary influences; most of the New Englanders sympathized with the revolutionary cause and many of them gave to it their active support. The break with the Atlantic seaboard colonies on the outbreak of war, however, effectively isolated the New England group and led to a considerable strengthening of British influences. Organized religion as a result gained a greatly increased importance as a force supporting the British connection. Efforts to establish a powerful ecclesiastical-religious structure and to capture the West India trade were not unrelated phases of the general struggle to build up in the Maritime Provinces after 1800 a political system secure against attack by the United States.

In the St. Lawrence waterways region, the western movement of American population after 1790 breached temporarily the isolation of the British colony which had resulted from the Revolutionary War; people poured across the border to form the new province of Upper Canada and to bring into being the settlements of the Eastern Townships. But barriers to communication provided by language and culture made it possible for the Roman Catholic Church to maintain its strong position of control among the French Canadians in Lower Canada (especially in face of the threat to the political security of the province as a result of the operations of French agents in the United States) while the precarious political situation in Upper Canada where the vast majority of the population was American led to a vigorous effort to build up the influence of an established Protestant ecclesiastical system. The War of 1812 served in Upper Canada, as the Revolutionary War had done in Nova Scotia, to cut off any close contact with the United States. After 1815 a British influence that tended on the whole to be traditionalistic and illiberal became predominant. Anxiety on the part of the growing overseas population to maintain its political attachments intensified the dependence upon religious attachments. Religion operated as a powerful force in checking the spread of liberal influences from the United States and from Britain; in return, it secured the support in the colony of those interests identified with the British connection. Failure of the rebellion in 1837 completed the political and religious isolation of the colony that had its beginnings in the American Revolution and the War of 1812.

Of even more crucial importance in the preservation of the religious influence in Canadian life was the failure of outside liberal movements to gain a hold in the country in the period from 1850 to the close of the century. This was the period in Great Britain and the United States that witnessed the growth of almost literally hundreds of rationalist, free-thinking societies. Scarcely one such society made its appearance in Canada before the closing years of the century. Instead, the period witnessed the emergence of powerful new religious denominations, the Methodist Church (Canada), the Presbyterian Church in Canada, the Church of England in Canada, and the Baptist Conference of Canada, fused out of smaller and less politically effective religious bodies. Nationalism served to emphasize, as colonialism had done earlier, the need of limiting contacts with liberal-revolutionary movements outside the country. The Civil War in the United States was for Canada, in effect, the fourth phase of the revolution that began with the War of Independence in 1776 and continued into the War of 1812 and the Rebellion of 1837. Confederation, as an effort to consolidate politically scattered communities which in themselves had few means of resisting encroachments on the part of the powerful neighbour to the south, grew, like the Constitutional Act and the Act of Union before it, out of forces of counter-revolution in the country. Lacking new frontiers for expansion the Canadian nation in the years after 1867 was able to gather strength through isolation. Within such a community, thus turned in on itself, religion faced no real challenge to its authority.

Developments in Canada since the turn of the century have been too complex to make possible any easy generalization respecting the strength of religious influences. In large areas of Canadian life, especially since the First World War, there has been a steady move away from a religious point of view. Nevertheless, the influence of organized religion in the country has perhaps never been stronger. Union of the Presbyterian, Methodist, and Congregational churches in 1925 has been followed by the development of new forms of interdenominational co-operation which have enormously strengthened the influence of Protestantism. At the same time, there has been a strengthening of the Roman Catholic ecclesiastical structure. Because of the political pressure they are able to exert, both Protestant and Roman Catholic churches have secured a degree of state support which provides them with many of the privileges of establishment. No political party in the country could survive if it openly attacked either of these churches.

International developments of the past quarter-century have had the effect of intensifying some of the conditions of insecurity of the Canadian national community. Preservation of national independence has involved a rejection of such anti-religious ways of thought as those associated not only with the American revolutionary tradition but with the revolutionary tradition of Russia. Canadians have not felt sufficiently secure in their national attachments to cultivate an attitude of tolerance. At the same time, developments within the country have led to a growing provincial or regional isolationism. Threats to the autonomy of French Canada have had the effect of increasing dependence upon the leadership provided by the Roman Catholic Church, while the growing political strength of French Canada in turn, has made English-speaking Canada more conscious of its Protestantism.

As a result of this continuous dependence upon the influence of religion in resisting outside political and cultural pressures, it is almost possible to think of the development of the Canadian community as having taken place within a closed theocratic-ecclesiastical system. The Canadian frontier has never been, like the American frontier, an area of unrestricted economic development. Rather, it has developed under what might be described as conditions of monopoly control. One of the important forces securing such control has been organized religion.

As all monopoly control tends to do, that of religion has placed a sharp brake upon the economic growth of the country. It has done so directly where, for instance, the church has been actually able to direct the movement of population and to prohibit any sort of economic endeavour which has threatened the religious interest. Out of such control there has developed at most a sort of theocratic monopolistic capitalism. But religion also, indirectly, has served to retard economic enterprise. The promotion of the religious interest in itself has involved a weakening of the economic interest because of the fundamental antagonism of the one to the other.

In the first place, the heavy drain upon the material resources of the country in maintaining institutions of religious worship has weakened the economic energies of the population. Church buildings have had to be erected, a body of religious teachers supported, and a decent portion of people's time devoted to performing the necessary rites and ceremonies of religion. The fundamental economic problem of a new country such as Canada has been that of mobilizing a sufficient supply of capital and labour to exploit fully its available resources. Where a large share of the capital and labour of the society has been diverted to the support of religious establishments the problem of securing a sufficient surplus to promote economic growth has been considerably intensified. The economic costs of religion cannot be easily calculated, but there would seem little doubt but that they have borne heavily upon various areas of the country at different times. In French Canada heavy ecclesiastical taxation in one form or another has meant that the capital required for the establishment of industry has come to a considerable extent either from outside capitalist groups, from the state, or from the church itself. In English-speaking Canada the burden of maintaining a religious structure has also made itself felt. In the colonial period, governmental, military, and ecclesiastical establishments made about equally heavy demands on the resources of a poor pioneer population, and, although the growing wealth of the country since the middle of the nineteenth century has made possible the easier financial support of religious institutions, the economic costs of religion in the way of large buildings, denominational colleges, missionary organizations, and salaried ministers have vastly increased. In poorer sections of the country where the resources of the population are limited, as for instance in certain parts of the Maritime Provinces, financial contributions to religious bodies have probably continued to be a factor in retarding economic growth.

In another closely related way, the religious interests of the population have tended to obstruct economic interests. Religion has given support to an attitude of mind, and a governmental policy, which has placed a check upon that kind of economic and social mobility conductive to the development of capitalism. Churches are essentially status institutions, and this has meant that the organization of religion has served to maintain status distinctions that have had no meaning in terms of economic endeavour. The strength of the aristocratic tradition in Canada owes much to the influence of religion. In Roman Catholic Quebec the notion of a socially superior class based upon family connection, education, and, usually, the ownership of land has been rooted deeply in the teachings of the church; there has been an aristocracy of old families that has proved itself on the whole inept in promoting new forms of economic enterprise. In English-speaking Canada, if the relation between religion and the class structure has been less obvious, it has been little less important. Church establishment in colonial times placed a considerable dependence upon a close alliance with a privileged upper class that lacked the imagination or inclination to take any sort of lead in the economic development of the country, and, although the formal disestablishment of the church weakened the religious support of such a class system, the organization of religion has continued to be sufficiently powerful to maintain to some degree the status distinctions of a religiously oriented rather than economically oriented society. By nepotism and other means church bureaucracy has succeeded in securing to the proper people positions of social distinction in the community. To the extent that such has been the case, and economic success as a result has not been the determinant of social worth, the economic ambitions of the population have been weakened.

Again, with respect to the moral results of its teachings, it would appear that the influence of religion has not been wholly favourable to economic development. The other-worldliness of the highly religious has resulted to some extent in an attitude of indifference to such worldly obligations as the payment of debts. If the judgment of various observers is to be trusted, business honesty has not been characteristic of religious populations. Rather, such business honesty has developed when people's positions in the community have become dependent upon social judgments in terms of secular values of worth. The development of capitalist economic enterprise, therefore, has involved the building of an ethical system opposed in many ways to that of religion. This has been successfully done only where the economic interest has gained dominance over the religious.

Finally, the influence of religion has checked the growth of that sort of rationalist attitude of mind favourable to economic activity. Economic success depends upon a clear appraisal of the relation of means to ends. Religion has tended to a confusion of this relation which inevitably has been carried over into the field of economic activity. It is scarcely correct to assume that religious-minded populations have successfully kept separate their religious and their economic attitudes and have been able to act perfectly rational outside the province of religious conduct. That has been possible only where emancipation from religious controls has been secured to some extent. Where religion has operated as a dominant force in people's lives, irrationality has tended to be characteristic of their way of thought and behaviour in general. Thus the effect of the religious influence has been to retard the development of that kind of coldly calculating mentality that has made for economic success. A readiness to place dependence upon divine intervention, as upon luck, is perhaps a necessary quality of the good gambler but not of the good business man.

If the effect of the religious influence generally has been to check economic growth, there would seem no reason to believe that any particular set of religious doctrines has been of importance as a factor in the economic development of the Canadian community. Essentially, the religious influence exerted through Protestantism in Canada has been no more favourable to the promotion of economic enterprise than the religious influence exerted through Roman Catholicism. If Roman Catholicism has appeared to offer a greater obstacle than Protestantism to economic growth, that has been largely because the religious influence has found stronger support in the Roman Catholic than in the Protestant ecclesiastical system. Where the Protestant religious organization has been strong the Protestant population has tended to be as economically unprogressive as the Roman Catholic population.

It has been the character of instability of the Protestant religious organization that has chiefly accounted for what difference there has been in the influence of Protestantism and of Roman Catholicism upon economic development. Where the Protestant organization of religion has faced continuous attack from schismatic sects, the religious influence of Protestantism in general has been weakened. It is true that the growth of new religious movements has tended to a strengthening immediately of the religious interests of the population; such movements have grown out of deep emotional experiences that have served to emphasize the importance of spiritual values of life. Ultimately, however, the effect has been to weaken the influence of religion by weakening its denominational supports; by producing divisions within religious organization the sects have destroyed some of religion's authority. It has been this indirect result of sectarian religious activity that has been so important in relation to economic development. The religious influence as such, exerted by the sects, has been no more favourable to economic growth than that exerted by the old, established, ecclesiastical bodies.

Thus, with respect to the effect upon economic development of the costs of supporting religious services, there has been no fundamental difference between the church and the sect forms of religious organization. It is true that the sects have not made as large financial demands upon the population as the more elaborately organized ecclesiastical bodies, but this has been so mainly because they have operated in areas of society that have not been able to support more expensive forms of religious organization. It has been "good business" in a sense to get along with cheaply constructed church buildings and low-paid religious teachers; a church that made greater demands had little chance to survive. The areas in which religious sects have grown up have been those that have had no surplus of capital and labour to be placed at the disposal either of expensive religious establishments or of new forms of economic enterprise. Only after such a surplus has appeared have the economic costs of sectarian religion become important in relation to economic development. With the increase in the wealth of the community, sectarian religious groups have sought to build about themselves elaborate ecclesiastical structures. But their primary influence as movements of religious separation has tended to the defeat of their ultimate purpose as religious institutions. Resentment of ecclesiastical taxation which they have cultivated among their followings in meeting the competition of more richly endowed religious bodies has persisted even after they themselves have become dependent upon such taxation. The result has been that the economic costs of religion have tended to fall below the level that the community has been able to afford, and the surplus of capital and labour that has accumulated has found an outlet in the development of economic enterprise.

Similarly, new sectarian religious movements, in their effect in weakening the traditional class structure of the community, have only indirectly favoured the growth of new forms of economic enterprise. Such movements have grown up in areas of society where class lines already had broken down; they have been a means of giving people who have had no definite status within the community a feeling of being important. This has meant that, rather than giving rise to a non-religiously oriented class system, they have created a class system in which the spiritually elect stood against the non-elect, and which rested accordingly upon a religious foundation. A social class that bases its claim to superiority on its special piety is not the sort of class that is likely to take a lead in promoting economic growth. Only after the influence of religion has been weakened as a result of division has the class system that sectarianism has created shifted from a religious to a secular basis. The spiritual elect of the sectarian society has very easily transformed itself into a class of economic entrepreneurs when the early enthusiasm of the religious revival has passed; the behaviour of such a class has been free of the controls of an institutionally powerful ecclesiastical system.

Again, with respect to the effect of their teachings upon the moral values of society, new sectarian religious movements only indirectly have favoured the growth of economic enterprise. These movements have grown up on what might be called the moral frontiers of society; they have developed out of conditions of moral breakdown where traditional standards of behaviour have no longer commanded respect. The task performed by them has been that of reawakening the moral sense of the population by bringing the moral problem into close relation with the problem of personal salvation. Thus their moral teachings, concerned almost wholly with the sin of man, have tended to be very largely other-worldly in emphasis. Within the moral system of the religious sectarian society there has been little room for the development of ethical standards associated with such worldly problems of behaviour as business activity. Yet the religious teachings of the sect have not provided a solid basis on which to erect a system of moral values; only when religious teachings have been caught up within a powerful religious organization have they been able to retain their moral force. It has been here, in the effect of weakening the organization of religion, that sectarian activity has contributed to the development of a system of moral values free of the religious influence. Once the extremely rigid controls exercised within the closed sectarian religious group have broken down, moral values have shifted easily from a religious to a secular basis. In this way the business ethics of capitalism have grown out of the moral teachings of religious sectarianism.

Finally, sectarian religious teachings scarcely have promoted that rational attitude of mind so essential for the successful prosecution of economic affairs. Rather the sects, growing up among those sections of the population that have placed little reliance upon reason, have tended to promote a state of general irrationality through their highly emotional appeal. Yet, paradoxical as it may appear, the ultimate effect often has been to encourage such highly rational forms of behaviour as business activity and scientific experiment. If religious fanaticism has resulted in a flight from reason, it also has resulted in a flight from the well-tried teachings of the church. Thus, whereas the irrationality produced through the influence of an ecclesiastically organized religion has rested upon a solid foundation of superstitions, myths, and dogma, the greater irrationality produced by religious sectarianism has tended to be converted into a rationalism the moment the hold of organized religion has weakened. It has been this indirect effect of sectarian religious activity in breaking through the walls of traditional beliefs and freeing the minds of people for more rational ways of thought that has given to it such importance in promoting economic development.

One of the distinctive characteristics of the development of the western world has been the maintenance of a condition of continuous instability in the organization of religion as a result of the rise of new sectarian religious movements. This has been particularly true of the United States where the failure to build up an elaborate ecclesiastical system supported by the state has been largely owing to the strength of the sectarian spirit in American religious life. This characteristic of religious organization has accounted in part for the rapid growth of American capitalism. With a religious organization not sufficiently strong to divert the energies of the population along channels of endeavour of advantage to the religious interest, such energies have found release in capitalistic activity.

A significant difference can be found here in the religious development of Canada and the United States. Canada, it is true, has had its sectarian religious movements as has the United States, but they have operated much less as a force weakening the hold of organized religion. The reason has been that Canada in a sense has not been able to afford the price it has been necessary to pay for religious division. Political pressures have forced the community to come to the support of organized religion and such support has placed a definite limitation upon sectarian activity. With the collective weight of the community brought to bear upon them, the sects have been forced either to retreat behind a wall of isolation or build themselves into an integral part of the community, or else they have been extinguished. Thus they have tended rather quickly to seek denominational supports by aligning themselves with the state and with the traditional institutions of the community. By accommodating themselves to powerful political and cultural interests they have come to secure strong support from such interests.

To some extent this was the case with respect to the development of the church in French Canada. Under Jesuit leadership, Roman Catholicism assumed in the beginning something of the character of a sectarian religion at war with the society about it. The uncompromising opposition to the fur trade led to the growing divorce of the church from politics and trade and to its isolation as the church of the habitant population. The steady decline of the religious influence in the colony after 1700 was indicative of the growing weakness of the social supports of Roman Catholicism with the expansion of commerce. But the precarious military situation forced the state to come to the support of religion even at the expense of trade, and the dissolution of the Jesuit Order paved the way for the accommodation of the church to the secular community. The effect of the British conquest was to accentuate dependence upon religion in maintaining the separate community identity of French Canada and thus to secure even more completely the secula⁻ rt of religious organization. The narrow, separatist churc' 1 developed out of the frontier situation under Jesuit leadership grew into the socially and politically powerful church of nineteenth-century French Canada.

Similarly, in the Maritime Provinces, the rise of new sectarian religious movements, rather than weakening, resulted in the end in actually strengthening the Protestant church as a religious force in the community. The Maritimes shared with New England in the great awakening of the mid-eighteenth century, but, whereas in New England the resulting religious division led to the dissipation of much of the evangelical religious energies of the population and to the growth of strong liberal movements, in the Maritimes religious division was checked through political pressure and much of the religious fundamentalist outlook was preserved within the organized church. In New England, Unitarianism as well as Newlightism grew out of Congregationalism; in the Maritimes, only Newlightism survived the break-up of the Congregational churches. The counter-revolution following the Loyalist migration intensified dependence upon religious organization and forced the Protestant sectarian churches to identify themselves with colonial political interests in the colony. The formal alliance of Methodism with the English Wesleyan Conference was paralleled by the increasing dependence of the Newlight Baptist movement upon English Baptist leadership. Thus the break of the Methodists and Baptists from their American frontier origin, while it involved a shift from their earlier narrow sectarian position, did not involve a weakening of their religious influence. What the establishment of the British connection meant was a considerable strengthening of the denominational supports of religion and, in the end, a consequent strengthening of religion itself. The Protestant sectarian churches came to derive almost as much support from the colonial tie as the established church, and joined with the latter in resisting the spread of liberal influences into the area, either from Britain or the United States.

In Upper Canada, likewise, the religious sects that grew out of the great revival after 1800 were able in a way that they were not in the United States to preserve their original religious influence. In a sense, the effect of the War of 1812 was to perpetuate in Upper Canada the ways of thinking of the American frontier. By 1815 the western movement of American population had pretty well pushed beyond avenues reaching into the Canadian colony, and the later Upper Canadian society might have been expected to be increasingly affected by currents of thought reaching out from the East. It was this line of contact that was broken by the war. Upper Canada inherited the strong religious tradition of the American frontier but shared in little of the equally strong rationalist tradition associated with the great eastern universities and with the political and social thought growing out of the American and French revolutions. Paine was read in the United States but not across the border. Instead, the increasing British influence after 1815 brought to the sectarian churches the support of the whole colonial political system. The break of Canadian Methodism with American Methodism, and its alliance with English Wesleyanism, signified the shift to a position of accommodation to conservative political forces. Upper Canadian radicalism, with its ties with American and British radicalism, gained little support from religious movements that earlier had fought the established political-ecclesiastical order. Egerton Ryerson of the Methodist Church joined with Bishop Strachan of the Church of England in building up a politically powerful Protestant church that could command the support of the state. Isolation of liberal forces with the failure of the Rebellion of 1837 secured the dominant position of ecclesiasticism in the colony.

From 1850 until the opening of the West towards the close of the century the strength of forces of national consolidation was so great as virtually to prevent the growth of any free sectarian religious movements. The armed might of the state was brought to bear to crush the revolt of Louis Riel from the Roman Catholic Church in 1885. Small sects sought survival through isolation, as for instance the Mennonites in Manitoba and the Mormons in Alberta. No important religious denomination emerged out of a sectarian movement which grew up in the country during these years. Only the Salvation Army gathered any real strength as a force of religious separatism and, in its case, developments after the turn of the century, particularly the First World War, had the effect of making it an integral part of the community structure as a sort of social welfare institution.

It is still too early to determine how successful those religious sectarian movements that have grown up since 1900 will be in building themselves into powerful religious organizations with the support of the community behind them. The way in which the religious movement founded by William Aberhart in Alberta became caught up within a provincial political movement suggests that provincial political forces may become as important as are national forces in supporting a theocratic-ecclesiastical system. The Social Credit Government of the province of Alberta became virtually dedicated to the preservation of a religious fundamentalist outlook. The effort of the government of Ontario to introduce religious teachings in the public schools and the very active measures taken by the government of Quebec to oust the Jehovah's Witnesses and other sects from the province offer further examples of the growing support of ecclesiasticism by provincial political interests.

The close alliance between the state and the church in Canada has preserved more fully the influence of religion within an established ecclesiastical system and thus checked the free play of economic forces in the country. In contrast with the United States, the sects have been much less important in breaking down the hold of organized religion and thus in releasing the energies of the population for economic pursuits. Rather, the sects have been drawn into the theocratic-ecclesiastical structure of the community and have served to increase resistance to secular forces. This has been most evident within isolated ethnic-religious communities in the country such as those of the Mennonites, Doukhobors, or Hutterites. Here the conditions established by the simple sectarian organization of religion, the frugality and industry of the population, and the taboo upon expensive luxuries would seem such as to have encouraged economic enterprise, and yet these communities, though they have been agriculturally prosperous, have not produced a class of successful capitalists. Farming has involved no challenge to the religious way of life, but capitalist enterprise has. Thus, while the organized religious community has promoted collectively large-scale capitalist undertakings, as, for instance, the co-operative enterprises established in the Doukhobor communities in British Columbia, it has prevented individual members from acting as free economic agents.

Not all religious bodies in Canada have been as successful as the isolated ethnic-religious groups in building the organization of religion into the total community structure. In large areas of the Canadian society, division, in spite of efforts to check it, has served to weaken the influence of organized religion and to make for the strengthening of economic forces; it has been within such areas that the great capitalist enterprises have grown up in Canada. But even where emancipation from religious controls has extended furthest a sharp limitation has been placed upon activity of a purely secular character. Canada has been, and remains, a fundamentally religious nation. No great political or social upheaval in the country has served to break the close ties with a past which placed a great emphasis upon religious values of life. Insecurity has forced a dependence upon isolation, and in isolation the hold of tradition has been preserved.

PART III

Formative Influences in the Development of the Canadian Society

CHAPTER XI

The Canadian Community and the American Continental System*

RECENT STUDIES of Canadian-American relations, particularly in the social field, have served to give emphasis to the importance of the continental environment in the development of a common way of life on the North American Continent. Indeed, one is almost tempted to begin a paper such as this with the bald assertion that the Canadian community is but a pale reflection of the American community, and that if the reader wishes to learn something about it he need only refer to the extensive body of literature relating to social institutions and social behaviour in the United States. Nothing, it would seem at first glance, could be said about the Canadian community which has not already been said about the American.

Certainly, in many ways the Canadian community has been a northern extension of the American; population movements and the sharing of a common environment have led to a close similarity in social development. Exploitation of their North American resources has been a joint enterprise of the two peoples. There has emerged not two separate cultural systems—an American and a Canadian—but rather a number of distinctive forms of community organization, related more to underlying conditions of economic life than to political developments.

*From *Canada*, edited by George W. Brown (Berkeley and Toronto, 1950), pp. 375–89. With permission of the publisher. The original title read: "The Canadian Community."

On the Atlantic Coast, exploitation of the fisheries early led to the development of a form of community organization—the fishing village—which differed little in New England and Nova Scotia. In the continental interior the trade in furs made much the same social demands whether the traders were operating out of Albany or Montreal. The timber-lumbering industry of New Brunswick and the Ottawa Valley grew up in close relation to that of Maine, Vermont, and, later, Michigan and Wisconsin. The agricultural settlement of New Brunswick, the Eastern Townships, and Upper Canada was part of the great western movement of agricultural peoples which led after 1790 to the occupation of Upper New York State, western Pennsylvania, and the new states of Ohio, Tennessee, and Kentucky. The discovery of gold in the Fraser River Valley in the 1850's followed the discovery of gold in California, and the mining camps in British territory differed little from those which had grown up in the American West. Wheat farming on the plains of Canada gave rise to a society much like that which developed out of wheat farming on the plains of the United States. Out of the Industrial Revolution there grew up in English-speaking Canada cities which had little to distinguish them from those which had grown up across the border.

The forms of community organization which developed in Canada represented the adjustments of the population to their North American environment. Like similar forms across the border, they were the products of social experiments forced upon a people faced with new conditions of living. The effort to build societies on a common front brought the populations of the two parts of the continent close together. Though their cultural heritages were different, particularly before 1760, cultural differences tended to disappear upon settlement in America. The move from the Old World to the New, and from one area of the New World to another, often involved an almost complete break with the past. The very character of the settlement of America made for little continuity in the development of forms of social organization.

The settlement of America did not take place gradually. Rather, there were long periods when movements of population came almost to a halt. Wars and political uprisings, lack of transportation, ignorance of resources or failure to develop technological means of exploiting them, speculation in land, and the resistance of large economic organizations such as fur-trading companies to developments which threatened their monopolistic positions were some of the factors which held back the spread of population across the continent. When the barriers to migration did break down, the movement of population tended to be a flood. New means of transportation, technological developments in methods of production, realization of resources hitherto unknown, the up-swing of the business cycle, or sudden climatic changes were sufficient to attract attention to new areas of the continent and to set under way a mass movement of people.

Thus the settlement of America might be thought of as having taken place in a series of great "rushes." The sudden occupation of the Fraser River Valley after 1857 and of the Klondike after 1897 by gold seekers are two of the best examples of such rushes in the settlement of Canada, but other areas—the St. Lawrence Valley after 1660, the Annapolis Valley and the South Shore of Nova Scotia after 1760, the St. John and Miramichi valleys and the Great Lakes region after 1800, the Red River and Assiniboine valleys after 1880, the western prairies and the industrial city after 1900, the Canadian Shield after 1920—were occupied in much the same fashion by mass movements of population. It is true that settlement began long before the mass movement set in, but the simple forms of social organization established by the pioneers were swept aside by later comers. With thousands of bewildered people suddenly thrown together, strangers to one another and to the environment, pressing problems had to be solved hurriedly. New conditions forced an abandonment of traditional ways of thinking and behaving. In many respects the population began anew the task of building up a social system.

It is true that the loss of the Old World social heritage was offset in some degree by borrowings from the culture of the native. In North America, however, the native culture played no such role as in South America, where social continuity was secured through the absorption of the old society by the new. In North America, for the most part, the white man looked upon the Indian as a nuisance to be got out of the way; the Calvinist doctrine of predestination, in particular, offered an easy justification for the ruthless extermination of a race who were not of the elect. Only here and there, chiefly where the Roman Catholic attitude towards the native tended to prevail over the Protestant, were efforts made to draw upon the experience of the aboriginal inhabitants. In Canada there was no such military slaughter of the Indians as in the United States, but deprivation of their means of livelihood and the spread of disease served as effectively to decimate the Indians and to place them in a position of subjection. In much of Canada today Indian placenames are all that is left to remind one that the land was once occupied by the red man.

This sharp break with the past has accounted for much that is distinctive in American life. Out of the new societies growing up in America have come the challenges to Old World ways of doing things and Old World ways of thinking. Such societies have been the chief breeding grounds of the great American economic, political, social, and religious movements. The break with the cultural past has been evident in the development of the Canadian as of the American community. Movements of social reform have spread from one side of the border to the other. Canada has shared with the United States in the frontier revolt against established society.

Geography has drawn the two countries together socially, yet there are many striking differences between them. Powerful forces have operated to bring about a distinctive development of many important aspects of Canadian society. The influence of these forces was most evident in the frontier—the very area where a common way of life showed most signs of developing. In the United States— or in that part of America which later became the United States— few restraints were imposed upon the opening up of new areas of settlement. Population moved in freely, and there was little interference from the outside in the building of the new society. People were left largely to rely on their own resources. In Canada, however, the risk of absorption by the southern neighbour was too great to permit the unrestricted development of new areas of settlement.

The frontier was a great leveller in a political as well as in a social sense; it tended to destroy Old World political loyalties and thus to weaken Old World political attachments. The movement for the political independence of the British colonies in America before 1774 was a reflection to some extent of the separatist political tendencies of the frontier, but the political independence of the colonies, especially after the collapse of the French Empire in America, involved no great danger of the intrusion of a foreign power. For Canada, however, such intrusion was always a real danger. Before 1760 the lines of the French Empire reaching into the interior of the continent lay exposed on the south to attack from the English-speaking colonies. After 1760 British control of the interior through the St. Lawrence was similarly challenged by the independent-minded Atlantic seaboard colonies and, after 1784, by the new Republic of the United States. The Quebec Act of 1774, the American War of Independence, the long struggle after 1784 for control of the western posts, and the War of 1812–14 revealed the intensity of the conflict for lines of communication reaching into the interior. Outlying settlements in British North America, in New Brunswick, Upper Canada, the Eastern Townships, and the Red River Valley, on the Pacific Coast, and even on the western prairies, faced the threat, as had the earlier French settlements, of absorption by their neighbour to the south.

Because of this threat the grip of political authority could not be relaxed within new areas of settlement in Canada as it tended to be south of the border. The Canadian frontier grew up within the protective custody, first, of the French colonial Empire, then of the colonial Empire of Britain, and finally, after 1867, of the Dominion itself. Thus the fur-trading posts of New France, the fishing villages of Nova Scotia, the lumbering camps and agricultural settlements of New Brunswick and Upper Canada, the mining towns of the Pacific Coast and of the Klondike, and the prairie farm communities of the West did not develop merely as economic areas of production and exchange; they were also important outposts of Empire or nation. Defence constituted, along with trade, a determinant of lines of community development and forms of social organization. An army, or at least a special constabulary force, usually followed close upon the heels of the frontiersmen; indeed, many of the earliest settlements, for instance that of the Richelieu Valley in New France and of Perth in Upper Canada, were affected by military organization. Other agencies, particularly the church, played an equally important role in maintaining political control in frontier areas. The result was to make for the more orderly development of the Canadian than of the American frontier. The radical departures from accepted practice which were characteristic of the behaviour and thinking of American frontier populations in political organization, justice, family life, cultural relationships, and religious organization were less evident in the Canadian frontier population. The conservatism of the country as a whole operated as a powerful force in checking innovations.

In political organization the spirit of revolt and experimentation has not been lacking. Support of the revolutionary cause by large numbers of Nova Scotians and French Canadians in 1776, the movement of political disaffection among many Upper Canadians during the War of 1812–14, the Gourlay agitation and the rebellions in Lower and Upper Canada in 1837, the rise of the Clear Grit movement after 1850, the Red River Rebellion of 1870 and the Northwest Rebellion of 1885, the defiance of Canadian political authority by miners' associations in the Klondike in 1900, the rise of farm political movements in western Canada after the First World War, the Winnipeg general strike in 1919, and the growth of the Social Credit movement in Alberta and of the C.C.F. movement in western Canada and industrial Ontario after 1932 are indications of the strength of the challenges to constituted authority. But such movements of revolt, in contrast with similar movements in the United States, were arrested before they could make their influence significantly felt in the political life of the country.

In the United States, support of political reform offered a means of strengthening the political structure of the nation; the Republic was in effect a product of revolution, and movements of political reform after 1784 served to sharpen politically the divorce from the Old World and to make American institutions more distinctive. In Canada, however, reform movements threatened to draw the population more closely to the southern neighbour and to weaken if not destroy the political ties of Empire or, after 1867, of nation. This was true even when such movements drew their inspiration from the Old World, as, for instance, in New France before 1760, in Upper Canada during the 1830's, and in western Canada after 1920. The attack upon political institutions implied a challenge to constituted authority, and the danger was great that a state of confusion would lead to the intervention of the southern neighbour. William Lyon Mackenzie and Louis Riel are obvious examples of reform leaders who, though advocating ideas only partly American in origin, found themselves leading movements which derived much of their support from across the border.

Thus the effort to build up a political system in Canada which would remain independent of the United States involved the imposition of strong checks upon revolutionary tendencies. New France was isolated from revolutionary France through the building up in the colony of a powerfully centralized political and ecclesiastical system. The British colonies and, after 1867, the Canadian nation were similarly isolated from outside revolutionary influences by the maintenance of a strong system of political control, supported by the church, a privileged upper class, and, before 1870, the British army and navy. Whereas the American nation was a product of the revolutionary spirit, the Canadian nation grew mainly out of forces of a counter-revolutionary character.

In the development of institutions of law and order, similar forces of conservatism operated to restrain the influence of the frontier. Areas developing beyond the reach of the law have not been unknown in Canada. In the fur-trading interior of New France, the transient fishing settlements of Cape Breton and the east shore of New Brunswick, the lumbering camps of the St. John, Miramichi, and Ottawa valleys, the shanty towns of Irish canal-workers, the mining camps of the Fraser River Valley and the Klondike, and the congested areas of the growing cities, widespread lawlessness and disorder developed. Crime was an expression of the emancipation of the population from the traditional controls of an Old World society. Efforts to enforce the law assumed the character of interference from outside; the authority of the police and the courts was challenged by that of the gang, the vigilante committee, and the mob. Yet, in contrast with the United States, such challenges to constituted authority were never strong enough to lead to a general breakdown of law and order.The fire-arm was much less important in Canada than it was in the United States in defending the frontiersman from the North American Indian and from his fellow frontiersman. Seldom in the Canadian frontier did force pass out of the hands of the state. The Vigilante Committee organized in San Francisco in 1857 or the gang rule of Soapy Smith in Skagway in 1897 has no true parallel in Canadian experience.

The reason was that frontier settlement in Canada rarely extended far beyond the reach of the military forces of Empire or nation. The United States had no pressing reason for providing military protection to outlying settlements; border warfare, whether with the Indians, the Spanish, the Mexicans, or, before 1760, the French, was left mainly to the settlers. The vulnerability of the Canadian frontier, however, forced early attention to problems of defence, with the result that law-enforcement agencies could usually rely upon the support of military forces. Thus about the fur-trading posts of New France, in the agricultural settlements of New Brunswick and Upper Canada, and in the shanty towns of Irish canal-workers the army played an important role in maintaining order. In the isolated fishing settlements of Nova Scotia, policing was a function of the navy. A force of Royal Engineers put an end to lawlessness in the mining camps of British Columbia. Settlement of the western prairies and the gold rush to the Klondike took place under the close control of the North West Mounted Police. Even in Canadian cities, serious threats to law and order have been met by the decisive use of force.

The result was to establish a tradition of respect for the institutions of law and order. The population generally did not feel the need of taking the law into its own hands through mob action or the organization of vigilantes. There was lacking that intense jealousy of local rights which in the United States made it difficult for federal forces to intervene. The way in which the North West Mounted Police came into being was in striking contrast with that of the Texas Rangers. In the United States the frontier bred a spirit of liberty which often opposed efforts to maintain order. In Canada, order was maintained at the price of weakening that spirit.

The institution of the family similarly has found support from conservative forces in the Canadian community. In the family, as in other forms of social organization, the disturbing influence of the frontier made itself felt. The rapid increase in the Canadian divorce rate in recent years is a reflection of family disorganization which is closely related to urban growth and the weakening of puritan values. Before the turn of the century few divorces were known, but family disorganization as a social phenomenon reaches back to the beginnings of the Canadian community. By its very character the frontier tended to be a society of men: the fur-trading post, the lumbering camp, the agricultural settlement, the mining town, the ranching community, and even the manufacturing city (as distinguished from the more mature urban community with a diversity of economic interests) were made up predominantly of men in the age group from eighteen to forty. In such areas, large sections of the population lived entirely outside the family system, and there developed such substitute forms of social organization as prostitution and the partnership of two men to meet needs ordinarily satisfied within the family. The disorganizing effects of such developments upon the mores of the community were evident, for instance, in the rural society of New France brought into close contact with the fur-trading frontier, the agricultural settlements of New Brunswick which grew up alongside timber and lumbering camps, the old fur-trading and governmental centre of Victoria which served during the gold rush as the disembarking point and supply centre of the mining population, and the urban community developing in relation to manufacturing and the new northern frontier of mining and pulp and paper. The two world wars have

only accentuated the effect upon family life of the disorganizing influences growing out of conditions within the Canadian
community.

The much lower divorce rate in Canada than in the United
States, however, indicates a greater stability in family organization,
which has been as true of the past as of the present. The restraining
influence exerted upon Canadian frontier development had the
effect of limiting the degree of emancipation from moral values.
Controls of social class and the church lent strong support to the
controls of a traditional morality. There was less readiness to
accept unconventional forms of behaviour in matters relating to
the family. Whereas in the United States the frontier spirit of experimentation led to a modification of forms of family life and to
a tolerant attitude towards deviations from traditional moral
standards, in Canada such a spirit was severely checked through
the pressure of strong forces of social conservatism. Frontier patterns of revolt against the controls of a formal family system, as for
instance among the *coureurs de bois* of New France or within the
bohemias of the urban community, tended to be confined to the
peripheral areas of society and to have little effect upon behaviour
generally.

The strength of the puritan tradition in Canadian society has not
been unrelated to the strength of the aristocratic tradition; the spirit
of equalitarianism generated within the frontier situation, like that
of libertarianism, was greatly moderated by the opposing spirit of
conservatism. Canada shared with the United States in the great
democratic movement, with its almost fanatical emphasis upon the
principle that all men are equal. The frontier provided unfavourable
ground on which to build an elaborate structure of social classes,
which broke down under the influence of the common experience
of frontier life. The social worth of the individual was measured in
terms of accomplishment rather than in terms of family background.
Thus, in New France, seigneurs had difficulty in maintaining a social
status which set them apart from the lowly habitants or, indeed,
from the bush rangers. In the new agricultural settlements of the
Maritime colonies, the Eastern Townships, Upper Canada, and,
much later, the western prairies, upper-class families were forced
into close social association with families of lower standing, and
differences in social worth quickly disappeared along with differences in economic worth. Even more, in such highly mobile areas
as mining towns and industrial cities, an inherited class structure

tended to disintegrate in the face of powerful forces of equalitarianism. Yet, in spite of the strength of such forces, the aristocratic principle has persisted as an important organizing influence in Canadian society.

The strength of the military interest in itself served to emphasize the importance of class distinctions. Because the frontier was usually garrisoned by military forces, there was present from the beginning a strong influence operating against democratic tendencies. The military emphasized and lent support to distinctions in status. In the town of Quebec under the French régime, and in the British colonial centres of Halifax, Fredericton, Kingston, York (Toronto), and Victoria, the army or navy, with its officers in smart uniform, gave the local society a colour and dash which were lacking in American frontier communities. Even in the new Canadian frontiers, the Klondike, the western prairies, the industrial city, and the northern mining communities, the military tradition, as represented by the Northwest or later the Royal Canadian Mounted Police, had some influence upon social class relationships.

Efforts to strengthen the political ties of Empire or of nation led to deliberate attempts, through land grants and political preferments, to create and strengthen an aristocracy in the colonies of New France, Nova Scotia, Prince Edward Island, New Brunswick, Upper Canada, and British Columbia, and, later, in a less obvious fashion, in the Canadian nation. The democratic movement, it was felt, was liable to draw Canadian people closer to their neighbours to the south; and a privileged upper class was a bulwark of loyalty and conservatism. Though the economic forces of the frontier tended to the destruction of class differences, as, for instance, in the Upper Canadian backwoods community of the 1830's, the effect was neutralized in some degree within a political and military system of class privilege; many upper-class persons who proved unsuccessful as farmers obtained appointments in the government or the army. The frontier had two things of value to offer—land and offices— and both were reserved to an important degree for a privileged few.

The strength of the aristocratic tradition in Canada, though not easily measured, is revealed in the political attitudes of the population, the educational institutions, the patriarchal organization of the family, and the respect for old and established leaders. Though few Canadians would consciously subscribe to a society based upon class distinctions, the belief in the social superiority of certain groups underlies much of their thinking. There has been lacking in

Canadian experience that explicit rationalization of an equalitarian philosophy which in the United States was a product of revolution. The aristocratic tradition was too deeply rooted in the political philosophy of Empire to be destroyed by the equalitarian forces of the frontier.

In Canada, as in the United States, the frontier acted as a great melting pot of different ethnic cultures whereby the population was forced to conform to a common pattern of thought and behaviour. Though New France after 1660, Upper Canada after 1800, and the western prairies and industrial cities after 1900 were settled by people of diverse cultural backgrounds, a common cultural type soon emerged in these different areas. Assimilation proceeded even more rapidly in such highly mobile areas as the mining frontier. The breakdown of cultural differences on the frontier hastened the development of a single Canadian type.

Yet the persistence of ethnic differences suggests that assimilation did not proceed unchecked. The separation of the two chief cultural groups, the French-speaking and the English-speaking, offers the best example of the preservation of inherited ethnic loyalties within the Canadian cultural system, but ethnic separatism has not been a characteristic of the French Canadians only. Throughout English-speaking Canada there has been a similar tendency towards the preservation of inherited cultural attachments among English, Irish, Scots, Americans, central Europeans, and Asiatics.

Such a tendency has been a reflection of the colonial character of Canadian society. Assimilation in Canada meant an increasing conformity to American values of life and standards of behaviour. Efforts to check American influences in Canadian cultural life thus involved the strengthening of the supports of ethnic group loyalties. British colonial policy offered no real encouragement to the assimilation of the French-Canadian population, particularly after 1774, when assimilation would have meant the more rapid spread of American revolutionary ideas in the colony. Similarly, in Nova Scotia, New Brunswick, and Upper Canada the chief bulwarks against the growth of the American revolutionary movement were the Old World loyalties of the population; state support of an upper-class social system offered one means of keeping such loyalties alive. Since 1867, paradoxically, the security of the Canadian nation has depended upon discouraging a too strong Canadian nationalism. Preservation of English and Scots and Irish group loyalties served to perpetuate the colonial attitude of the Canadian people and thus to check the spread of American influence. In the United States the Briton hastened to become a good American; in Canada he has been encouraged to remain a good Briton. Nor has any vigorous effort been made to assimilate continental European peoples in Canada, except through the public schools; as with the French Canadians, the break of continental Europeans from their cultural past has tended to expose them to American influences. The maintenance of the political attachments of Empire or nation depended upon the cultural isolation of the population within the American continental system, and such isolation has been secured most effectively through the preservation of Old World loyalties.

Finally, the religious development of Canada, in contrast with that of the United States, has reflected the influence of strong conservative or traditionalist forces operating to check the influence of the frontier. In Canada, as in the United States, the frontier was a breeding ground of new churches and sects. The failure of Old World churches to gain leadership in frontier areas, and the weakening of traditional social values and forms of social organization encouraged the population to join whatever religious groups made their appearance. Sects developed naturally out of the frontier situation in response to the need for new and satisfying group loyalties. No Canadian frontier escaped the phenomenon of religious upheaval.

In New France, it is true, restrictions upon the settlement of Huguenots made impossible the development of any religious movement outside the Roman Catholic Church, but much the same sort of spirit as sectarianism found expression within the Jesuit Order. Later religious movements, both within and outside the church, have similarly tended to weaken the Roman Catholic ecclesiastical structure in Canada; schisms among central European Catholics in western Canada are recent examples of sectarian development. Among Protestants, of course, religious division has been much more pronounced. The history of Protestantism in Canada has been characterized by a series of religious upheavals which have precluded the development of unity within the church as a whole. Even to list the names of the sects which have appeared at different times would be impossible. Schisms within churches have been succeeded by new schisms to add to the confusion. The recent growth of movements such as the Pentecostal, Pentecostal Holiness, Nazarene, Apostolic, Church of God, Four Square Gospel, Christian and Missionary Alliance, and Jehovah's Witnesses demonstrates the continuing state of disunity of the Protestant body.

Nevertheless, a considerable degree of stability has been characteristic of the religious organization of the Canadian community. The large denominations have succeeded in maintaining a strongly influential position in spite of the weakening effects of religious division. Soon after Confederation the various branches of Presbyterians and Methodists came together in two great national churches. The Baptists, the Disciples of Christ, and even the Salvation Army and the Pentecostals gradually lost much of their extreme separatist character in accommodating themselves to the secular social structure. The union of the Methodist, Presbyterian, and Congregational churches to form the United Church of Canada in 1925 and the more recent formation of the Canadian Council of Churches mark a culmination of developments reaching back to the beginnings of Protestant religious organization in the country.

Powerful political and cultural forces served to support the denominational organization of religion and to check extreme manifestations of religious division. The church, as distinguished from the sect, closely identified itself with the interests of Empire or nation. By its very nature it depended upon the maintenance of the traditional loyalties. In offering support to established political attachments, it was able to command, in turn, a measure of political support. Thus the Roman Catholic Church in French Canada, the Church of England in the British colonies, and more recently the United Church of Canada enjoyed many of the privileges of a state church, whether or not legally established. Maintenance of the political ties of Empire or nation has depended upon the maintenance of a system of ecclesiastical control in the Canadian community.

Movements of religious division, on the other hand, have been viewed as threats to traditional political attachments. By its otherworldly appeal, the sect tended to deprecate the importance of such secular interests as the state; it sought the full and undivided loyalty of its followers. When the sect was American in origin, the political implications of its teachings were particularly disturbing. Lack of interest in the welfare of the state was assumed to be a disguise for attitudes of political disloyalty. Thus the full weight of the traditional political and social order was brought to bear, directly and indirectly, against the development of sectarian movements. The result was to make for the rapid accommodation of such movements to secular interests. The Newlight Baptists, the Methodists, the Disciples of Christ, and the Salvation Army early broke with the parent churches in the United States and shifted from a separatist position to seek closer ties within the Canadian community. Where such ties were not secured, as in the Jesuit Order in New France and the Riel group in the Northwest Territories, the sect was virtually outlawed by the state.

The effect has been to give a conservative character to religious organization in Canada. The hold of tradition has been strong, and new forms of religious organization and new types of appeal have received little encouragement. Fanaticism has been confined mainly to the fringes of society. On the other hand, Canada has been unfriendly to a too liberal approach to religious teachings; such movements as Unitarianism have made little headway. Religious organization has been built closely into the political and social structure of the community, and change has come slowly in the face of resistance from powerful interests identified with the established order.

The strength of the ties with the Old World is exemplified in the maintenance of the imperial connection. Canada has no revolutionary tradition. At no time in their history have the people turned their back on the past and placed their whole faith in the future. The lack of such an emotional experience has affected the development of all aspects of Canadian society. It is this which accounts for what is most distinctive in the national character.

CHAPTER XII

Education and
Social Change in Canada*

IN A PAPER concerned with the problem of education and social change in the twentieth century it is tempting to turn, as most other Canadian commentators have done, to the case of French Canada where developments of the past half-century have presented a striking example of how a tradition-bound educational system has failed to meet the needs of a rapidly changing society. Here the problem remains largely one of seeking to persuade educators who do not want to change that change is vitally necessary. In English-speaking Canada, in contrast, those who command the important posts of education, with only a few exceptions, have been persons who have clearly identified themselves with the cause of social progress and advancement. Almost every official release, of the various provincial departments of education, urges the importance of new and advanced methods of classroom teaching and school organization, and the boast is constantly made that in the nature of the school curriculum and the style of school architecture education is keeping abreast of the times. Under such circumstances, it might appear that there was little to be said about the problem of education and social change in English-speaking Canada.

Yet in certain respects, perhaps, the educational system of English-speaking Canada has been no more responsive to social change than the educational system of French-speaking Canada. An

*From *Transactions of the Third World Congress of Sociology*, 1956, vol. V, pp. 64–70. With permission of the publisher.

educational system may become a powerful force directed towards maintaining the status quo not only because of its command of the resources of the state or of the church and its elaborate and propaganda-minded bureaucratic organization but because every person in the community whose social position depends upon the education he received is in some way its apologist. The doctor of medicine, the lawyer, the engineer, the druggist, the minister of the gospel, and indeed even the minor civil servant, are possessors of certain special educational qualifications which entitle them to perform certain special services, and the education of which they were recipients can scarcely be repudiated without repudiating the claims which are made on the basis of that education. It is just here that education can operate so powerfully as a force of conservatism in society. Changing social conditions lead to a demand for new kinds of services and thus for new types of training but such changes tend to be strongly resisted by those with vested interests in old established forms of training. The greater freedom of the educator in English-speaking Canada from what might be called parochial influences has made it more possible for him than for his counterpart in French-speaking Canada to overcome the resistance of that powerful class within the community and within educational circles which has a stake in established forms of education, and to introduce change. Yet there is a point beyond which even the most socially conscious educators have not been prepared to go in the effort to adapt an educational system to changing social needs, and in this respect there has been no essential difference between English- and French-speaking Canada.

To the educator who likes to think of himself as socially conscious, whatever is directed towards the object of adapting education more fully to the needs of present-day society is considered desirable, but this may mean little more than making education serve better the interests of dominant cultural groups in society. Educational reform thus becomes a force in support of the established order of things. In a business culture such as ours, extension of the hold of rational forms of thought tends to become the end to which education strives. For the vast majority of the population an education such as this may well serve its best interests, but this may clearly not be true of certain sections of the population whose needs are not being taken care of within the dominant culture, and it is these sections of the population which are the most caught up in social change. Under such circumstances, the traditionalist, intent on cherishing values of the past and acutely aware of the danger of any slavish conforming to the present, may well prove the real radical in education.

In a new country like Canada, the development of which has been characterized by the sudden opening up and settlement of large, hitherto unoccupied land areas and by the equally sudden conversion of peaceful countrysides and small rural towns into great sprawling industrial cities, the problem of building up a social system which would meet all the various needs of the population has been very great, and the rise at different times and in different places of new movements of economic, political, social and religious organization indicates that the effort to establish such a system has not always and everywhere been wholly successful. In what might be called the outer fringes of the society, in the new farming, mining, lumbering and fishing communities and in the new growing areas of the industrial cities, large sections of the population have found themselves in sharp conflict with the dominant interests and social groupings of the established society.

Primarily, the problem of social organization here, as in all situations of social change, is one of the development of kinds of social needs which can be satisfied only by persons possessing a different kind of educational training from that which hitherto has been provided within society, but here the changes required in the form of educational training offered are of a sort which cannot readily be made within the established educational system. What occurs, where new movements of social organization take their rise, is in effect a revolt against the leadership of the established society and consequently, indirectly but in a very real fashion, against the kind of education upon which such a leadership bases its claims.

To persons economically and socially insecure, seeking within a new kind of social order a more satisfactory form of life, there are two things basically wrong with the leadership of the established society: it imposes upon the population for its support too heavy financial demands and it fails to provide the kind of leadership which is wanted. Both failings to some extent can be attributed to the kind of educational training of which it is a product. A long, expensive educational training makes necessary substantial rewards in the way of fees, salaries, or financial returns of other sorts while a training designed to fit persons to serve in the more favoured circles of society may have the effect of making them unfit to serve in less favoured circles. So it seems to those more socially harassed sections of the population which is offered, by the leaders of the old established political parties, by ministers of the gospel in the traditional churches, and by the representatives of such socially protected professions as medicine and law, cures for its political, spiritual, physical and litigious ills which while costly produce no certain results. To get the kind of government, spiritual solace, medical attention, or legal aid wanted, and which is not too costly, may involve breaking outside the social system established for providing such services and turning to persons who lack the kind of educational qualifications demanded within the society at large.

Thus, for instance, the farmers of Alberta in 1920, in seeking a change of government, entered into a political association which stipulated that no one could run for political office who was not a bona fide farmer. Fifteen years of Liberal rule in Alberta had demonstrated the extreme difficulty faced by anyone who had not come up through the usual channels of party preferment, beginning ordinarily with a career in law or small-town business, of getting anywhere in politics. At one stroke, in the election of 1921, all those persons who had what hitherto had been an accepted background of training and experience for politics were swept from office and an entirely new kind of leadership created.

Similarly, in Alberta again, in 1935, when the leaders of the United Farmers' party could now boast of fifteen years of education through political and administrative experience, there occurred, out of the desperation created by the great depression, a new sudden break from an accepted type of leadership. Newspaper interviews held with the members of the Social Credit administration were revealing of the kind of claims made by the new political leaders of Alberta. Almost without exception these new ministers of the Crown boasted that they were men completely lacking in political experience, in many cases previously so uninterested in politics that they had not voted, or subscribed to any newspaper or magazine; that until the truths of Major Douglas and Mr. Aberhart were made known to them they had been wholly ignorant of economic matters; that, indeed, they had none of the preparation usually expected of people entering into public life.

The significant thing about these two political movements in Alberta was that they based their appeal on their freedom from dependence on a leadership made up of men of education and experience. There was no apology that, because they were a new party, they had not yet got their full share of leaders with acceptable qualifications. Their virtue lay in the fact that the men they put forward for public office, being of simple tastes, would not expect the kind of material rewards accorded to persons of more accomplished attainments and, being comparatively uneducated and wholly inexperienced, would neither have been misled by the false teachings of, for instance, economics and political science as offered within the universities nor have been taught the arts of political corruption by service in a party organization. They were thus men who could be expected to serve the people of Alberta honestly and well.

Something of this sort of thing occurs with the rise of any new political movement, such as the C.C.F., the Union Nationale, and, where it seeks to make a popular appeal, Communism. The attack upon the entrenched positions of established political parties and institutions involves, to some degree at least, an attack upon that whole system of training upon which the leadership of these parties and institutions bases its claims. Thus Jacksonian democracy, as represented in Canada by various movements seeking a more direct control by the people of its political affairs, contained within it something of an anti-educational philosophy.

Even clearer was the attitude of hostility to an educational training which found expression in those new movements of religious reform the growth of which has been such a characteristic feature of the religious development of Canada. The new religious sects very deliberately turned to the leadership of men who had little or no academic or theological training. The less education a preacher had the closer to God he was believed to be. Thus, in denying the value of an educational training, the sects demolished virtually all those special claims of the established clergy as ministers of the gospel. The way was opened for the intrusion of the part-time local preacher and the itinerant evangelist who because he "lived off the country" expected no great material reward, and because he had no great education could be expected to have a firmer hold upon the simple truths of Christianity.

With respect to medicine and law there is no way of knowing to what extent certain elements of the population have turned to the services of persons lacking prescribed educational qualifications. Judging from newspaper reports, and from knowledge of conditions in such a city as Calgary, Alberta, in the 1930's the number of what might be called quacks practising medicine in various parts of Canada at different times has not been inconsiderable, but the strength of the reaction against the medical or the legal profession cannot be determined by the incidence of those sorts of acts which involve a breach of public regulations. Thousands of people, it may be suspected, in those areas of the community least economically and socially well off, stay away from doctors and lawyers except in cases of urgent necessity and turn for medical or legal advice to persons who, because they publicly make no claims to possession of the skills of the doctor or lawyer, cannot be apprehended by the authorities of the law. A reluctance to pay the fees exacted by the medical or the legal profession (the size of which is often exaggerated in the minds of such people) has much to do with this tendency to "shop around" and find someone who can provide the same sort of services at much less cost. In addition, however, there is, among such sections of the population, a deeply rooted distrust and suspicion of the kind of learning possessed by medically or legally trained persons. Getting "into the clutches" of the doctor or lawyer is something which strikes terror into the hearts of such people.

It should not be concluded from this that movements directed against the established leadership of society grow out of feelings of unconditional hostility to education. There is, among people caught up in such movements, an ambivalence in their attitude to education as, indeed, there is in their attitude to many institutions of society. Such people may have an overwhelming desire to secure for their sons and daughters that education which will provide them with the kind of opportunities enjoyed by young persons in more favoured social circles and thus may be insistent that nothing is too good— and thereby too modern—in the way of educational institutions. More than that, such people may develop an enormous faith in "education," meaning by education that which offers easy and immediate solutions to the kind of problems they face. Such attitudes to education as these may be combined in a way not entirely contradictory with one of distrust and suspicion. The very same person who wants his son to become a lawyer, or who joins a study group to learn more about the legal problems of, for instance, trade unionism, may be highly distrustful of lawyers or lawyer-politicians, and that on the grounds of the kind of training they had received.

It is easy for the apologist of an established educational system to take comfort in the view that this failure of certain persons to recognize the value of an educational training is a result of ignorance and that all that is necessary is to reveal to them some of the "truths" of which the educated person is a recipient. It was this sort of thinking which, in the Alberta election of 1935, led one of the old parties to bring into the province a professor of economics to expose the falsehoods of Social Credit and another of these parties to arrange for a series of radio broadcasts to be given by its intellectually most able leader on the unconstitutionality of the Social Credit programme. Nothing could have been better calculated than either of these two acts to convince the Alberta electorate that the old party leadership of the province, with all its learning, had nothing to offer it. The truth was that, given the kind of economic and political ills this electorate was suffering at the time, the old party leadership, wedded to certain economic, political and constitutional doctrines currently being taught in the universities, had nothing to offer it. Likewise, it would appear evident that in those areas where the old established churches or such professions as those of medicine and law have come under attack, the reason has been that they were not able to offer cures (given the uncertain definition of what a cure really is) of the kind of spiritual, physical, or legal ills being suffered by certain people.

One might well question thus some of the sociological assumptions underlying discussion of such a movement of educational reform as that in French Canada. Wedded as many of them have become to a functionalist theory of society, sociologists, like psychologists, have been too much inclined to stress the importance of processes of adjustment and integration at the expense of processes of conflict and disorder as forces of change in personality or social organization. To build bigger and better equipped engineering schools, to crowd classics and philosophy out of the school curricula to make room for the social and natural sciences and to introduce programmes of teacher training are thought of as steps in advance in making over the educational system of French Canada. Like all persons in economically and socially insecure positions, the French Canadian is faced with the problem of providing for the future of his son or daughter, and if the young French-speaking Canadian is to compete successfully with the young English-speaking Canadian he must have an educational equipment which is equal to the latter's. Thus the drive to "modernize" the educational system of French Canada, to make it conform to the demands of the dominant Anglo-Saxon culture. But the French Canadian, caught up in the changes taking place in his society, and seeking relief, turns to values of the past and to a reassertion of the simple truths of nationality and religion. It would be foolhardy to suggest that he is mistaken in doing so, considering what the dominant Anglo-Saxon culture has immediately to offer him. Rather the real radical in French Canada may well be that person determined to resist at all costs the values of this dominant culture.

What this means is that an educational system which seeks "to keep astride of the times" may fail to meet the needs of those people most fully exposed to forces of social change. That is not to say that the simple reaction of distrust of education offers any real solution in itself to the kinds of problems such people face. Nor is it to say that those expedients which may be resorted to as alternatives to an educational training represent any real advance in preparing people for positions of leadership in society. The establishment, within new movements of political, social, or religious reform, of various kinds of training schools such as labour or bible colleges, may lead, in certain particulars, to new and improved methods of training within the established educational system, but developments such as these, for the most part, are in the way of compromises forced upon movements if they are to survive in the social world in which they find themselves. The signifiance of the growth of an attitude of distrust of education lies not in the direct effect of leading to improvements in forms of educational training but in the indirect effect of giving support to movements directed against the established leadership structure of society. Change is forced upon the social system from without, by the repudiation of that form of educational training of which its leadership is a product. It is thus that reactionism may operate, within education as within other areas of social life, as a revolutionary force within society.

CHAPTER XIII

The Frontier
in the Development of the
Canadian Political Community*

IMPLICIT IN MUCH OF THE WRITING on Canadian political history has been the assumption that an entirely different set of forces have shaped the development of democratic institutions in this country than in the United States. Whether because Canada learnt from the political experience of nineteenth- rather than eighteenth-century Britain, or because the tradition of the country has been more British, Canadians have been thought less inclined than their neighbours across the border to experiment with radical political solutions to their problems. Rather, they have sought through an orderly process to adapt their political institutions to changing circumstances. Thus the distinctive Canadian contribution to the development of democratic political organization has been considered the working out of the principles of responsible government within the framework of a system of imperial, and later federal, control. The more radical principle of checks and balances, involving the separation of the executive and legislative functions of government, written into the Constitution of the United States, has been avoided as foreign to the spirit of Canadian political life.

*From *Transactions of the Royal Society of Canada*, vol. XXVIII, Series III, June, 1954, Section Two, pp. 65–75. With permission of the publisher. The original title read: "The Frontier and Democratic Theory."

That Canada has a political tradition more conservative than the United States would seem evident. This country remained within the British Empire, ultimately to secure separation by peaceful means; the people of the United States fought for and won their independence on the field of battle. The contrast today between the political institutions, and the informal processes of government, of the two countries reflects the different background of political development.

Concern to demonstrate the distinctiveness of Canada's political institutions, however, has led to a failure to recognize fully the importance of very similar forces in the political life of the two countries. The assumption that the Constitution of the United States grew out of the political experience of eighteenth-century Europe, while the constitution of Canada (that is, the unwritten part determining the form of parliamentary government) grew out of the political experience of nineteenth-century Europe, overlooks as Turner emphasized a half-century ago the extent to which the principles of American government reflect very directly the political experience of American frontier peoples. What this paper seeks to demonstrate is that Canada shared in the revolutionary tradition of this continent which found its fullest expression in the American War of Independence and the principle of checks and balances written into the American Constitution, that, however, geography favoured the maintenance in this part of the continent of the controls of an Old World imperial, and later of a close federal, system, and that the effort to maintain these controls in face of the continuous threat of the expanding revolutionary community to the south led to the development of a form of government directly opposed to the principles of political organization growing out of the frontier experience of Canadian peoples. Thus what has been thought of in Canada as an orderly process of adapting political institutions to changing circumstances has actually represented an effort to hold in check the kind of democratic forces which were growing up from within the Canadian community. Responsible government developed in reaction rather than in response to the true democratic spirit of the Canadian people.

For the three centuries of its history the North American Continent has been a breeding ground of economic, political, social, and religious experiments of various sorts. Such was particularly the case during the latter half of the eighteenth and the first half of the nineteenth centuries. These one hundred years witnessed not only the Revolutionary War of Independence but most of the great utopian experiments in economic, political, and religious reform. It was not an accident that it was on the North American Continent that the ideas of the English utopian, Robert Owen, and the French utopian, Charles Fourier, were tried out or that on the Euro-Asiatic Continent were tried out almost a century later the ideas of the German utopian, Karl Marx. Great land masses present problems of control. The ineptness of political administration where distances are great breeds political discontent and offers opportunities for the growth of revolutionary movements. On the North American Continent political authority was established only in face of almost continuous resistance on the part of the population in outlying areas. The American people fought not one but many wars of independence. Thrown onto their own resources, the populations of isolated areas or of areas of new economic growth organized their own systems of control and, when central authority sought to establish itself, movements of revolt quickly developed. The committee of safety, the territorial convention, the bill of rights, a locally issued currency, and encouragement of smuggling and tax evasion afforded means of politically organizing the frontier and of securing its autonomy in relation to outside government bodies.

It was this insistence upon local autonomy, this separatist spirit, which was the dominant characteristic of those revolutionary or reform movements which grew up in the interior parts of the continent. Such movements sought to build the new society not by making over the old, but by separating from it. The reason, of course, lay in the economic and political weakness of the frontier community. The thirteen small, scattered, English colonies of 1775 could not hope to reform the British Empire but they could escape its exactions by separating from it. Similarly, the few Mormons settled on the desert wastes of Utah one hundred years later could have little hope of transforming to their liking the society of the United States (though the founder of the Mormon sect, Joseph Smith, did for a time aspire to the American presidency), but they could retreat from that society and secure their isolation by establishing a strong form of local theocratic government, a distinctive and to the outside world morally repugnant family system, and their own banking and currency system.

There was something of this intense localism, an almost sectarian exclusiveness, in all American reform movements of the frontier.

The dominant urge of frontier populations was to be left alone, to escape the exactions and restrictions of outside political authority. This was not because the frontier was poor but because it was rich. As politically virgin territory, it offered almost unlimited opportunities for office seekers from the outside; its virgin natural resources invited economic exploitation. It was in the struggle for the control of these two things of value on the frontier—office and land—that there developed much of the resistance to central government. Reform on the frontier was directed against such social evils of the outside world as political patronage, the payment of excessive salaries to governmental officials, economic monopoly, a stringent money supply, exorbitant interest charges, and burdensome taxation. Remedy for the ills of the frontier was sought in the effort to develop its own means of exploiting its economic and political resources.

It was no easy task for the central authorities to hold in check these separatist movements, to put down what amounted in effect to revolts against the state. Such movements had enormous advantages in geography and in the fanatical zeal of their leaders and followers growing out of strong feelings of righteousness. Where few qualifications for office were insisted on, an unlimited supply of people to fill positions of leadership and trust was available. Frontier conditions made for great mobility of agitators, self-appointed prophets, and organizers. On the other hand, the difficulties of policing, the ineptness of officials unfamiliar with local conditions, and the limitation in the supply of trained personnel handicapped severely governments seeking to impose their authority from the outside. When force was resorted to, a rebelling population, by delaying tactics, by hit-and-run raids, and by scattering when faced with a force more formidable than its own, could make the cost of defeating it so great as to discourage any determined effort directed to such an end.

Yet it would not be correct to say simply that the state was powerless to deal with frontier movements of revolt in America. The fact was that in that part of the continent which became the United States the authority of the central government was seldom employed with any resoluteness of purpose in putting down such movements. The American political society tended to be highly tolerant of the non-conforming elements of its population. The very weakness of the military forces of the country until recent years has been a reflection of such tolerance.

The constituted political authorities in the American society had no reason to be greatly concerned about movements of political separatism except when, as in 1776, they threatened to carry the population out of the British Empire or, as in 1860, they threatened the dismemberment of the Union. Rather, until recent years at any rate, such movements have constituted an important means of extending and strengthening American society. The major task of that society has been the conquering and occupation of a continent. In undertaking that task, it faced no organized political community on the continent as powerful as itself. There were, however, two serious claims to the continent which had to be destroyed if the Manifest Destiny of American peoples was to be realized.

The first, of course, was that of the North American Indian. Experience had demonstrated the costliness of trying to subdue the Indian by open warfare and the use of regular armies. The Indian enjoyed the advantages of all frontier people: great mobility, thorough knowledge of the terrain, and familiarity with the kind of weapons and tactics most suitable for frontier warfare. In challenging the claim of the Indian to the continent, accordingly, reliance was placed upon the resourcefulness (and unscrupulousness) of the white settlers. Treaties with the Indians solemnly entered into by the government were disregarded by these land-hungry settlers, and resistance on the part of the red man was used as an excuse for wars of extermination. The advance of American white society on the continent took place by means of this continuous pushing back and destruction of the native by people who took the law into their own hands. The same result would have been secured in the end, and at much less cost in human life, had the central government maintained a greater degree of order on the frontier, but only by delaying the advance of the white man's civilization. By tolerating the frontier settler's exercise of a large measure of independence, by granting in effect a large degree of autonomy to frontier communities, the American society was able that much more speedily to complete the occupation of the continent.

The second important claim to the North American Continent was that of the overseas empires. In the effort to destroy this claim, the interests of the British governing authorities before 1760, as of the central governing authorities of the united colonies or united states after 1776, were closely identified with the interests of the American frontier population. With no standing army on the continent sufficiently powerful to challenge the French Empire in America before 1760, and no navy sufficiently powerful to challenge the British Empire in America after 1776, the claims of the American political society to the continent were most successfully championed by the advancing frontiersmen fighting on ground on which the advantages were on their side and often through acts of warfare which were formally repudiated by the responsible governing authorities. Frontier armies or border raiding parties played an important part in the French-English wars, the War of Independence, and the War of 1812–14, while the two later invasions of Canadian territory, by the Patriots in 1838 and by the Fenians in the 1860's, were carried out entirely by armed forces of this sort. Spanish and French claims to the southern part of the continent were attacked by military forces of a similar character.

The invasion of territory outside the formal jurisdiction of the American political society was not simply an act of aggression of a land-hungry people. Frontier populations were land-hungry, but land hunger became closely identified with an interest in political reform. To wrest territory away from the control of France, Britain, or Spain was to "liberate" not only the territory but the inhabitants from the control of an Old World empire system. Here was to be found the significance of the revolutionary movement in the strengthening of the continental claims of the American political society. Wars with neighbouring communities assumed something of the character of wars of independence. In terms of the local scene, for instance, there was little essential difference between the border fighting in the Seven Years' War, the Revolutionary War, the War of 1812–14, and that which took place after the Canadian rebellions of 1837. In all these cases, the drive to liberate Canada came largely from what was then the American West, and in all of them, important support was obtained from within the Canadian community. Frontier populations on both sides of the border faced much the same problems and readily joined forces in protesting against the exactions and restrictions of outside political authorities. Within the continental situation, such movements of protest meant inevitably the weakening of the position of the overseas empires and the consequent strengthening of the position of the American political society.

Until at least the present century, thus, American expansionism and American reformism were closely linked to one another. The doctrine of Manifest Destiny found important support in the doctrine of revolutionary republicanism; or, to look at the matter from the other side, the isolationism of the American Republic was born out of the isolationism of the frontier and was a natural response to a situation where the nation felt no real threat to its position within the American continental system and craved no allies. What this meant was a form of government based upon the principle of a separation of powers and a limitation of centralized authority. Though in the writing of the Constitution of the American Republic powerful conservative interests, identified with sound finance and the promotion of overseas trade, did succeed in securing certain safeguards against the development of a system of political irresponsibility, the separatist-isolationist spirit of the American political community was too strong to be effectively checked by particular constitutional expedients such as the method of the election of the president or federal senators. American political theorists may have read Blackstone and Montesquieu, but the form of gevernment they devised was one which reflected very directly the frontier political experience of American peoples.

In Canada there was not lacking among the people a frontier political experience similar to that of American peoples. Developing as the American frontier did through the spread of settlement into the interior of the continent, the Canadian frontier offered an almost equally fertile field for the growth of movements of a reform or revolutionary character. The insurrection of the *coureurs de bois* and the generally unco-operative attitude of the population during the period of the old régime, widespread disaffection in Nova Scotia and Quebec during the American Revolutionary War and in Upper Canada during the War of 1812–14, the rebellions of 1837, the Irish riots and the Clear Grit movement of the 1850's, the Red River and Northwest rebellions of 1870 and 1885, the development of militant miners' associations in the Klondike following the gold rush, the Winnipeg general strike in 1919, and the rise of the western agrarian political movement in the 1920's and of the Social Credit movement in the 1930's afford examples of efforts upon the part of Canadian people to create for themselves a better world in which to live. As across the border, these movements were essentially separatist and anti-authoritarian in character. They grew out of the feelings of isolated people that their problems were peculiar to themselves and could only be solved through their own efforts. Thus the resort to similar forms of political organization and instruments of political expression designed to limit the authority of central governments: the committee of safety, convention, bill of

rights, election of executive as well as legislative officers, group representation, referendum, and recall.

But whereas in the United States the development of separatist
political movements meant freeing the expansive energies of the
frontier and thus strengthening the political society as a whole, in
Canada it meant exposing the frontier to forces of American expansion and threatening thereby the separate political existence of the
Canadian community. The Canadian frontier lay alongside the line
of advance of the American, and, while it could be reached only
with great difficulty by armed forces moving out from the established centres of government, it could be swiftly invaded from across
the border or from it Canadian rebellious forces could as readily
withdraw to American territory. John Allan, William Lyon Mackenzie, Joseph Papineau, and Louis Riel found refuge in the United
States when rebellions they had led in Canada failed, and new rebellious uprisings were plotted on the other side of the line with the
aid of American sympathizers. What this meant, therefore, was that
any assertion of greater independence on the part of the Canadian
frontier society drew it closer to the American and paved the way
for its ultimate absorption.

Had the advantages of geography been all on one side, of course,
no effort to maintain in the northern part of the continent a politically separate community would have been successful. But though
American expansionism threatened Canadian lines of communication with the interior, no American liberation movement was sufficiently powerful to completely destroy in this part of the continent
the claims of a rival political power. Canada maintained her separate political existence but only by resisting any movement on the
part of her population which had the effect of weakening the controls of central political authority. The claims to the interior of the
continent were staked not by advancing frontiersmen, acting on
their own, but by advancing armies and police forces, large corporate economic enterprises and ecclesiastical organizations, supported
by the state. The Canadian political temper, as a result, has run
sharply counter to the American. Those creeds of American political life—individual rights, local autonomy, and limitation of executive power—which have contributed so much to the political
strength of the American community have found less strong support
within the Canadian political system. Canada sought political
strength through alliance with the North American Indian and the
support of ties which bound her people to the Old World and to a

highly centralized federal system. In turn this meant a political system which emphasized the responsibility of governing authorities and tended to concentrate power in the hands of the executive. In this respect, it is easy to exaggerate the change which came with the establishment of responsible government in Canada. The two-party, cabinet system of government grew out of those conditions of rule in Canada which required the maintenance of a highly centralized political community and, as such, it stood sharply opposed to the separatist principles of political organization growing out of the frontier experience of the Canadian people. In the 1830's the Canadian frontier community found its true champions in Joseph Papineau and William Lyon Mackenzie. Responsible government came not as the climax but the anticlimax to the long struggle in Canada to secure the reform of colonial institutions. It represented an accommodative movement in the political organization of the Canadian community.

That is not to say that reform thought has developed no strength in Canada. The American revolutionary movement has made its influence felt in spite of strong forces of resistance which have been built up. Important also has been the influence of overseas reform movements and particularly the great reform movements of nineteenth-century Britain. But if the effect of such influences has been to soften the character of Old World political toryism in the country, the effect of powerful conservative forces has been to convert the harsh and politically irresponsible radicalism of the frontier into more accommodative forms of reform thought. Canadian reform, as a result, has displayed a less uncompromising spirit than American reform; it has sought more to rebuild the old society than to separate from it.

Enough perhaps has been said to indicate the nature of some of the forces which have determined the character of development of the political institutions of this country. It is not the purpose of this paper to examine in any detail recent political developments which have taken place in Canada or the United States. The fact, however, that the United States today appears to be more intolerant of radical political movements than Canada or her other immediate neighbour, Mexico, may seem strange in the light of what has been said above.

If this is so, the reason in part would seem to lie in the changed position of the United States in world affairs. Until about the turn of the present century, as this paper has attempted to demonstrate, the main energies of the American people were directed towards the occupation of the continent and in the carrying out of this task reformism and expansionism were closely linked. Facing no serious threat to its political existence, the American society could tolerate the growth of noncomformist movements and the growth of such movements contributed to the extension of American territorial claims on the continent. Faced now with a threat to its national existence, and that from another continental power which has linked closely together forces of expansion and reform, the United States would appear to have turned its back on its revolutionary tradition and to be seeking strength by consolidation of the forces of the state. Canada, by withdrawing less from the Old World society in the past, is now perhaps more able to infuse into her society something of the reform spirit developing strength outside the country.

To say this, however, is to risk exaggerating the difference between the political temper of the United States of today and of the United States of the past. The American people are perhaps no more intolerant of nonconformity within their midst than they ever were. What they are intolerant of, as they have always been, is any interference in their affairs from the outside. The attack of Joseph McCarthy upon Communist influences in the government of the United States was a clear and genuine expression of the American frontier, isolationist spirit. It was no accident that McCarthy came from the Middle West and represented an ethnic-religious minority population in the United States. His attack was directed not against poor, downtrodden people crying for a voice in the affairs of the state but against powerful political leaders, of unquestioned social respectability, largely of Anglo-Saxon background. Critics outside the country might well pause to consider not the intolerance which found expression in McCarthyism but the tolerance which made it possible for McCarthyism to develop. In Canada it would be hard to conceive of a state of political freedom great enough to permit the kind of attacks upon responsible leaders of the government which have been carried out in the United States. More careful examination of the American community in general, and perhaps of the academic community in particular, would probably reveal that, in spite of the witch hunts in that country, the people of the United States enjoy in fact a much greater degree of freedom than do the people of Canada. We could scarcely have a witch hunt when we have no witches!

Such considerations suggest the need for caution in the use of such terms as radical and reactionary. A student of Social Credit in

Alberta is quickly made aware of the fact that here was a movement which from one point of view could be thought of as radical, from another point of view as reactionary. The same would seem to have been true of the McCarthy movement in the United States. It is not sufficient to say that these were movements which went "bad," because of their unfortunate leadership or for some other reason peculiar to themselves. What appears evident is that all those movements which grew out of the American—or Canadian—frontier were of this character, radical in the sense that they involved a break from established political practice, reactionary in the sense that their efforts were directed towards the creation of a more simple, primitive type of political world.

The farm movements of the western United States or of western Canada, for instance, sought the reform of political institutions not in a strengthening by more subtle means of the responsibility of the governors to the governed but by the development of simple, direct means of popular control over government. Thus the convention, referendum and recall, election of public officials, rotation of offices, and group representation were intended to weaken the executive branch of government and thereby strengthen the voice of the people in the affairs of the state. As instruments of political separatism, such forms of popular government were highly effective. They afforded a means of mobilizing the resistance of a population, often geographically remote and isolated, to a political authority which failed to give adequate expression to its interests. It is in these terms that must be viewed, for instance, the U.F.A. experiment in political democracy—convention rule and group representation. By giving to the convention what was hoped would be the decisive voice in determining, within the provincial sphere, the personnel of the cabinet and the legislative programme of the government, and by giving to the constituency associations control, in the federal sphere, of the voting behaviour of Alberta members of Parliament, a form of government was devised which promised to destroy party discipline and bring to an end cabinet domination over the legislature. The significance of such a development lay in its effect in weakening the influence of Ottawa in Alberta. By breaking from the federal party system, and by undermining the whole system of parliamentary government both in Ottawa and Edmonton, the people of Alberta, at least theoretically, were given a dominant voice in the governing of their own affairs.

What eventually became evident, however, even to some of the U.F.A. leaders themselves, was that a form of political organization devised to strengthen the control of the people of Alberta over their own affairs had the effect of seriously weakening their control over the affairs of the country at large. In Ottawa, the members from Alberta, acting as delegates of the people, were forced into a position of political irresponsibility. They could not be held accountable for any actions of the Government, or for any actions of that party which on defeat of the governing party would succeed it. Even more than this, to the extent that convention rule really operated, the governing authorities in Alberta were placed in a politically irresponsible position. They could not be held accountable for acts dictated by the convention. Examination of the behind-the-scenes role played by Henry Wise Wood in the U.F.A. provincial conventions reveals how readily such an instrument of popular government could have been manipulated by an unscrupulous leadership to serve its own ends. That it was not so manipulated and that convention rule was as little damaging as it was in Alberta were largely owing to the high idealism which characterized the leadership of Mr. Wood and to the good sense, tact, and intellectual strength of the province's second U.F.A. premier, Mr. Brownlee.

The truth is that the forms of political organization which grew out of the frontier experience were not well designed to secure the effective, continuous control of the population over its affairs. Immediately, the revolt from outside authority did lead to an increased control over matters of local concern, but such a result was secured at the price of destroying some of the most important of the safeguards of political organization against the concentration of power in the hands of irresponsible leaders or groups. Such an effect was not intended, of course, but the insensitiveness of frontier democratic theory to the importance of executive responsibility meant inevitably a failure to provide the conditions necessary for effective democratic control.

We have been too much inclined perhaps to exaggerate the political intelligence of frontier populations. It comes hard to one brought up in Alberta to suggest that the people of that province who thought of themselves as in the vanguard of reform actually had only a limited appreciation of the complexities of modern government and no great understanding of the conditions necessary for the preservation of individual rights and a sense of community responsibility. In a cultural sense, the frontier was not a rich and progressive but a poor and retarded society. Its effort to break from the old political and social system of which it had been a part and to create a new system of its liking involved the disowning of a heritage which it had in large measure lost and the building anew of a political and social life with tools fashioned out of its rough and limited experience.

This fact becomes evident when it is recognized that the political reform movement was only one of many forms of frontier protest. Religious sectarianism, vigilantism, medical quackery, mob rioting, tax evasion, smuggling, and political apathy were other means of resistance by a frontier population to the interferences of an outside society in its affairs. What was apparent in all the various kinds of movements which came out of the frontier was an underlying attitude of irresponsibility with respect to the affairs of the larger community. The frontiersman was a difficult person to govern in that he was not prepared to accept the normal obligations of a member of society. One of the primary objects of convention rule, as the U.F.A. sought to establish it in Alberta, was to make the individual a bad party man and thereby in a sense a poor citizen. In the emphasis of Social Credit upon results rather than means, poor citizenship in the form of lack of concern for the actual management of political affairs became almost a condition of membership in the party.

If what is said here is true, one is forced to the conclusion that the development in Canada of parliamentary institutions of government within the framework of the British imperial, and later the Canadian federal, system represented a more enlightened approach to the problem of government in the modern world than did the development of those forms of political organization which found expression in the constitution of the United States. Canada can assume a more responsible and thus more effective role in world affairs than can the United States not because its government is less responsive to the people but because its government's freedom of action is not continuously hampered by the behaviour of irresponsible parties and groups. In this sense, McCarthyism did represent a reactionary force in American political life.

In another sense, however, McCarthyism might be thought to represent a progressive force. By bringing about a break from established practice and forms of organization, the frontier separatist movement had the effect of weakening the hold of tradition upon men's thoughts and actions and thus in making possible a more rational approach to society's problems. There is nothing paradoxical in the fact that religious sectarianism, though in its teachings intensely hostile to science, did much nevertheless to further its growth. The very violence of the sectarian break from traditional forms of thought meant that it was not easy for those caught up in its teachings to fall back into old, accepted ways of thinking once their religious fervour had cooled. Such persons were able as a result to embark upon new and what might be considered socially dangerous lines of thought. Thus did Protestantism contribute to the growth of science and to the development of new forms of economic enterprise. In a similar way, it may be argued that the frontier political protest movement, though reactionary in terms of the ends it sought to accomplish, has been progressive in terms of its ultimate effect upon the organization of society. A native son of Alberta might well take comfort in the view that once the people of that province learn wisdom their inclination to go on trying something new will result in their contributing in a very real way to political advancement. Critics of the United States need to recognize that a country which has so little respect for the past is perhaps the country most able to learn what the past has to teach.

PART IV

Sociology and History

CHAPTER XIV

Sociology, History,
and the Problem of Social Change*

ON THE ANNIVERSARY OF THE PUBLICATION of Darwin's *Origin of Species* it is appropriate to turn at this time to a consideration of the problem of social change. The development of the theory of evolution reflected a growing general awareness one hundred years ago of the fact of change, in the biological, physical, and social world. In the century before Darwin, concern in the social sphere had been largely with the basis of political and social organization and with the relation of the individual to society and, more specifically, to the state. The sociology of Thomas Hobbes was a sociology of social order. In contrast, the sociology of Herbert Spencer was a sociology of social change. Social evolutionary theory, drawing on the data of anthropology, and borrowing its analytical tools from the physical and biological sciences, developed as an explanation of man's social past, of the progress of his society from a primitive to a civilized state.

Though among continental social theorists there was much less readiness to accept the evolutionary thesis, with its strong overtones of individualism, gradualism, and belief in progress, the sociology which they developed was no less challenging to a conception of a static social order. Indeed, with little tendency to distinguish between the social sciences, history, and philosophy, the continental attack on the problem of change could be bold and sweeping in character. Thus emerged that body of work, in general terms

*From the *Canadian Journal of Economics and Political Science*, vol. XXV, no. 4, Nov., 1959, pp. 389–400. With permission of the publisher.

described as philosophy of history, with which have been associated such distinguished names as Hegel, Feuerbach, Marx, and, more lately, Spengler.

Yet today on this continent, one hundred years after Darwin, there appears in the work of sociology little concern with the problem of social change. Indeed, a glance at any one of a great number of introductory textbooks in sociology will reveal that so little is this problem integrated into the general body of sociological theory that it can only be dealt with in a chapter by itself, invariably tacked on at the very end. American sociologists have tended to restrict themselves to the investigation of kinds of problems which have involved the consideration, only within a very narrow range, of the fact of change. Concern has been largely with the way society operates as a functioning system. Thus library shelves have been well laden with studies relating to the family, the community, racial and ethnic relations, social stratification, the professions, labour and other types of occupational association, forms of mass communication, and the like, but few empirical studies will be found that are directed to an analysis of the phenomenon of social change.

To say this is not to suggest that there should be a return to the nineteenth-century search for grand laws of social evolution or social development. Better sociology is being written today largely because sociologists have succeeded in ridding themselves of the false conceptions and illusory ambitions of their nineteenth-century namesakes. By concentrating attention on clearly observable social phenomena, by seeking by painstaking methods of research to determine the nature of the relationships among the different elements which make up society, an enormous advance has been made within the past half-century in the sociological understanding of the world in which we live. Certainly there could be no quarrel here with the view taken by Talcott Parsons that the development of an adequate theory of social change must await the development of a theory of the social system.

Unfortunately, however, or so it would seem, this great advance in the development of the method of sociology has not taken place without the building into it of a bias which has made almost impossible the growth out of an interest in the problem of social order of an interest in the problem of social change. The eyes of sociology are geography and chronology. To view society as an ordered social system, account clearly has to be taken of the spatial dimension, and in the development of sociological method on this continent scrupulous regard has come to be paid to techniques designed to determine the facts of society as they are found in space. But, if social order can only be viewed within the spatial dimension, social change can only be viewed within the dimension of time. Change in society takes place in time. It has a chronology. Yet the use of the chronological method, dealing with facts in any sort of temporal sequence, appears to the sociologist as a task properly belonging to the historian. If historical facts are to be used at all, it is felt, they should be provided by the historian and not by the sociologist.

Where in the grand manner of a Harry Elmer Barnes the sociologist has made of the historian a hewer of wood and drawer of water the result has been to produce poor history and poor sociology; few sociologists would subscribe today to such an unprofitable exploitation of the labours of their historical colleagues. But the repudiation of such an abuse of historical knowledge has not led sociologists to turn to historical research. It has led to an ignoring of almost everything that has to do with history.

Given the kind of environment in which American sociology grew up this perhaps is understandable. To the mid-West sociologist of the 1920's there was nothing terribly exciting about the past of America. It was scarcely necessary to look back to the centuries that had gone before to seek an understanding of the slums and the gangs, the racial riots, the public immorality of the Chicago of W. I. Thomas, Robert E. Park, and Ellsworth Faris. The pressing problems of American society were problems which had their origin in developments of the very recent past. Chicago a hundred years before was nothing but a name on a map. To have turned to an examination of the way in which civilizations are born and develop would have involved a colossal waste of the resources of American sociology.

But the result of this was to get American sociologists into the habit of looking at their society here and now rather than in the past, and the techniques of research they employed became primarily adapted to this task. In the search for leads, in the development of their analytical tools, they turned, not to history, but to anthropology and psychology, and the dependence of sociology on these two sister disciplines has steadily strengthened over the years. Indeed, in Harvard University, the closeness of the tie found recognition in the establishment of the new Department of Social Relations, linking together sociology, social anthropology, and social psychology.

There is no attempt here to belittle the gains to sociology which have come from this association. Only the mention of such names as Malinowski, Radcliffe-Brown, and George Herbert Mead is sufficient to suggest the greatness of sociology's debt to its sister disciplines. But one effect of this close tie of sociology to anthropology and psychology has been to strengthen the bias in sociological method directed towards the investigation of problems of social order rather than social change.

A half-century or more ago anthropology encouraged a sweeping approach to the study of the societies of primitive peoples. It was for long committed to the evolutionary theory, and in seeking support for this theory it had no hesitation in speculating about the origins of primitive forms of social organization or the way in which these forms had evolved or changed over time. Nor did it have any reason for not welcoming forces bringing about the change of primitive society to a more advanced state. The belief in progress was strong, and whatever, therefore, appeared to contribute to the break-up of the old, custom-bound society was viewed as ultimately to the advantage of the peoples concerned. Thus the early anthropologist marched hand in hand with the colonial administrator and church missionary in the effort to civilize primitive man, to reform or rebuild his society.

But that was in the day when few anthropologists did fieldwork and knowledge of the primitive world was based largely on speculation. Once fieldwork was undertaken it quickly became apparent that theories of change which had developed on the basis of speculation could find no support in the facts. Primitive societies have no history in the sense of having a body of written records relating to their past. Thus the anthropologist, once he became concerned about scientific method, had no means of ascertaining the nature of the development of the society under investigation. His study was limited to the society as he saw it before him and, within such a perspective, the spatial dimension assumed enormous significance and the temporal dimension appeared of little account. What seemed to require explanation was not how the society was changing but how it was holding together, operating as a functioning unit. There was much about it which at first glance made little sense in the way of religious practices and beliefs, forms of family organization, taboos, rituals, and ceremonial functions. Such elements took on meaning, however, when they were examined in relation to the whole complex of the culture. What the anthropologist discovered was a social system, an order made up of independent and functionally related elements. Thus was developed the social theory of functionalism.

The personal involvement of the anthropologist in the life of primitive peoples gave to this functional theory thus developed a strong moral force. Fieldwork revealed that the changes that were being forced on primitive society through contact with the white man were exacting a heavy price in the demoralization of primitive peoples. What the colonial administrator or church missionary failed to realize, or so the anthropologist was led to argue, was that to interfere with primitive society at any particular point meant upsetting the whole delicate balance of relationships among its various parts. However repugnant to the outsider certain social practices or beliefs might appear to be, such practices or beliefs were functional to the society in the sense that its survival was dependent on them.

Thus, in his concern to protect primitive peoples from the misguided efforts of reformers and do-gooders, the anthropologist became something of a propagandist for the status quo. Not all anthropologists, of course, so followed through the logic of their functional theory. The old interest in evolution was still sufficiently strong to prompt the development by an anthropologist such as Robert Redfield of a new, and skilful, interpretation of the process of change of primitive society from a folk to a civilized state. But in the application and elaboration of the functional approach, the anthropologist tended to find himself arguing, both out of the logic of his theory and out of his feelings, in support of the view that, since all the elements of primitive society contributed to its survival, to destroy any of them would result in its weakening or disruption. Change thus came almost to assume the character of a nasty word in anthropology.

In psychology, a similar kind of bias has tended to become rooted in functional theory. If the anthropologist, concerned for the welfare of primitive peoples, has reason for viewing with disfavour anything which upsets their society, even more has the psychologist, concerned for the mental health of people generally, for viewing with disfavour anything which upsets individual personality. The psychologist tends to like that which makes for the better adjustment of the individual, for the fuller integration of his personality. A person living in harmony with his environment becomes the end of therapeutic psychology. Conflict is thought of as a destructive force in the development of personality. Organization is set over against disorganization as a measure of psychological well-being.

No psychologist, of course, is so naïve as to suppose that a well-adjusted individual is one who slavishly conforms to his social environment. Yet because his inquiries tend to be carried out within a limited social situation such as that of a clinical laboratory or schoolroom, the term well-adjusted tends to assume this meaning. Investigation is confined to an examination of the adjustment of individuals to an environment which is treated as constant. To seek to examine how the environment itself undergoes change, how indeed it is changed by individuals who have failed to adjust themselves to it, would require the use of very different techniques of research on the part of the psychologist. The psychologist, in a word, would have to become a historian.

To say all this is to imply no criticism of anthropology or psychology as such. Certainly, in the case of psychology, the terms order and disorder have a very real meaning when applied to human personality. When, however, the way of thinking of the anthropologist and psychologist, and their techniques of investigation, have been taken over by the sociologist, the effect has been in sociological thinking to lead to an over-emphasis on such processes as socialization and social integration, to the neglect of processes of social change. The sociologist has been too much inclined to impose on his own material the limitations which are inherent in the material of the anthropologist and psychologist. Non-primitive societies, unlike primitive societies, do have a history, and they are not confined, as is the individual personality under investigation by the psychologist, within the four walls of a clinical laboratory. Yet the sociologist has tended to proceed as if both of these things were characteristic of his society.

Indeed, Talcott Parsons, in urging the importance of the small group approach to the study of social processes, seeks in effect deliberately to impose on his materials the limitations which are inherent in the material of the anthropologist and psychologist. By subjecting the small group, assembled within the laboratory, to investigation, much certainly can be learned about the way people sort themselves out in society, come to accept certain roles, and develop some sort of social hierarchy. But such a microcosmic society is a society without a history, or with a history covering a span of time no greater than the investigation itself. And, by the very nature of the situation created, such a society starts out as

indeed not a society at all and ends up (unless the individuals
selected for the experiment are stubbornly anti-social in character)
as one possessing form and a sense of order. What is being studied
is the process of social formation but not of social change. Forces
which might operate to arrest or even reverse the process of group
formation are effectively excluded by the laboratory's walls.

As the functional theory has been developed within anthropology
and sociology since the day of Malinowski and Radcliffe-Brown, it
has been given a much more dynamic meaning. It has been made,
particularly by such sociologists as Robert K. Merton, a theory of
social change as well as of social order. And yet, or so it seems,
there persists some sort of blockage or bias in sociological thinking
which results, when the theory is put to work, in imputing to society
a static quality or a character of order which it does not possess.
The twisting of the meaning given to certain terms may be only so
little but its cumulative effect can determine much of the character
of the work done in sociology. Thus in the use of such terms as
survival, integration, and equilibrium there is suggested the idea
that, unless certain conditions are fulfilled, society will not survive
or will cease to be fully integrated or in a state of equilibrium. In
reality, two people cannot interact without there being a society,
and all societies, by virtue of the very fact that they are societies,
are integrated and in a state of equilibrium. Thus, for instance, it
cannot make sense to talk about a society such as that of Toronto
in a state of equilibrium or disequilibrium, of integration or disintegration. Something may be happening to this society: it now can
boast Sunday baseball and movies, cocktail bars, and people speak-
ing many tongues. But the society is as completely integrated, as
fully in a state of equilibrium, today as it was twelve months or ten
years ago. It is just a different society.

The trouble would appear to be, in the use of the functional
theory, that society has been stripped of the attribute of time and
assigned boundaries which in fact it does not possess. Because of the
extreme isolation of Radcliffe-Brown's Andaman Islanders, and the
slow rate of the change taking place in their social relationships, it
was almost possible to think of the various patterns of behaviour
and modes of thinking of the people, within the particular area
inhabited and at the time these patterns were observed by the
anthropological fieldworker, as making up *the* society. Actually,
however, the Andaman Islanders were never wholly cut off from
contact with other people, and though social relationships were

changing slowly they were nevertheless changing. Thus, even in such a simple social situation, no attribute of the culture could be thought of as functional to the society in the sense that it was essential to the society's survival. Certain items of culture secured, obviously, the survival of one kind of society: the society which got recorded in the anthropologist's field notes. But by the time the anthropologist was ready to leave the field, a different kind of society, even if so very slightly different, had come into being; and the items of culture which were clearly functional to the society which had been observed were not necessarily functional to this new society.

If this was true of the society of the Andaman Islanders, it is, of course, even more true of our highly complex and rapidly changing Western society. Here it is impossible to speak with exactness of any one society as over against another. People live and work, and eat and sleep, in a great number of different societies. Where lines must be drawn, as for instance between the country and the city, we are forced in the end to resort to an arbitrary statistical index; that is an urban society which has a certain specified density of population. No man can be certain when he is acting as a member of a family, an ethnic group, a church, or a nation. And affiliations which appear clear today may by tomorrow become confused or radically altered. Every day we awake to participate in what in effect is a different society.

Nowhere perhaps is this more apparent than in the area of social class, and in perhaps no area of sociological analysis has the sociologist been more influenced by the functional anthropologist in treating what is under examination in static terms. There is a mounting body of literature in sociology relating to social class but almost all of it is posited on the naïve Warner assumption that society can be divided up into a number of different classes, three, nine, twenty-seven, or a number still larger, and that these different classes possess a character of fixity. What has been developed is a sociology of social stratification but not of social class relations. Society can be ranked in terms of some sort of hierarchy just as it can be ranked in terms of age. The eleven-year-old boy recognizes himself as an eleven-year-old, and in certain situations this precise age of his will be important in determining the kind of social relations in which he becomes involved. Similarly a man's rank in the hierarchical structure may determine the time he eats his evening meal, and whether he calls it supper or dinner. But in the total complex of social relations in which he is involved, class affiliation may have no social significance whatsoever or the nature of the affiliation may vary widely depending on the particular situation he finds himself in. What Warner does, for example in the case of Newburyport, Massachusetts, is to treat the society he is examining as an entity and an unchanging entity at that. Thus there can be no allowance for the fact that people participate not within one social class system but in a great number, forming and reforming in different and changing situations. Nor can there be any allowance for the fact that the social class relations which do develop in various situations give expression, in no small degree, to feelings of animosity, developing at times, indeed, to the point where, by rebellion or revolution, the existing class lines in society may be destroyed. One can read almost everything that has been written by American sociologists on social class without once coming across the nasty word "conflict." Emphasis is placed on social class as a system of order, not as a force of social division, of social change.

What, therefore, can we mean by such terms as survival, integration, or equilibrium when they are applied to a society such as ours? The swinging door on the old-time saloon clearly had a function or purpose; it made it possible for the lonely passer-by to see what was going on inside before committing himself to enter. It contributed to the survival of the social system of the saloon. But it did the social system of the family no good, or that of the church. Looked at from one vantage point, such an item of culture, therefore, would have to be considered as functional to the society, from another vantage point as disfunctional, to use the term made current by Merton. Certainly, in a community like Dawson City, in the boom days of the gold rush, the saloon did much to give the population a sense of social belonging, of being part of society. It was clearly a force of social reorganization. But it was also a force of social disorganization in its effect in weakening within the society traditional values of behaviour and forms of organization.

What becomes apparent, the moment we turn to the examination of any item of our culture, is that it is both functional and disfunctional at the same time, that is, it contributes to the survival of certain forms of social relationship while weakening or destroying other forms. If such is the case, how then can functionalism be made a useful theoretical tool in the analysis of society? The answer lies in seizing on what appear to be, at a particular point of time and within a defined area, the most distinctive features of a society and building these into a theoretical model. It is in these terms that Talcott Parsons conceives of society as a boundary-maintaining social system. Thus, for instance, the society of Dawson City, let us say on January 1, 1900, with boundaries clearly fixed by geography, could be thought of as a boundary-maintaining social system. Defined in this fashion, its distinctive features could be described and the conditions necessary for its survival determined. Now, conceivably, the functional significance of a social institution such as the saloon could be empirically established. Given the nature of the social system thus defined, it was probably more sensible for the population to spend its leisure time fraternizing about the bar and the gambling table than in struggling to maintain some form of religious worship or some kind of family life. Beliefs or habits which placed a heavy emphasis on the importance of religion or family values might well be found on investigation to be disfunctional to the society, caught up as they were in types of behaviour which assumed the character of being queer or, in extreme cases, pathological.

What must be made clear, however, about such a theoretical model is that it has had imposed on it two important limitations. It has been fixed in terms of its boundaries and it has been fixed in terms of time. For consideration of the problem of social order, it is essential that there be these limitations. There can come no sociological understanding of how man relates himself to man, and builds of these relationships the thing we call society, unless we are prepared for purposes of analysis to impute a quality of permanence to what in reality is highly impermanent and indeterminant.

But if these two limitations on the theoretical model of the social system are not kept clearly in mind, such terms as survival, integration, and equilibrium, as used in the functional theory, can play treacherous tricks. Once attention is shifted from the problem of social order to the problem of social change, what we are searching for are not the forces operating within the society to secure a boundary-maintaining social system but the forces operating within the society to bring about the breakdown of such a system. Change in society is spread over the horizon of time and over the horizon of space. It is of various sorts and takes place at all different levels of social organization: in the ecological ordering of man and his social institutions, in the forms of social interaction in which he becomes involved, in his ideas, ideologies, and values of life. No facet of our society exists whose origin could not be traced back to the beginning of man. And social changes taking place today will not really have run their course until human civilization vanishes from the earth.

What more then can we do than simply chronicle the changes taking place in our society and rely on our descriptive powers to make such a chronicling appear interesting and worth while? Much social history is written in this manner and from it we can learn a good deal about how people lived in the past, how they changed their habits, their manner of dress, their style of housing, their ideas of what constitutes the good life. But clearly there can come in this way no understanding of the process of change in society. There are patterns of social change. Changes in one area of social life are related to changes in another. The task of the student of social change is the searching out and systematic analysis of these relationships.

In doing so, he must obviously have some place to begin and some place to end. Otherwise, every Ph.D. thesis having to do with change would tiresomely trace its way back to Adam and Eve, and, however narrow the original focus of attention, searching for the relationships between the different facts relating to the change under consideration would involve reaching into all four corners of the earth. If there is to be a systematic analysis of the process of change, the sociologist must have some sort of theoretical frame of reference.

Such a theoretical frame of reference is provided by functionalism, and more specifically by Talcott Parsons' conception of the boundary-maintaining social system. To say this may appear strange in the light of the argument thus far advanced in this paper. But if we want to grasp what happens to a thing undergoing motion we must somehow get a look at it when it is still. Though society is never actually in such a state of stillness, it can be conceived to be at certain points in time, the point at which the analysis of change begins and the point at which it ends. Snapshots, in a sense, are taken of the society, but snapshots which are then touched up by the artist to bring out more clearly the distinctive features of the object. What we seek is to get to know as far as possible what the society was like before undergoing the change we are examining. And what it has come to be like after having changed.

In such a context the functional theory takes on dynamic meaning. Analysis begins at that point where the society has been fixed in its boundaries and in time. Such a society is considered as being in a state of equilibrium. Thus the changes taking place in it can be thought of as a movement from a state of equilibrium to a state of disequilibrium and, eventually, at that point where the society has once more been fixed in its boundaries and in time, to a new state of equilibrium. In these terms, we can talk about survival and integration, disorder and disintegration.

Such a fixing of society in its boundaries and in time, at the point of departure and at the terminal point of the analysis of social change, is not so arbitrary as at first glance it might appear. If we are engaged in the examination of a society undergoing change, it requires no great knowledge of it to discern the approximate point at which the change became pronounced and the approximate point at which it had pretty well ceased. Thus, to turn to an actual example—the town of Newmarket some twenty-five miles outside of Toronto—a few casual inquiries made around and about the town will reveal the fact that something began to happen there about ten years ago which in the years since then has been transforming the character of the community. People began to move out to Newmarket from Toronto in great numbers, to build for themselves on the town's outskirts vast subdivisions and new shopping centres. Today Newmarket is in the process of becoming a suburb of Toronto. Eventually, and in years not far distant, it will become an integral part of the Toronto urban community.

Here, obviously, the analysis of the changes that are taking place begins with the town as it once was. For certain purposes, the inquiry could be extended back to the establishment of the town at the beginning of the last century, to the changes wrought upon it with the changing character of the larger community during the nineteenth and early years of the twentieth century. Certainly we would want to know something about the forces that made the community the kind of community it became. But to understand the nature of the changes taking place in the community today, the impact on it of the suburban movement of population, it is scarcely necessary to go back beyond a point in time ten years or so ago. What we want to know is what the community was like before there was any substantial movement out to it of population from the city. We seize on this point in time as our starting point, and seek to discover what, at that time and within the limits of an area that can be fairly clearly defined, were the distinctive features of the society. The society of Newmarket at that point in time is thought of as a boundary-maintaining social system. The analysis of change thus involves the examination of those forces bringing about the disintegration of this social system, its transformation into something different, first partly small town, partly suburban, later almost completely suburban, and, finally, though that time has not yet come, into a social system purely urban.

Implied within such a framework of analysis is the notion that it is possible not only to define in fairly clear terms the nature of the society as it once was and the nature of the society that it became but to identify the main force of change. In the case of Newmarket, the assumption is that the invasion of the community by people from the city has had something to do with the way it has changed. Of all the facts relating to the community, none stands out so clearly and obviously as this one. It would appear only sensible, therefore, to begin with it as the jumping-off point in the analysis and seek to relate all the other facts of change about the community to it. Thus the study of Newmarket becomes a study of suburbanism, of the impact on the society of a small Ontario rural town of the suburban movement of population.

But if the student of social change in his analysis of a situation such as this prefers to start somewhere else, with, for instance, the rise of the birth rate after the Second World War, or the increased concern of urban people with the kind of environment in which their children were to be reared, the results achieved would be equally revealing. It is not the task of the social theorist to seek to discover whether social change is caused by the thoughts men hold, the tools they employ, or the way they order their economic lives. Much too much ink has been wasted in debating what comes before what. It is not what causes what but what is related to what that is the concern of the social scientist. A wheat farmer thinks as a wheat farmer and a South Carolina cotton picker is not likely to develop a religious philosophy as sophisticated as that of an Oxford don. When Turner wrote his classic on the frontier in American history he put his finger on what was a very obvious fact about the development of American society: that there was a relationship between the frontier experience of American people and the forms of social organization they developed and the thoughts they came to hold. Only a very curious reading of Canadian history could lead one to deny that Canada had no frontier or that there was no relationship between the Canadian frontier and the development of the Canadian society. It would be tantamount to arguing that because the sun has no means of compelling me to walk on the shady side of the street there is in fact no relationship between my so walking and the sun's existence. There is nothing deterministic about social science though a good many historians and humanists seem to think there is. Perhaps, indeed, it is not unfair to suggest that no one but a determinist can read into what the social scientist is trying to do a deterministic philosophy. If we believe that princes and kings, or what some are pleased to call the higher values of life, determine man's destiny on earth we cannot but view with dismay any effort of the social scientist to treat these things as only some among many elements within a vast system of interrelationships.

To the philosopher must be left the task of searching out the inner meaning of change in society, of discovering those laws which determine the course of history or the future progress of man. To the social scientist belongs the much more modest task of trying to discover how one thing is related to another, of formulating principles of economic, political, and social organization from the examination of the way in which people behave, think, and feel. Although, as the economic and social theorist have demonstrated, there is a value in seeking out logical relationships within a purely theoretical model, the test of the validity of the social scientist's principles, in the end, is whether they are founded on fact.

Thus the development of a sociology of social change involves the examination of societies in change. To say this seems almost trite. And yet, or so this paper has argued, it is just such an examination of societies in change which the sociologist has not been prepared to undertake, except to a very limited degree. We cannot become students of change without becoming historians. It is only by looking at what has happened to societies of the past, and over time, that the sociologist can derive the data on which to build his principles of social change.

To say this is to raise the question of what are the proper limits of sociological as over against historical investigation. So long as the task of history was conceived of as simply that of discovering and making known the facts of the past, and the task of the social sciences that of discovering immutable laws of human conduct rooted in nature, the distinction between them rested on a logical basis. History had nothing to gain from the social sciences and the social sciences had nothing to gain from history. But we have moved a long way from Darwin and the naïve conceptions of nineteenth-century history and social science, and nothing today would appear to set off these disciplines from one another other than the biases and prejudices inherited from the past. The search for the nature of the relationships among happenings in society, the explanation of what occurs by comparing a particular occurrence with other occurrences, is the task which the historian performs and it is a task which must be performed by the sociologist the moment he turns to examine the process of change in society. All facts relating to man's conduct, of the present or the past, have a character of uniqueness in the sense that acts are performed by individuals at particular times and places. But the moment we recognize these facts as facts they lose their character of uniqueness. We can only talk about a horse if we have seen more than one horse, and similarly when we speak of revolutions and wars, and princes and principalities, it is clear that we have formed in our mind an image of what these things are by looking at more than one of them. In method, sociology must come closer and join forces with history. Would it, however, be impertinent to suggest than in theory it is history which should come closer and join forces with sociology? One might wish that sociologists like Talcott Parsons, in the development of their sociological theory, would take time off to do empirical studies of a historical nature. But one might also wish that more historians would turn for a brief spell from their historical writings to an examination of the work of sociological theorists.

CHAPTER XV

History and
the Sociological Method*

IN A PAPER written twenty-three years ago, entitled "Sociology and Canadian Social History," I argued for a greater use of history by the sociologist. What was said in that paper by way of criticism of sociology was largely directed at what seemed to be certain dominant characteristics of the discipline as it had grown up on this continent. Developing in reaction to the philosophical tradition of nineteenth-century European sociology, American sociology, so it seemed, had moved so far in the direction of being concerned about scientific methods of investigation that it had lost the capacity to deal with the really significant problems of a sociological character. Too much of the research being done was directed simply to the end of testing the methodological tools being employed. The result only too often was the reporting of things already known about society or, if not known, of such a trivial character that they were scarcely worth being made known. Theory as well as research suffered from this concentration upon the study of small, narrowly defined problems of a sort which lent themselves readily to the use of certain approved methods of scientific inquiry. In particular, there was an almost complete failure to grapple with the major problems of historical development.

However justified may have been such criticism of American sociology twenty-three years ago, there would seem to be little basis for similar criticism today. Sociological method, with its vastly im-

*Presented at the World Congress of Sociology, Washington, 1962. Published with permission of the International Sociological Association.

proved techniques of investigation, has been made to grapple with problems of almost unlimited scope while theory building, as undertaken by a Talcott Parsons, has become a task which knows no empirical bounds. With this development in theory and method has come a greatly strengthened interest in the use of history. There are few sociologists today who would subscribe to the view that the sociological method limits investigation to the contemporary society. There is nothing in history any longer which would be considered beyond the reach of sociological analysis.

The growing literature in the field of sociological history attests to how effectively history has been made to serve the ends of sociological analysis in the work of a number of American sociologists. To mention the names of Reinhard Bendix and Sigmund Diamond should not be taken to imply that the list could be quickly exhausted.

Yet what was said twenty-three years ago with reference to the anti-historical bias of American sociology may not be wholly inappropriate today. Though there has been much talk in recent years about the importance of history to sociology, it is perhaps not unfair to suggest that a good deal of this talk has come from sociologists who themselves have done little or no history. It is now fashionable to pretend an interest in history and so long as such an interest demands nothing more than making use of work already done by the historian it can be subscribed to at no great cost. The question has to be asked, however, whether a good many American sociologists have not become so unhistorical in their way of thinking, and in their methods of investigation, that, in turning to history, they find themselves unable to become sufficient of historians to make effective use of what history has to offer. In effect, the sociologist too often wants to use history without doing history. However much he may talk about the importance of history, the conviction remains strong that there is a difference between sociology and history, that is, between the method of the sociologist and that of the historian.

Park and Burgess had stated this difference, in their textbook which has now become a classic in sociology, as one between *natural history* and history and, though the difference would not be expressed in this way today, the notion that there is a difference persists. What the historian presumably is interested in are the facts of history; what the sociologist is interested in is in the way these facts are related in some sociologically significant pattern. It is unnecessary to argue here how impossible it is to logically distinguish between these two exercises. If pressed, probably no sociologist could be found who would insist upon such a distinction. Yet implicitly, whenever they turn to history, many sociologists proceed on the assumption that such a distinction in fact exists.

The result only too often is that the sociologist will not let himself do in the study of past society what he is quite prepared to do in the study of society here and now: be guided to his theory by the facts he discovers as well as to the facts by the theory he has formulated. He will not let himself do this because its doing appears to involve turning himself into an historian. He may, in the manner of the grand theorist, so enclose himself in the armour of his theory that only that part of history which fits into his analytical and empirical framework is taken notice of; the theoretical boxes are filled before the task of historical investigation is begun. Or he may, like the functional anthropologist, avoid entirely the tangled problem of motion or movement in history by making a study of a society or institution of the past fixed in time. More usually, however, resort is had to what is called the comparative historical method, where developments in one place or time are compared with developments in another. Here the sociologist appears to be exploiting to the full what history has to offer while still avoiding the awful charge that he has become an historian.

There is no suggestion here that great gains have not come from any of these sociological approaches to history. But involved in all of them is the danger of taking on faith a part of the history used. The result can be a gross distortion of the facts upon which the sociologist bases his generalizations. Indeed, what were some of the worst faults of the nineteenth-century evolutionists, in the methods they employed, appear in the work today of some of those sociologists who in this fashion have turned to investigation of the historical past. It is perhaps in no way surprising that when Talcott Parsons seeks to incorporate within his general theory a theory of change it is upon the sociology of Herbert Spencer that he largely relies. Spencer was no historian, and with the example of biological evolution before him he perhaps can be forgiven for viewing change in society as being one in the direction of increasing structural differentiation. But by building the process of structural differentiation into his model of social change, Parsons from the very beginning seriously limits the range of historical investigation. Among the changes taking place in society can be discerned certainly changes in the direction of increasing structural differentiation. But so also can be discerned changes of the very opposite character. The fact that the model used excludes consideration of changes of this latter sort cannot be taken as sufficient answer to the charge that what is offered is a distorted picture of what is happening to society as it changes over time. Movements in the direction of increasing structural differentiation (and as well social integration) are intimately related to movements in the opposite direction and any theory of change must be able to account for one type of movement as well as the other.

Among those sociologists who make no claim to having a general theory of change there is, of course, no such effort as that represented by the sociology of Talcott Parsons to fit all the facts of history into a tight theoretical framework. The problems of investigation undertaken are of a much more modest character. Here what is sought are theories of social organization or development of what a Merton would call "the middle range." Work of this sort thus appears much more defensible than that undertaken within the framework of a general theory.

What cannot be overlooked, however, is that there is here involved, in the effort to select out of history only that part which is considered sociologically relevant, the same danger of forcing the facts of history into a preconceived theoretical framework. The sociologist, acting on the assumption that the peculiar method of sociology is that of comparative analysis, only too often leaves the important task which must be done before comparative analysis can be undertaken—the task of discovering what are the facts of history —wholly to the historian.

Thus can occur that curious joining together of comparative sociological analysis with the most conventional kind of historical analysis. This is not the place to attempt an assessment of work done by the historian as such but this much certainly can be said, that only a small part of that work has been directed towards the investigation of problems of concern to the sociologist. The result is that the latter, where he limits his investigation by the method of comparative analysis, only too often finds himself relying upon what is far from complete information. Meanings of facts change when viewed within a different kind of context. What to the historian may not have been recognized as a fact, or if recognized considered so trivial that it was not taken notice of, may to the sociologist be a fact of enormous significance. Yet such a fact lies buried, unknown to the sociologist, if reliance is placed upon only those facts which come to be reported by the historian. What this can mean is the building up of a body of sociological generalizations on the basis of comparison when what is being compared is not really comparable.

Efforts to examine over a period of time reaching back into history the relation of social class to voting behaviour afford an example of the hazards involved in this type of comparative sociological analysis. Here the sociologist approaches his task with a fairly good idea of what social class means in his contemporary society and so long as he confines himself to an analysis of the relation of class to voting in this society he can avoid getting into trouble. Not only is his definition of social class based upon a very substantial knowledge of present-day societies but he can be expected to revise it, in the course of his investigations, if new facts come to light. The moment, however, he turns to history his definition no longer is amenable to change for the reason that he now makes himself dependent upon this definition for selecting from the facts of history—as set forward by the historian—those which he considers relevant to the problem at hand. The almost inevitable consequence is the formation of conclusions about the relation of social class to voting behaviour on the basis of facts which have come to be known through the employment of two very different definitions of social class, the definition of the historian and that of the sociologist.

If Canadian history can be taken as representative, it is not hard to see how seriously misled the sociologist can be who proceeds in this fashion to make a comparative sociological analysis of the relation of social class to voting behaviour. Canadian history has tended to be written as if social classes were something almost which did not exist. There are a number of reasons for this. The historian's bias which leads him to place a heavy emphasis upon the role of ideas and leaders may be one. Another is that the techniques of investigation upon which he relies result in a failure to distinguish clearly between the interests of social class and those other much more prominent interests such as regionalism and religion. But whatever may be the reasons, the fact certainly is that what the historian has done offers no clear picture of the part social class may have played in the forming of men's thoughts and actions in the Canadian political society of the past.

On the other hand, the techniques employed by the sociologist in the study of contemporary society tend perhaps to exaggerate the role played by social class. A man's position in the status hierarchy is something which can be measured, and the temptation thus is strong to seize upon such tangible attributes in seeking an explanation of why people behave in the way they do. Be that as it may, certainly few sociologists can be accused of giving insufficient recognition to the fact of class in the organization of society about them. What this can mean, however, the moment the sociologist seeks to draw comparisons between the role of social class in society of the past and its role in present-day society is the forming of generalizations on the basis of very different kinds of facts. Even more treacherous can be the effort to cast the comparative net beyond the society of one country and treat as meaning the same thing what the historians of different countries have written about social class. To compare the role of social class in the political development of two or more countries assumes a knowledge of the history of these countries such as the sociologist is scarcely likely to have if in his investigations he has strictly limited himself to the problem at hand.

This is not to argue, of course, that the sociologist, in the manner of the antiquarian, should allow himself to be guided by no theory in his historical investigations. Nor is it to argue, indeed, that in turning to history he should not attempt to take advantage of work already done by the historian if by chance what the historian has done serves fully the purposes of sociological analysis. In the end, sociological historian and historian may become one, and, where that happens, the division of labour which results would naturally be on the level of generality of analysis. But this clearly is far from the case today. Historians have not become sociologists and as a consequence sociologists, seeking to use history, have no real choice but to become historians.

It is no answer that the sociologist has no time to do the painstaking task of historical research and that in the interests of an economy of effort it is better that this part of the task of historical comparative analysis be left to the historian. It involved a lifetime of work on the part of the late H. A. Innis to rewrite the economic history of Canada, but economic theory, particularly as it relates to problems of economic development, would be vastly poorer today if work such as his had not been done. It is perhaps no exaggeration to say that what is written into the textbooks of sociology comes almost wholly from the study of contemporary societies, literate and non-literate. The consequences are certain serious misjudgments about the character of society and social change.

The effect in developing within sociological theory a static bias, where emphasis tends to be placed upon the phenomenon of social order at the expense of the phenomenon of social change, is a consideration which need not be gone into here. Of greater concern is the nature of the theory of change which has come out of the way many sociologists have approached the task of historical investigation. Parsons is not alone in his use of a kind of nineteenth-century evolutionary theory to account for the character of change over time. There is in the work of a number of sociologists a curious mixture of the sociology of Spencer, Weber, and Durkheim which becomes particularly pronounced the moment there is a turning to consideration of developments taking place in the past. It was a crude kind of Spencerian sociology which got written into the Park and Burgess notion of *natural history*, but even today, if it is not Spencer alone, it is a compounding of his ideas with those of Weber and Durkheim which determine in large part the nature of the theory of change in much American sociology.

Thus comes the emphasis in the study of American society upon the role of values as a conservative force in social development. Values as they find expression in written records and the speeches of public men appear as something which change little over time. If attention is fastened upon such values, what Americans believe today seems not greatly different from what they believed almost two hundred years ago when, having got rid of the British with their aristocratic notions of government, they proceeded to establish the institutions of their society on the basis of principles of liberty and equality. Change as it has taken place since in these institutions can be made thus to appear as involving little more than the giving of fuller expression to the basic values of American life.

It is in terms of such a conception of change in American society that what had been elaborated as a theory of social order with a heavy dependence upon Durkheim has been made into a theory of social development with a heavy dependence upon Spencer. In particular, the sociology of Talcott Parsons would appear to have undergone a transformation of this character. This is not the place to argue whether any useful purpose can be served by the effort to erect a general theory of society in the manner undertaken by Parsons. What must be noted, however, is the fact that the Parsonian theory maintains at best its character of generality only in so far as it has to do with the problem of order in society. The moment it becomes a theory of change rather than order it loses its character of generality and takes on a highly particularistic reference. It is a theory which accounts for certain kinds of changes taking place in society but quite clearly not for other kinds.

Given the high rate of growth and general prosperity which has been characteristic of American society in recent years, it is perhaps not surprising that sociologists such as Parsons should mistake as general patterns of change in society certain developments taking place within their own. Something of the same sort of mistake had been made in their different ways by Marx and Weber, and, of course, even more by Herbert Spencer. Thus in the treatment, for instance, of such social phenomena as bureaucracy or social stratification, there is the implicit assumption that what is being looked at is a reflection of tendencies or patterns of change in the organization of society in general. It is hard not to believe that American society compared with other societies represents in some fashion or other a higher stage of development in forms of economic, political, and social life.

The difficulty in part comes from the failure to look at the society of the United States as an integral part of a larger society. It is easy enough to believe, for instance, that wide differences in income and styles of life between social classes, and class conflict, are disappearing if attention is confined to the example of American society. Nor is this impression little corrected if what consideration is given to societies in other parts of the world is in the way of comparing these societies with the American rather than treating them as part of the same society. It is in this manner that account can be taken, for instance, of the kinds of developments taking place in Latin America or in the newer nations of Africa without any modification of the conception of development occurring in the American society. No attempt is made to examine what is happening outside the United States as a response to what is happening within and to explore the possibility that social class conflict now finds expression less through the existence within American society of social classes with sharply divided interests than through the existence of such classes within the larger society of which American society is a part. To a very considerable extent the United States has become an area of residence of a privileged social class. To find the people living "across the tracks" it is now necessary to look beyond the boundaries of the United States.

Much the same can be said of power and the bureaucratic organization of society. To talk of a power vacuum and to describe society in terms of an impersonal bureaucratic structure operating almost automatically without any manifest exercise of power may appear to make sense to an American looking at the state of politics and the organization of economic life within his own society but to a Canadian residing across the border from the United States conscious of the might of the neighbouring republic and of its large industrial and financial corporations there can be little doubt where power resides. What American sociology perhaps needs more than anything else is a new Frederick Jackson Turner to call attention to the importance of the forces developing within what has become the new frontier of the western world. A greater recognition of these forces would result certainly in a more sceptical treatment of conclusions regarding the nature of bureaucratic organization, social stratification, and such other features of modern society drawn from the study of the society of the United States. There is the very real danger that a whole generation of American sociologists will be misled by Parsons' insistence on treating American society as a boundary-maintaining social system.

It is not ethnocentrism alone, however, which accounts for this failure on the part of a number of American sociologists to recognize that what they are treating as developments of a general character are in fact developments of a highly particularistic kind. The determination to view society as an orderly social system has led to an unwillingness to look beyond those nice comfortable segments of the American society itself where talk about integration and consensus appear to have some meaning and examine within the same theoretical framework those areas of the society that are characterized by disintegration and conflict. A sociology of deviance has been made to account for what it is in the society that is not liked. Thus emerges a conception of change as development in the direction of increasing rationality in human affairs. It is this sort of conception of evolutionary change which has largely determined the way in which a number of American sociologists have approached the study of the development of their society.

It would be beyond the limits of space imposed on this paper to attempt to indicate the kind of things the sociologist can learn from history if prepared to explore all the various avenues of historical investigation without regard to where those avenues may lead. But this much perhaps can be said. What he almost certainly can learn is that what has happened in society in the past was not greatly different from what is happening now. There has always appeared to man something mysterious about his past and from this feeling many sociologists have not escaped. What spreads back behind—the society of the past—seems much more forbidding than what spreads before his eyes—the society of the present. Thus methods of investigation which are used with great confidence in exploring the society today come to be considered inadequate when there is a turning to an exploration of the past. What now seems to be required is not a theory to guide the way but a theory which will determine the precise route to be followed. Even Barrington Moore, Jr., though arguing valiantly the need for the sociologist to make greater use of history, feels nevertheless compelled to advance as a condition of such use a general sociological theory of historical development. Long scorning history, sociology is perhaps now in danger of expecting from history more than it has to offer.

In the end, the chief contribution which can be made by investigation of a sociological-historical character may be that simply of calling into question many of the theories about society now held. But if this is so, it is as it should be. History has not one social theory to offer and the study of present-day society another; which is simply another way of saying that there is no such thing as a theory of social change as such. In studying the past the sociologist must find himself doing nothing different from what he is doing when studying society here and about. And he must expect no more miraculous results from his investigations. There is no theory to be discovered which will unlock the gates of history. The most any theory can do is guide the investigator to certain historical facts. If such a theory is not to be made a dead thing, investigation must be pushed on to other facts and to the development of other theories.

What this means is that there is nothing in history that the sociologist can safely disregard. If he is to use history he must be prepared to do history without fear of being charged that he has become an historian. There are involved, of course, perils of no inconsiderable sort. It is easy to get bogged down in historical facts. But so as well is it easy to get bogged down in facts about society of the present. There can be no abandonment of theory in investigation of a historical or non-historical character. But, on the other hand, there can be no enslavement to it.

This paper began with a reference to American sociology as it was twenty-three years ago. It can well conclude with a similar reference. In their concentration upon the problems of the immediate society about them, sociologists of that time had essentially sound instincts. The whole vast society of the United States was a problem area and particularly that part of it of which Chicago was the centre, and it would have been strange indeed if American sociology had assumed a character very different from what it did. The sociology of Park has led naturally to the sociology of Parsons with the kinds of changes which have taken place within American society over the past quarter-century. There has grown as could be expected an increasing concern with the character of the forces which have shaped this society. Out of micro-sociology has developed a macro-sociology. The new approach has given emphasis to new kinds of limitations not too unlike those that were characteristic of the sociology of the "grand theory" of the nineteenth century. The growing interest in historical investigation has been a welcome consequence of the new macro approach but it is in the type of historical investigation undertaken that the limitations of this approach most clearly show up. This paper has been concerned with these limitations. It can scarcely overlook, however, the importance of the advance which has been made. Whatever the limitations of some of the work now being done, there has come from the new strengthening interest in historical investigation a greatly strengthened sociology. And the move forward is not likely to stop at the point of advance now reached. It is hard to believe that the sociologist who has turned to history will remain for long so little curious about the facts of history that he will be content to leave to others the task of historical research. The sociologist who uses history is almost bound in the end to find himself doing history.